The girl who waited 100 years
By
Chris Cutler

Dear Jon

I hope you enjoy
reading my first book

Lots of love Tod xxx

For Ariane.

Ariane is a real person. Her ice cream parlour
existed when this book was written. Maybe it still does.
You will have to go to the Périgord to find out. It did not
on the dates referred to in this novel because it is a work
of fiction. All other names, characters, businesses,
places, events, locales, and incidents are either the
products of the author's imagination or used in a
fictitious manner. Any resemblance to actual persons,
living or dead, or actual events is purely coincidental.

Part 1
The cuckold

Chapter 1
Dordogne, France
Winter 1943

I look at myself in the mirror. I am naked. I like most of what I see. My hair is too short, but immaculately groomed. My skin is pale. I am meticulous about shielding it from the Dordogne sun. Before the invasion my one extravagance was savon de Marseille. Now, if I can get soap at all it is coal tar. It smells of petrol. Even in this hateful war I make sure that my skin is soft enough to be the envy of the girls in the village. Some try to date me. I am not interested. They think I'm homosexual. I'm not, I'm a girl. To emphasise the point I push my penis between my legs. Clamping with my thighs I stand straight. All I can see is a triangle of pubic hair. I am Francine not Francis, or perhaps Francesca. That is pretty too. Am I pretty? Jean thinks so. They say he is homosexual. That's silly, he's married. I'm sure he loves me more than he loves her. He said so. He kissed me. We even made love the night I thought he had been killed. It hurt. If I had a vagina it would not. I relax my thighs and let my genitals escape. Thinking of Jean has given me an erection. My penis looks worse when it is swollen. When I was young I thought about cutting it off. I was scared I would bleed to death. I take one last look at my naked body then start to dress.

Not my sister's clothes, I have to go out. We have information on a German patrol. Until his disappearance the Italian mason was our source. He arrived before the war. There was work then. Now there is none. People wonder where he gets his money. It is obvious. Every faction in the village has paid for his information at some point. Some support the Vichy regime and hate the Jews. They welcomed the Germans, even when they took direct command. We are close to the demarcation line. The resistance is active. Even they fight amongst themselves. The Gauchists and Gaullists hate each other with a passion almost matched by their mutual hatred of the Germans. With so many factions it is no wonder we were invaded. Our group has news of a German patrol. Jean and I volunteered to ambush them. I slip from the house without waking my family. I have not told them of my work in the resistance. They know of course, but do not speak of it. War makes families do that. I do not speak of my love for Jean. What a village doesn't know it guesses. I don't care. I can't speak of who I am, so people guess. I let them, even when the guess is untrue.

I take the path beside the Templar house that was commandeered by the Germans. There's only one guard, and he is asleep. Out of sight of the house the track narrows. It is pitch black. Jean is betrayed by a tiny red dot which brightens momentarily. The smell of tobacco will betray us both. I take it from his mouth and crush it into the soft earth. Then I kiss him. We do not speak. We acknowledged our love and acted upon it. I am empowered. He takes my hand and leads me to the ambush point. We lie down. My heart is beating so loudly I'm sure he can hear. The night is cold, the earth damp. He pulls me towards him as I hoped he would. There is no German patrol. At one point we hear shots far away, here silence. He holds me closer. We must have fallen asleep. I am woken by the click of a pistol being cocked. Hunter becomes hunted. The boots are not German. Looking up I recognise their owner. With relief I whisper the name. "It's us, Jean and Francis, we were..."

"I know what you were doing. Regular little love birds aren't we?" The heavy Sud West accent is unmistakable. The noise is deafening as the pistol is discharged. I turn my face towards Jean's. It is not there. Most of it is splattered across mine. I barely have time to register this when there is a second crack.

Cambridge, England
Autumn 2020

In pride of place against the wall is an old damaged wooden box. It could easily be mistaken for an ammunition box. The condition suggests it is a relic of the Great War. The lid was removed to display the contents. Save one it contains all the elements of a concert 'cello. Instead of the polished rosewood body there is a crude pine box. Notwithstanding it is capable of producing a tune. It is a wedding present to Susan from her mother-in-law. Strictly speaking she is not Peter's mother. It is complicated. Everything about the Cartwright family is, let's say, unconventional. The sepia picture that accompanied the instrument shows French soldiers. The peaked caps and long coats identify the period. Wattle panels retain the walls of the trench in which they sit. The picture is posed to convey a reassuring message to relatives. Life is normal; the men are enjoying an impromptu concert before seeing off the Hun. Only one soldier in the photo returned. He died from his injuries soon after.

Peter props his bicycle against the railings outside the tiny terraced house, running his fingers through his hair to mitigate the effects of the helmet. His pale blue linen shirt is crumpled with darker patches under the arms and in the small of his back. It is a sunny autumn evening; he has left his jumper in his study. When cycling he was too hot; now the damp patches make him shiver. Automatically he locks his bike removing the saddle. His father never locks anything in Saint Etienne d'Isle. South West France and Cambridgeshire are different worlds. He compared the two buildings. In front of him was a tiny Victorian town house. The entire house could fit easily into his father's barn. The front garden is big enough for a bicycle or wheelie bin, but not both. Instead of opening the front door directly into the living room, Peter squeezes down a side alley into the back garden. It is as small as the house, but it at least provides somewhere private to sit outside. Susan is indoors. The early autumn sunshine has gone. It is getting chilly. She has to be careful these days. Her long hair is tied back loosely. She wears a stretch fabric string top under a pale pink knitted cardigan. It no longer reaches the top of her trousers. This leaves a small band of naked flesh which Peter finds irresistible.

Erwin jumps on to her lap where he perches precariously. He kneads the swollen stomach hoping for a second supper. Susan needs to pee. She holds Erwin's paw absentmindedly, moving the tablet to one side so she can continue reading. Tail erect Erwin places his anus centimetres from Susan's face blocking her view of the tablet. Not unkindly she places him on the floor so she can go to the loo. The bathroom was built in the fifties as a ground floor extension. It takes space the garden cannot afford. It is however a vast improvement on the privy at the bottom of the garden. The advantage of a downstairs bathroom is that there are two bedrooms upstairs. The second is Susan's music room. Peter would like it for his study. He gave it willingly to Susan. He likes giving her things. His latest gift kicks her bladder. Her call of nature becomes an imperative. The greeting Peter was looking forward to is delayed. She plants a quick kiss on his lips before pushing past him. "Sorry, I'm desperate." As soon as she can she continues through the open door. "Your cat is asking to be fed." She doesn't mean to sound cross. She doesn't mind cats.

She comes back into the living room drying her hands. Peter picks up the tablet. She smiles at him. "Sorry about that, now I can say hello properly." She puts her arms round his neck and pulls him as close as the baby allows.

"What are you reading?" he asks when he can speak again.

"Your thesis, I don't understand it but I've marked up a few grammatical errors. The formulae you will have to get one of your fellow geeks to check."

"I could explain it to you."

"It would send me to sleep."

"After supper then. Did you get a chance to do anything?"

"There's tabouleh in the fridge, and our own lettuce and tomatoes."

"Shall we eat in the garden?" He asks.

"It's getting a bit cold, that's why I came in."

"We'll eat on our laps then."

"Peter, I don't have a lap any more. I'll lay the table." They are both trying to avoid this fall back option as the dining room table doubles as Peter's desk. She balances the books on an already overstocked bookshelf. He will complain that she had moved his stuff but she doesn't care, he should have tidied it himself.

After supper Peter's contribution is to take the plates to the kitchen. "Shall I explain my thesis to you now?" He asks.

Susan laughs. "You like explaining things don't you?"

Peter looks hurt. "What's wrong with that? I'm a lecturer. It's my job. Besides, if I can explain it to you I will be able to explain it to undergraduates."

Now it is Susan's turn to look hurt. "That's not fair. You didn't understand my thesis."

"You explained it to me and then I did."

Susan laughs. "Now you sound like Winnie the Pooh!"

"And what's wrong with that?"

Susan hugs him. "Nothing at all. I'll do my 'cello practice then you can explain all you want."

Peter loves it when she plays. The notes feed the emotional side of his brain while he exercises the logical side. "I'll check my emails while you practice."

Peter searches for something in the pile of papers Susan moved to the window sill before supper. Fauré's first 'cello sonata floats down from a bygone age. Peter remembers this being played at his aunt's wedding. Then he knew who had played it whilst Susan did not. They were sitting together at the long table under the balcony. It may have been why she had chosen to learn the 'cello. She was certainly affected by the piece. Others at the wedding feast were more impressed by the girl in period costume who mysteriously appeared to perform. Susan wondered at the time why she had not joined the wedding party after playing.

Susan comes downstairs. "That was beautiful." Peter congratulated her.

"It's getting harder to play."

Peter is puzzled. "I thought practicing was supposed to make it easier."

"It does. It is being pregnant that makes it harder. I have to hold the instrument so far in front of me my arms are not long enough!"

Peter laughs. He closes the laptop and sits beside her. "Story?"

She smiles. "You can't wait to be a dad can you? Will you read Pooh stories to our child like your dad did to you?"

"Of course."

"I'll read too" said Susan. "You only seemed to have one story when you were little. I want our baby to be different."

Peter nods. It is a fair point. Susan lies on her back with her head on his lap. "Now tell me my story" she smiles.

"Don't you want me to explain my thesis?"

"The Cartwright phenomenon? No Peter, not tonight. Tell me again the story of how you came to live in France."

Chapter 2
The Accident
February 2007
Dordogne

"It was spring half term. Mum had seen a house online. She was waxing lyrical about it. Looking back I think the enthusiasm was a bit forced."

"Why do you think that?" Susan had heard the story many times. It reminded her of her father's bedtime stories. Notwithstanding her familiarity with the story she thought it only polite to ask such questions. At the very least it proved she was still awake.

"Why do I think she overdid the enthusiasm? Because of Stuart. None of us knew then what we know now. She wanted to show she was not just going along with dad's plan, but that she embraced it. I don't think she did, I think dad had finally got fed up with mum having the best of both worlds. He wanted her to make a choice between him and her boyfriend. Moving to France forced the choice." Susan didn't ask any more questions. She let him tell the story. Soon her rhythmic breathing showed she was sleeping.

13 years earlier

Father and son drove from Reading to Southampton and took the overnight ferry. John was not sure his own car would make such a long journey. They parked at Southampton and collected a hire car in Caen. This meant taking public transport from the docks at Ouistrehem. It was already nearly midday when they started their journey in earnest. The damp, rich fields clung possessively to the overnight mists. With a ten-year-old navigator John advanced through the Normandy forests to Alençon and then Le Mans. John explained to his son that they were crossing the Loire valley towards Tours. Peter knew. He was learning about France at school. They were following the demarcation line between occupied France and Vichy France. Normandy orchards gave way to Loire vineyards. For Peter the novelty of explaining the history of France to his father wore off. The active decision to be bored sustained him from Poitiers to Angouleme, then he slept. At Angouleme John headed inland. He crossed the demarcation line towards Périgord Vert, chased by an incoming storm.

Peter's sleeping was soporific. John battled his own tiredness. He should have stopped. He was so nearly there. He lacked the fluency of French to concentrate on the talk radio stations. He flipped to a music channel. The music was not to his taste so he clicked off the radio and took a large gasp of air as he tried to ease his aching back. It could not be much further. The satnav assured him it would be ingratiatingly helpful as soon as it found a GPS signal.

SHIT!

A reflex act of self preservation jerked the steering wheel causing the car to lurch sideways. Nearby, in a reciprocal act a boar pushed with its good leg ensuring just enough of its body cleared this new adversary to suffer only a glancing blow to its haunch. This deflected him from his target bolthole sending him up the road to the next gap in the undergrowth. John had just time to register this before the car slid to a halt. The emergency braking was assisted by two offside wheels finding a ditch on the left.

Peter was suddenly wide awake. "Daddy, did you just say shit?" Clearly this was much more important than almost being killed. John restarted the engine. A few attempts at letting out the clutch and attempting to return all four wheels to the highway revealed that his problem might extend beyond justifying the use of Anglo-Saxon to a ten year old boy. He opened the door and negotiated the ditch. The result of the recent contretemps between car and boar had clearly favoured the former which showed only minor damage. The boar however was winning the mobility stakes. It was nowhere to be seen, the car, without help, was going nowhere.

Help, as luck would have it, was not far away. A brace of hunting dogs appeared closely followed by their owners driving an impossibly old Citroen van. A man emerged from the passenger side. "Putang con!" The curse, uttered in a heavy Sud Ouest accent was delivered amongst a stream of words spewed out in a mixture of French and Occitain. John caught the word "cochon" combined with much pointing, thankfully not at him. "Mon cousang va vous aider" The hunter jerked a thumb over his shoulder before following the dogs, cursing the beast that had not had the decency to die where it was shot. John found his sympathy lying with the boar that nearly killed him and not the cousin who was busy extracting his car from the ditch. The latter had already produced a rope which he was expertly tying to the cars. He had clearly done this before. Whilst his saviour was detaching the rope John asked for directions. He was only 10km from his destination. He quickly gave up trying to understand. He hoped that driving off in the direction the Frenchman was pointing would suffice. He did manage a "merci beaucoup" and a hand shake. Omitting this petite politesse when they met had almost prevented his rescue.

"I'm hungry." For a ten-year-old this could equally be "I'm bored". Eventually the novelty of tubes of crisps and sugar coated chocolate peanuts wore off, even if you were ten. Ideologically opposed to junk food at home, for some reason car journeys were subject to an amnesty. It was an exception of which Peter took full advantage. "They've all gone."

"Then you can't be hungry".

"Well I am." Yet again child logic trumped adult. Miraculously the GPS found a signal. It told them to turn into what looked like a field. By now John was past caring. Triumphantly the satnav announced "you have reached your destination" in a singsong voice. There were three houses. The most remote was to be their base for the next week's house hunting.

Reading, England

Cathy was at home, waiting for Stuart to finish work. She inhabited two worlds. For more than ten years she had been flipping between them. At first John did not know. When he did, he didn't mind. That was what Cathy told herself. Lately she started to suspect he did mind. She was looking at a photograph of the house she hoped John had gone to France to buy. The gable end was lit by the setting sun. The rustic stonework looked warm and safe, like a golden retriever sunbathing in the garden. An old roof undulated uncertainly over what was now a living room. Skylights had been added. Cathy guessed this was the master bedroom. Below the French windows were open. A wrought iron garden table and chairs gleamed white with fresh paint. A second part of the house stood behind the poised rustic elegance. Taller and narrower it pressed against the first. It reminded Cathy of a wedding photo. The groom pressed against his bride who had taken pride of place in the foreground. Cathy could not imagine how the tall part of the house interacted with the lower. The dignified, comfortably broad living room was her she decided; the tall gangly bit behind was John. Between the two a chimney escaped like a phallus from the lower roof continuing up the second gable end. Definitely John, she thought. The kitchen was another addition. Like Peter, it was added much later.

Cathy's daydreaming was interrupted. She heard nothing, feeling only a sudden drop of temperature. She shivered. It was the precise moment the boar struck the car in France. Fifteen years later Peter, now Professor Cartwright, tried to explain this to his wife. "Our world is governed by complex mathematical laws. These laws include an uncertainty element of which we are mostly unaware. We live predictable lives and minimise risk. That means we minimise the role of random events. The exception is during an accident. That is when matter behaves unpredictably. Dad and I could have been killed that night. Clearly we were not. The possibility of a different outcome was so likely it gave birth to a parallel universe. The one in which we died separated from the one in which we lived. When universes separate, those affected experience a similar dissonance." The Cathy who had just become a widow split from the one who had not. She described it as 'someone walking over her grave'.

Cathy shook off the thought; she had quite enough juggling her two worlds in this universe. Stuart would be here soon; she went upstairs to get ready. She no longer gave much thought to her behaviour. As a child she had been stripped of all morality. Had she thought about it she would simply say it was payback. Now she was an adult she no longer had to please her father so she pleased herself.

Dordogne

The part of the house John could see in the car headlights bore no resemblance to Cathy's picture. He had phoned to warn the owner they would be very late. Unimaginatively she left the key under the mat. With the two adjacent houses empty and the nearest village 5km away it would have made little difference if she had not bothered to lock at all. John's only thought was to get Peter indoors and into bed. He fell asleep directly after claiming he was hungry. He woke when the car stopped but was not letting on. Experience taught him that feigning sleep would mean Daddy would carry him indoors. This saved him the effort of waking properly and walking.

This proved more difficult than usual. The stairs were so narrow that even without a ten-year-old boy in his arms John had problems. At one point the headroom was so low he had to resort to all fours. This house was built for jockeys, not rugby players. Peter decided, for his own safety, to wake up and was first to the bedroom. He stood smiling beneath a mop of hair. He was wearing his favourite Mario Brothers tee shirt over new denim jeans, several sizes too large. His toes peeped from the hem. "Which bed is mine?" Before John could answer he was struck on the forehead with such force it almost sent him back down the stairs. He entered the room gingerly, fumbling on the wall for a light switch. His assailant was poised to repeat the punishment if necessary. The beam was barely four feet off the floor. Peter found it extremely funny, John considerably less so. He pointed to the single bed under the eaves. At least by the bed in the middle of the room John could stand, once he had negotiated the man trap. The suitcase was still in the car. "No teeth, straight to bed". This was a rare privilege that Peter exploited with glee. He quickly stripped and slid between the sheets. "Story?"

"Of course, Winnie the Pooh?"

"Of course." Peter thought for a moment. "When will I be too old for Winnie the Pooh?"

"Never. Nobody is ever too old for Pooh"

Meanwhile in Berkshire Stuart arrived immediately after Cathy's 'turn'. It was an expression she had learned from her grandmother, it made her sound quaintly old fashioned. "You just heard my car without realising it. You have some daft ideas sometimes." That was the nearest Stuart got to sympathy. He had plans for this evening. He lost no time putting them into action.

Back in the Dordogne parenting duties complete, John pulled his mobile from his pocket. At first he hesitated in phoning Cathy at this late hour then realised he was an hour ahead of her. She would still be awake and would be wondering why he hadn't phoned. He wondered how much to say about the accident, and what she would later learn from Peter. "Hello?" The voice sounded thin and distant. "Did I wake you?"

Before she could say 'no' a slight noise in the background answered the question. John's stomach churned. "We've only just got in, I'm shattered. I'll call again in the morning." He hung up. Carefully he placed the phone on the bedside table, a sense of intense fatigue overwhelming him. Kicking off his shoes he lay on the bed. Drawing strength from the sight of a sleeping ten-year-old boy he closed his eyes and became a child himself. The last thing he heard was his mother's words. "Go to sleep now, you'll feel better in the morning."

Peter's breathing drifted into his dreams, joined by a rustle of leaves that heralded the rain. The steady drumming of rain gave way to the rhythmic swish of wipers and the soporific whine of a car engine. A sudden crash and Chabal, in a French blue rugby shirt glared through the window. John instinctively clutched the ball to his chest. A whistle blew. The Beast shook hands and thanked John for the game. Now he was in his local. Tree weaved through the crowd holding three beers and a cider above the heads of the post-match crowd. John and Horse took their pints. Ferret pulled a face and removed the kebab skewer from his cider. What's this? Tree grinned. Sorry, didn't you want the olive? The three forwards never missed an opportunity to take the piss out of a scrum half. Drinking with the pack was by appointment. John and Tree played second row. The latter's nickname an unimaginative reference to his height. Horse was a prop. His nickname was obvious once you had showered with him. When he had a bad game, which was most weeks, he was downgraded to Donkey. John was known as OM ever since his Buddhist beliefs were discovered. Today he was not up to the usual rugby banter.

"What's up OM?" asked the ever perceptive Ferret

"Woman problems"

"Women's problems? I didn't know you were a back, you on the blob?" Tree laughed at his own joke.

"John, she's not worth it" Horse entered the man-counselling session with all the subtlety you would expect from a prop.

"Yea, you can do better than that" added Tree, sobered by the lack of response to his vulgarity. Ferret finished eating the olive before adding "Can't see what she sees in him." This was typical of John's rugby mates, high on support, low on advice. It is remarkable that men who are perfectly happy to shower together find it so difficult to undress emotionally. John pushed them out of his dream.

He slept as long as possible to blunt the numbing depression of waking reality. He met Cathy at the University Buddhist society. Fresh from an all-girl's school with no boyfriend she was every male student's wet dream. John fell in love and grabbed her before anyone else had the chance. Following the Buddhist philosophy they both became vegetarian and learned meditation. He regarded himself and Cathy as two souls created as one when the Universe was created. It never occurred to him that she might not feel the same, or that he might be wrong. They married as soon as they graduated. The only cloud on the horizon was children. It took a long time for Cathy's biological clock to wake Peter.

Chapter 3
House hunting

John woke, briefly hoping he was mistaken about the phone call last night. In his heart he knew he was not. He had no desire to call again and reopen the wound. In times of trouble such as this he felt his mother beside him. Now she had temporarily passed from this world she was freer to be with him in his time of need. "Everything happens for a reason" she said. Raising a family on her own was not easy. For most people the swinging 60's were nothing more than a musical revolution. In the shires divorcees were still reviled; she had to be strong. It mattered not that her husband had been unfaithful; in those days you put up with it and kept your vows. Not mum, she made her children her world filling them with simple truisms. She had been wrong about feeling better in the morning. Was she wrong about everything happening for a reason? In his heart he knew she was not, he just did not know the reason. If he was being honest she was right about the feeling better bit too. He hadn't killed Peter by falling asleep at the wheel. He had managed to get them safely to the holiday cottage. The overnight rain had stopped and the sun was out. Turning over he looked at Peter. Watching his son sleeping always brought him peace, lightening his darkest thoughts. The bed was empty.

Stooping to avoid the beam that attacked him last night he negotiated the stairs. Whatever other issues he had with Cathy he was going to have to tell her that her dream home was a nightmare. Peter was sitting at the table. He had fetched the laptop from the car. "What's the Wi-Fi code?"

"Good morning Peter, how are you?"

"Good morning dad, how are you, what's the Wi-Fi code?"

"I've no idea, have you looked in the book on the table?"

"What book?"

"There's always a book in holiday homes. It tells you stuff like that." Peter grabbed the book before John had a chance to open it. He flicked past emergency telephone numbers, fuse boxes and how not to get scalded in the shower. Eventually he found what he was looking for. "I'm in, thanks dad."

John picked up the book and found directions to the nearest bakery. "I'm going to get bread and croissants, I won't be long."

"Can I have your card?"

"No."

"Why not?"

"Because you will use it to buy power-ups."

"But dad, I'm stuck on this level"

"Tough."

"It's not fair"

"Life's not fair." He had played his end of discussion card. John picked up the car keys and turned to go.

"Pain au chocolat, I don't like croissants" Peter's eyes never left the screen.

"Magic word?"

"Please."

There was a small group of children waiting silently in the lay-by opposite the baker. They moved respectfully to one side as he approached. English school kids would have glared defiantly, daring him to run them over. He got out of the car, practicing his "bonjour" as he did so. He felt as if he had stepped into a time warp. One of the girls had pigtails and a leather satchel with double shoulder straps. John smiled and crossed the road.

The village bakery had been in the Mason family for three generations. Their son and daughter showed little interest in continuing the family tradition. Her daughter studied music, first in Bordeaux, now Florence. Her son studied economics and moved to Paris. Mr Mason was good at what he did but he had been doing it too long. The hours were long; they were both past retirement age. With children uninterested in baking, the options were sell or close. The shop did not make enough money to sell. Closing would mark another milestone in the decline of a rural village. The children waiting for the bus were already too few to maintain a school. Without bread there would be no shop. With no shop what few families that remained would move elsewhere.

"Bonjour" Mme Mason smiled. Winters were hard in an area that relied on tourism. She was smartly dressed in a clean apron with her long, slightly thinning hair tied back in a bun. Her husband emerged from the back of the shop, his low toque concealing a bald head. He dropped an armful of baguettes into a basket and returned without a word. Customer relations were his wife's department.

"Bonjour, il fait beau aujourd'hui." John's rehearsed greeting resulted in what appeared to be a description of the weather in these parts since Napoleon last visited. This was followed by a detailed prediction for the coming week. He hoped that concluded the niceties and he could now buy something. "Deux croissants et deux pain au chocolat s'il vous plait"

Mme Mason placed them in a bag "Voilà, deux croissants et deux chocolatines"

"Excusez moi?"

She pointed to the baguettes then to a bar of chocolate. "Pain, chocolat. Ici on dit chocolatine" she beamed at him. For a moment John wondered if she was joking. He decided she was not.

"Ah, bon. Er, une baguette s'il vous plaît, et une..."
He squinted at the label on the round loaf behind her
head. "Une boule, er..." He made chopping gestures with
his hand.

"Tranché ? Bien sûr". She ran the loaf through a
machine that made the whole shop shake. It was clearly a
family heirloom. "Avec ça ?"

"Excusez moi?"

"Do you buy something more?"

"Oh no, er non, merci"

"Sept cinquante s'il vous plaît. Seven and fifty
please" He handed her a note, picked up his purchases,
put them down to take the change and picked them up
again.

"You want a poche?"

"A pocket?"

"Une poche, a small sac"

"Oh no, I'm fine, ah, non merci. Au revoir"

"Au revoir monsieur." She held up her hand in a
gesture to wait. "Vous êtes, you are staying at...?"

"Oh, er, La Brusse." He pointed up the road.

"Ah Mrs Jones. You buy?"

"Maybe, probably not, it is a bit..."

"Expensive? Yes, she thinks she is in England"

"No, well yes, that too. No, it is too..." He pointed
to the bruise on his forehead.

"Mon dieu! Yes I see, you are too big for the house!" She beckoned him back with a conspiratorial wave before lowering her voice. "It was not well done. She used foreign builders. Jean-louis would have done it much better. She is selling because she has a boyfriend and has moved in with him. He is married, but his wife has gone away. C'est la vie."

"Yes. Thank you, goodbye, er, merci, au revoir." John stumbled out of the shop. He had given Mme Mason just enough gossip to last till lunchtime.

The morning ritual of coffee and croissants was completed. In Peter's case it was chocolate milk and chocolatine. John had to decide what to do. Proceed as planned he concluded. He put last night down to fatigue, and a delayed reaction to the accident. He did not believe he was wrong about the phone call, he simply told himself he was overreacting. Cathy had agreed to move to France to rekindle their marriage. Maybe she had called Stuart to say goodbye. That was unlikely but he decided to press ahead with their plans anyway. He did not know what else to do.

John lined up a string of estate agents, one for each day, leaving a day free at the end for second visits. He had spent so much time recently drowning in a whirlpool of emotions he revelled in the structural certainty of his plan. Peter, now he had the Wi-Fi would quite happily have stayed behind. Dad put his foot down. This was going to be Peter's home too; he had to say what he liked about each house and make his own check list. "It's got to have a swimming pool"

"It won't have a swimming pool"

"Why not?"

"It would be too expensive"

"This one has a swimming pool"

"Have you seen it?"

"No, let's go and look." They eventually found it behind a hedge. It was an above ground pool slightly larger than a hot tub. They missed it at first because the surrounding grass had grown taller than the pool.

"OK, but it must have a trampoline."

"You already have a trampoline."

"It's in England."

"Then we will bring it with us."

"Can we do that?"

"Of course"

"Cool"

House hunting was a bit like internet dating. Each house ticked most of the boxes, but you knew as soon as you met it was not going to work. As soon as he parked outside the first house he knew it was a non starter. The barn was enormous. Peter was fascinated by the huge wine fermenting vat. There was no garden, the land, now left fallow, started at the back door. It had once been planted with vines. Either they became diseased or the owner became too old to keep up the labour intensive tasks involved with small scale viniculture. Wine growing was no longer commercially viable due to competition from the Bordeaux and Bergerac regions. John only asked out of politeness. The main road, the lack of front garden, the quarry lorries, all condemned this one before he opened the door.

Most properties he was offered were marked "a rafraîchir". It was the French equivalent of needs redecorating. It was also estate agent code for "total wreck, needs complete gutting." After a few visits John knew the signs. If the roof was leaking the chances were that rain had rotted structural timbers. The other thing to look for was saltpetre. These stone buildings were built without foundations or damp courses. If natural chemicals were leeching out of the stone it meant it was often damp. In a predominantly dry climate this spelt trouble as there may be a high water table or underground spring.

Peter didn't like any of the houses, seeing them as they were, not what could be made of them. When John asked which he preferred he picked one that had already been renovated. John hated it. They eventually found one that backed on to a river. The village was pretty. The house wasn't the wreck most of them were. As a trade off it was smaller than the others. Plenty big enough but still, it is all relative. The agent left them to find their own way home. This took them past a paper mill less than a kilometre from the house. Questions about flooding and the factory knocked the house off the 5 star rating.

They soon reached the last day of new viewings. Thursday was sightseeing, then Friday for second viewings. Thiviers is a little market town north of most of the tourist attractions. There is no "beauty spot" premium and the surrounding villages offer good value. The agent, given the brief of a house in the country had prepared a selection of isolated houses and barn conversions. Peter was outside, looking in the window. "What about this one?" It was within their price range so John asked for it to be added to the list. As much as anything it was to acknowledge Peter finally becoming engaged in the process. The other houses rolled by in quick succession. For once the agent thought she would get home on time. They drove back via Saint Etienne d'Isle to see the extra house. "It's not in the country like you asked, it is bang in the middle of the village" explained the agent. To John a village of 50 inhabitants was the country but he wasn't going to argue.

They parked in Place de l'Eglise. As John got out of the car a tiny movement just caught the periphery of his vision. Before he could turn his head it was gone. The building in front of him was familiar. Every life that anyone ever lived exists somewhere outside time. To those experiencing them within a temporal frame this includes those that had not yet happened. John was not remembering being here before; he was remembering being here in the future. The agent misinterpreted his silence. "Well that's it; if you don't want to look inside I can drop you back at your car. We can pop in to the office now or tomorrow if you want to get back." She meant because I want to get back.

John woke as if from a dream. "No, I want to see inside, shall we go round the back?"

"Oh, yes of course. Jump in, I'll drive you to the back entrance."

"No you go; I'll go down the passage by the barn and in the side gate. I'll meet you by the back door."

The agent was taken aback. They were sole agents. "Has someone else shown you this house?"

"Not exactly"

The front dated from la belle epoch before the Great War. It was quite ostentatious, with a balcony. The wrought iron balustrade featured the initials of some long forgotten owner. They had presumably been musical as along with their monogram were representations of musical instruments. On the other hand the back was an old farm house. The original stone steps to the back door had a smithy sign incorporated into the stonework. On the anvil was carved 1733. He didn't need to, but John let the agent show them round. As he entered each room he hesitated. Sometimes he walked past a door that he would stop using. At other times he nearly walked into a wall where there would later be a door. The bedroom opened on to the balcony. Whilst most of the rest of the house was heavy with the weight of history, this room was light and fragrant. It was as if someone had left a vase of fresh jasmine and lavender on the mantelpiece. There was a movement on the balcony. The martinets had not yet returned. Something else took flight the instant they entered. John opened the French window. To his left was another that took him back into an as yet unexplored part of the house. Otherwise the balcony was completely empty.

John turned back into the room, trying to identify the fragrance. He was going to be happy here; happier than he had ever been. That vanquished the demons that were following him. He was not sensing Cathy's presence but his own contentment. Surely that meant she would move with him to France and they would again be happy together.

Chapter 4
The house

John could not get the house in St Etienne out of his head. He did not articulate the idea of a future memory, but had someone asked he would have compared it to meeting Cathy. He just saw it as love at first sight. Today was their day off from house hunting. Tomorrow was set aside for second visits. John would have paid the asking price yesterday just to be allowed to stay. His sensible side said play it cool or you will finish up paying too much. It was true that it was overpriced compared to the others he had viewed. He also knew that old houses were money pits. He expected to pay at least as much again for the renovation.

He took another gulp of coffee. "Peter, today is your day, what do you want to do?"

Peter was already multitasking eating, drinking and playing computer games. He added to the list by talking with his mouth full. "Finif fif evel"

"Don't talk with your mouth full. I didn't understand any of that, and look at me when I talk to you."

Peter tried to sigh. He found he couldn't with so much food in his mouth. He took another swig of chocolate to wash down the croissant. He had finished both his chocolatines and pinched one of dad's croissants. To comply with the third part of the request he paused the game. This better be important. "Finish this level". He delivered his answer with a tone of exasperation ten-year-olds reserve for parents incapable of understanding basic child needs.

Not an option. Look outside. The sun was shining. Even in the microclimate of the Dordogne, Mother Nature hunkered down for winter. In the last few days she woke, shaking off a light dusting of snow. Summoning the sun she took advantage of the fast lengthening days to remind us that spring was just around the corner. The cranes answered the same call. They were on their long trip from North Africa to northern Europe. John spotted them on his way to get croissants. Circling like lost souls, they honked mournfully. Peter finally detached himself from his task of assisting the Mario brothers in their quest to rescue the hapless princess. "What's that noise?"

"Cranes"

"It sounds like birds."

"Cranes are birds, come and look." The birds were still circling as if unsure which way to go. Eventually one broke away. The honking grew to a crescendo as the others fell in line. In a perfect V they tracked across a clear blue sky towards the horizon.

"Why do they do that?"

"Well, most birds, like people find it easier to follow than lead."

"They took a long time to find a leader; I don't think any of them wanted the job."

"I think you are right. It is hard work at the front. You need to know where you are going."

"They looked like cyclists at the start of a race where everyone is trying to get someone else to go first."

"That's exactly what it's like. What do you want to do today?"

"Go canoeing!"

"I think it's too early in the season, you would get wet and be really cold."

"I'm never cold." It was true. Peter and Greg were best mates. They were both football mad. They often played street football after school. Even in January in the rain Peter only wore a T-shirt. When finally Greg gave up and went home Peter would come in, ball under his arm and a huge grin on his face.

John was not to be swayed. "You may not feel the cold, but I do. Anyway the canoeing doesn't start till Easter. What about Villars?"

"What's that?"

"There's a grotto there"

"I'm too old for Father Christmas. Anyway it's February, he will have gone home."

"It's not Santa's grotto, it's a cave where people lived in prehistoric times."

"Like Lasco? You said we went there when I was tiny"

"Yes, but Villars is smaller. There are stalactites."

"And pictures?"

"I think so."

"Ok, we'll go there."

"Great, I just need to pop in at the estate agent on the way

"But you said today was my day!"

"It is but this won't take long." They parked in the church square. Peter waited outside. He was disappointed there was no water in the fountain. Then he found the tap by the church door worked. Thiviers is on a pilgrim's route. The tap was there for the benefit of travellers. Today it served to wet a ten-year-old child and annoy his father.

"I don't think the seller will accept that offer. He has already reduced the asking price. Also there is someone else interested." He reduced the price on the advice of the agent. At the old price they failed to secure a single viewing in two years. The house had lain empty for some time before that. Now the roof was starting to leak. John did not believe there was another buyer.

"Can you ask? I might be able to go a little higher. It would depend on the survey, and quotes for the remedial work."

"I will say your offer is on the basis you will need to replace the roof. If that is not necessary then you may be able to go higher." The agent picked up the phone and had a brief conversation in French. "He has agreed to your offer if he can keep the land at the back."

John knew exactly why. With the rear access to the land the seller could build another house at the back. It would be one of those little modern bungalows loved by the French and loathed by the Ex-pats. "Absolutely not!"

"He owns the house next door which he rents. He says that the access to that house is over the land he would be selling."

"I don't mind moving the boundary so the common access road is on the smaller property. The rest of the land stays."

Another phone call. "He will think about it."

John felt he was winning this one. He guessed the owner knew the survey would show a new roof was needed. He did not know that the Mayor was requiring the owner to replace the roof. If he failed to do so he faced a compulsory purchase at a fraction of John's offer. "I leave on Saturday, my offer stands until then."

Back in the square he found Peter soaking wet. "How did you get so wet?"

"Water."

"I can see that. What were you doing?"

"Putting my hand over the tap to see how far I could squirt it."

"I can't leave you for five minutes..."

"What can I say? I'm a kid."

"Let's go."

"Can I have an ice cream?"

"What?"

"Over there, it says Glaces de Vaunac. Glaces means ice cream"

"It is February; I doubt they will be open."

"They are; I saw the lady."

They crossed the road and went inside. The logo on the glass was a boater and moustache in silhouette. Ariane looked up. "Hello, come in." It took John a second to register she had greeted them in English. Peter spotted it straight away.

"How did you know we were English?"

"It was a lucky guess. No, I'm joking. I heard you talking outside."

"Are you English?" asked John.

"No, I'm Belgian, my husband is English. Ah here he is!" Chris walked in. No boater, but he did have a large Edwardian moustache. "There, do you see the picture on the glass?" she pointed first to the logo then to Chris. Peter could not have looked more surprised if

Colonel Sanders had walked into a KFC. John laughed. "I'll have a coffee please, Americano. Peter, what do you want?"

"Do you do milkshakes?"

"Sorry no, but we do have hot chocolate."

"Ooh yes"

John whispered: "Magic word"

"Yes please. Do you have ice creams?"

"Yes, in little pots. In the summer we do cones too. In winter its pancakes and waffles."

"Ooh daddy, can I have a pancake?"

"Not if we are going to get to Villars in time for the English tour. We'll come back tomorrow."

"There would have been time if you hadn't spent so much time in the estate agents"

"Are you buying a house?"

"Yes in Saint Etienne."

"It's very old" chipped in Peter. "I bet loads of people died there".

"If you are interested in the local history, talk to Francine in the library she runs the Société patrimoine. It is a society that researches old buildings."

"Thank you I'll bear that in mind. Look we need to go, Peter, drink your chocolate. We will need to eat after; can you eat at the grotto?"

"I don't think so. There is a pizza place near the bridge as you go into Villars but I don't know the opening times. There is also a restaurant behind the church but again you would need to check."

"Thank you"

"If you are coming back this way we are open till seven. We do savoury pancakes too."

"We might do that. Come on Peter, we need to go."

"What about my ice cream?"

John sighed. "Did you say you do pots to take away?"

"Yes, they are in the freezer, do you want to choose Peter?"

"How did she know my name? Oh yes, she heard you say it!"

John sighed. "Hurry up and choose Peter!"

"How did you know my name? Oh yes, you're my dad!"

"You're asking for a clip round the ear, back to the car!"

"Thank you, enjoy your visit."

"Thank you; we will probably see you later."

The caves felt cold after the spring sunshine. Especially if all you were wearing was a still-damp T-shirt. Not that Peter was about to admit it. He refused to bring a jumper. John noticed the goose bumps and said nothing. When Peter started to shiver John took off his own jumper and gave it to him. Now it was John's turn to shiver. Peter trailed along behind. The jumper reached below his knees. The sleeves fell way below his hands. He looked exactly like Dopey from Snow White.

The guide explained this was a wet cave. Peter muttered "No shit Sherlock" and got a kick from his dad for his trouble.

"Unlike Lasco" continued the guide, pretending not to hear. "This means the cave paintings have been covered over the centuries by a thin coating of calcite. This protects them from the kind of damage that forced the original Lasco caves to close. When you see our pictures you are looking at the actual picture painted by someone over seventeen thousand years ago." She paused for effect. Lasco may be the big brother of French caves, but in this at least her family's grotto in Villars had the advantage.

"And finally, if you look up, you can see the chimney. That is where the water comes in. It is where the original caving club members descended on ropes in 1953. My grandmother, Marie Claire Ferres was in the party. Every year at Christmas, the local children gather and Father Christmas himself comes down the chimney."

"There you are" said Peter. "I told you it was Santa's grotto!"

Back out in the sunshine Peter warmed up by running round the gardens. John finally got his jumper back. Peter explored the reconstruction of a prehistoric settlement and practiced throwing spears at stuffed animals. John thought about the house. He could not explain the déjà vu. Would Cathy feel the same? He did not want to think about what Cathy might be doing right now. She had loved France when they came here eight years ago. He was banking on that - and the house. He hoped she would be blown away by it just as he had been. For years what she wanted was what he wanted. He assumed the converse was true. Lately that was not guaranteed. One day he would be forced to face reality. Today he still believed their souls could not be separated, even by death. The first salvo attacking his unassailable belief came when college friends Sandy and Al were splitting up. Friends were sure it would be Sandy and Al who stayed the course. John they said would soon wake up to Cathy's roving eye. They were wrong. Cathy wandered off but always came back. John was always there waiting for her. Sandi and Al moved to York. Neither couple had much idea what was happening with the other's relationship. It was easier to just assume things were as they had always been.

The split came as a surprise to John. When he told Cathy he said "It is wonderful to think that can never happen to us." It was an uncalculated remark he uttered simply because that was how he felt.

"Can't it?"

What is said cannot be unsaid. Her reply was just as uncalculated and so the more devastating because that was how she felt. If there is a road back it is a long one. He must find it for the road forward leads to the abyss.

"I'm hungry; can we go back to the ice cream shop for pancakes?" Once again Peter had rescued him from his dark thoughts. Living proof that what he and Cathy had was worthwhile and that worth fighting for.

Back home He decided to bite the bullet. He checked the clock and factored in the time difference. She would be home from work. "Hi Cathy"

"Christ, John, I thought you had died!"

"No such luck."

"That's a horrible thing to say, I'm missing you"

"Are you?"

"Please don't start that again, I'm really looking forward to moving to France."

"Are you?"

"For fucks sake John, I said don't start. You know I've always wanted to live in France, you know what I am giving up to be with you and Peter." She didn't say the name.

"I'm sorry Cathy, I love you."

"I know you do." When did 'I love you', 'I love you too' become 'I love you', 'I know you do'? He pushed the question away, she had said don't go there.

"Look Cat, I can't spend too much time, these roaming charges will end up costing me more than the house. Basically this gite is a non starter" He explained the architectural shortcomings of his interim pied a terre.

"That's a shame; it's your fault for being so tall! Did you look round Rock Gageac?"

Why was everything always his fault? He let it pass; he would only get another 'for fucks sake don't start again'. Also she was right, he could be over sensitive. "No the prices are way higher down there. You get far more for your money north of Perigeux."

"That's Perigord Vert isn't it, where the national park is?"

"Yes, but Saint Etienne is before you get to the park."

"Hold on, you're losing me. What is Saint Etienne?"

"It's the village where I bought the house."

"Christ, you don't hang about do you?" The first time she said that was on their first date. It had been a token resistance. Her voice had not changed in twenty years. He was still speaking to that young girl from the eighties.

"I haven't actually bought it. I saw it yesterday. It was Peter that spotted it in the window. Anyway, it's just perfect. I called back today to say we were interested and arrange a second viewing." He left out the bit about making an offer.

"Is Peter enjoying the trip?"

"Having a great time, we went to a grotto today. He wanted to go canoeing but they don't open before Easter."

"What's he doing now?"

"You have one guess." He held the phone out. Mario had found a good rock and was jumping up and down releasing a shower of gold coins. The repeated kerchings were clearly audible.

Cathy laughed. "I've bought him Mario in space. They've just released it. Put him on." John held the phone to Peter's ear.

"Hi mum."

"Hello sweetheart, are you having a nice time?"

"Yeah."

"What have you been doing?"

"Looking at houses. Dad bought a really old one. I bet it's got ghosts and secret passages and stuff."

"Lovely, I look forward to seeing it."

"Oh and Dad smashed up the car."

"WHAT?"

"I'll pass you back." Peter shrugged the phoned away

"It's ok, a boar ran in front of the car on the way down. The car got stuck in a ditch; a local farmer pulled us out."

"He said you smashed it up. Are you both ok?"

"We're fine. There's a bit of damage but I took out the excess waiver cover."

"That was lucky."

"Yes. Look, I better go. I'll see you Sunday. Love you."

"Love you too. Bye." She was gone, but she had said it. John told himself everything was going to be ok.

"Time for bed big fella. Don't forget your teeth."

"Just finishing the level."

Normality was returning to the Cartwright family.

Chapter 5
Buying

John woke feeling refreshed. For a long time he had a plan, but no route map to show him the way forward. Now he had clear objectives. Today at least, he felt Cathy was on board. After a quick breakfast he bundled Peter into the car. He had an appointment with the agent at ten but there was something he wanted to do first.

"Hello! Did you enjoy your trip to Villars?" It was still early, Ariane was just opening the shop.

"Yes thank you. Remind me the name of the lady who knows the history of houses."

"Francine from the Library. She should be there now."

"Pancake daddy!"

"I'm afraid they will be five minutes, the hot plate is still warming up."

John hesitated. "Can I ask you a favour? I'm in a hurry and I'd like to get to the library before I meet the estate agent."

"Do you want to leave Peter here to wait for the pancake?"

"Do you mind? That would be so kind."

"Not at all. See you later."

John went into the Library. The man behind the counter redoubled the attention he was giving the computer in order to avoid eye contact. The lady looked up immediately. "Bonjour monsieur."

"Bonjour, do you speak English?"

"A little, how can I help you?"

"I am looking for Francine."

"I am Francine."

"Wonderful, the lady at the ice cream shop said you knew a lot about old houses."

"Ariane? She is too kind. I am interested in the history of buildings, yes. It is my passion. You can say that?"

"Absolutely." John missed the sparkle in her eye as she said it.

"I am interested in a house in Saint Etienne. It's on the village square."

"Place de l'Eglise? That would be Mr Leclerc's house. It is a very important building." She noticed John's surprise. "Important for the village that is. Mr

Leclerc was the Mayor. There have been many Mayors in his family, Father, uncle, grandfather... They are I would say a dynaste"

"Dynasty, yes, I understand, I am visiting today. I was hoping you could tell me something about the house."

"Visiting? You are very lucky. The Leclerc family do not like people to go into their house. It is almost as if they have secrets."

"I would like to buy it."

"Buy? That is very lucky, for you and for Saint Etienne."

"How so? I don't understand. Why is it lucky for the village?"

"Nobody wants a ruined house in the middle of the village. Nobody will want to live in such a place."

"Can you tell me what I should be looking for?"

"That depends on what you want to find. If you want me to tell you if it will fall down I am not an expert. I can say parts were standing before the revolution. I expect they will still be standing when you and I are dead. If you want me to say which parts are original and which are new I will have to look. As I say, I have never been inside."

"If you want to look inside I can take you. I have an appointment with the agent in fifteen minutes."

"Sadly, as you see, I am working. I can come in my lunch break."

"Thank you. I will ask the agent if I can keep the keys and return them in the afternoon"

"It is I who should thank you. A tout a l'heure. See you later Mr…"

"John."

"Mr John"

"No, Mr Cartwright. But please call me John"

Ariane had given Peter two pancakes but only charged John for one. The agent was on a visit but had left the keys with the assistant. Everyone was happy. John could spend as long as he wanted at the house. Peter had a full stomach. Francine had the chance to look inside the house she had always wondered about. Also, she added as an afterthought, Mr Cartwright seemed like a nice person.

For a region where nothing was ever locked, the bunch of keys was enormous. Many were antiques but a fair few were cheap modern ones. The Leclerc family spent money to buy quality if it saved them money in the long term otherwise they bought as cheaply as possible. John was confused by the labels on the keys. It became easier when he remembered 'volet' meant shutter. Until you had unlocked the shutter you could not get at the door behind. He eventually got into a part of the house the agent had not shown him. He was in the tiniest kitchen imaginable. The floor was tiled; an enamel sink with one tap was set into the thickness of the wall. There was a gash along one wall where there had once been a solid fuel cooker.

Peter pushed past him. In front of them was the tiniest staircase imaginable. It was flanked by two doors. One led to a stinking toilet. The other was a room of similar size to the kitchen but with rotted parquet flooring. "I'm going up the stairs"

"Be careful, the may be rotten like the sitting room."

Eventually he returned. "There are two rooms upstairs like this. Above that is a loft. It is all tiny. On the outside it looks huge."

"Were there no doors leading anywhere else?"

"No, that's it. I'm calling it Sidrat"

"Why?"

"Tardis backwards. It's bigger on the outside than the inside".

John laughed wondering, not for the first time, at the imagination of his son.

Outside he facade started with the barn. It had a huge door rising two floors in height. The wood, as old as the barn itself, was bleached white by the sun of innumerable summers. Beside it was the tiny door they had just entered, followed by an equally small shuttered door. "That must go into the living room" said Peter.

"Yes I saw French windows on the inside."

"Because we are in France"

"Stop it, you are too clever by half"

"Sorry, which half would you like to be less clever?" Peter ducked to avoid John's raised arm which came down to hug him. "I love you Peter."

"Love you too dad. What's behind those big newer looking doors then?"

"That must be the garage. I've got a key, let's see if it works."

Inside the garage was as big as the kitchen was small. It could easily accommodate two family cars, but only if you cleared out all the ancient machinery and stored timber. A stone arch led into a workshop as big as the garage. It housed an enormous bright red boiler beside an even bigger plastic fuel tank. The pair sat, uncomfortable in their 20th century pedigree compared to the antiquity that surrounded them. To the right was another room. From the coolness and the earth floor they knew they were in the cellar. The shelves were packed floor to ceiling. Not just wine, bottled fruit of every description. Ancient labels long since eaten by snails left you guessing the jars' original contents. Leaving the cellar they found another door that presumably led to the back garden. It was locked. "There may be a key but I can't find it in the dark. Maybe I can open it from the outside."

They returned to the square just in time to hear a car pull up. Peter was impressed. If you fitted new suspension and oversized wheels it could compete in a monster truck rally. He was even more astonished at the tiny figure that climbed down from the cab. "Bonjour Francine!" John strode forward hand extended. He was learning to commence every encounter with a hand shake if not a kiss. Francine was in the habit of using the second form of greeting if it was not a total stranger. On this occasion she made an exception and took the outstretched hand. The English had a reputation for coldness although she could not believe that of John. "This is my son Peter. Peter, say hello to Francine, she has come to tell us all about the house."

Peter took his cue from his dad and held out his hand. "Enchanté."

"Oo la la, tu parles Français!"

"No, he is just showing off."

"Comme même if you come to live in France you will soon speak like me" She took a scroll from under her arm. "I have brought a map. It may answer some of your questions."

She unrolled the map. "You can see the front of the house is very new."

"It looks pretty old to me." John silenced Peter with a glance.

"I agree, but compared to the back it is new. It is 'm'a tu vu?' bourgeoise. I don't know how you say it in English"

"Posh." suggested Peter.

"Posh? What a strange word."

"Yes, it means Port Out Starboard Home."

"That's enough Peter, stop showing off."

"That's alright, il est mignon. Anyway this map shows the village square before the new front was built. The church is here of course. Where those houses are now, that was the cemetery."

John looked puzzled. "You said those houses were built on the graveyard. That is the end with the steeple. On this map the steeple is near my house."

"It is because the steeple fell down. It was in 1911"

Peter interrupted. "That's the year the new façade was built."

"How do you know that Peter?" His father thought he was showing off again.

"Because there is a date carved over the front door."

The adults looked at the door, then at Peter. "Well spotted Peter. Maybe one day you will be a detective" Francine fumbled in her bag. "I have photos of the old steeple. It was much shorter. When it fell they wanted to replace it with a bigger one."

"Why?"

"It had to be bigger than the church in the next village."

"I still don't see why."

"Because the priest was a man. Every man wants his penis to be bigger than the next man. If you are a priest your church steeple is your penis" Peter's eyes were like saucers. He had never heard a woman talk about penises in such a matter of fact way.

"That still doesn't explain why the steeple was put back on the wrong end."

"The mayor ordered it."

"The mayor ordered the priest to put the steeple on the wrong end?"

"Exact."

"How can he do that? France is Catholic, the Church would never allow it."

"John, France is not Catholic, it is, how do you say? Laic? Secular I think is the word. In fact even before the revolution, parts of France were Protestant and parts Catholic. There were wars. Bergerac was Protestant and Perigeux Catholic. Have you not read Cyrano de Bergerac?"

"No."

"You should. It is a beautiful love story, but very sad. I think love stories should be sad no?"

"No, I think they should be happy"

"You cannot have light without darkness, or happiness without sorrow. He was unhappy because he could not tell of his feelings to the woman he loved. At the end she finds out but now she is old and he is dying. Is that not beautiful?"

"No, that is sad."

Peter had had enough of this love nonsense. "Why did the Mayor want the steeple on the wrong end?"

"Because if they put a taller steeple on in the same place and it fell again, it would fall on the house."

"Is that more important than the church having its steeple in the right place?"
"It is if it is your house!"

They all laughed. "Now you can see other buildings here. That low building was a bakery."

"The village is very small, was it worth having a bakery?" John asked.

"It was very important. After the revolution it was the law that every village must have a bakery."

Peter piped up. "That's because the people were starving. When they complained to the King they had no bread his girlfriend said so what, they can eat cake instead. We learned about it in school. Then we went to see a musical called Les Miserables. They were miserable because they had no food."

"They teach that in English schools? I am impressed, first Rostand and now Victor Hugo. I came to talk about buildings and here we are discussing French literature!"

"I don't mind." John nearly added 'I love listening to your French accent' but stopped himself. He didn't want her to think he was flirting.

"You see the path beside the barn? It goes to the public well. The well is important in Saint Etienne. The story is that the Saint was visiting the village and stopped to bless the villagers. A young girl was not paying attention. The other women scolded her mother.

To this she replied 'my daughter cannot hear because she is deaf'. The Saint heard and called the mother to him. He baptised the child with the water from the well. Some of the water went into the child's ear and the child was cured. After that many people came to be cured of deafness" Peter was sceptical but said nothing.

"Can we go to the back of the house, I would like to look at the old building?"

"Of course." John led the way.

Francine pointed out parts of the ivy covered boundary wall: a beam socket here, a bricked up door there. "The wall is actually the back wall of a line of outhouses facing in towards the farm yard. You can check this by digging. I am sure you will find river stones or bedrock. That is more likely near the house as old houses were built directly on bedrock if possible." She found the well in the corner of the farm yard. Entering the back door to the barn Francine was excited to find the original stalls for four cows and space above for storing hay. Beyond the farm yard was a small outbuilding that was still standing. "That would be for the pigs" she said. Peter asked if the field behind the pigsty was where the cows grazed. "No, it was close to the house so more likely to be a vegetable garden." She pointed to a molehill. "Do you see how dark the earth is? That is because it has been cultivated for hundreds of years." She pointed to a clump of brambles. "Have a look over there, but be careful, I think it may be a second well."

"How can you tell?" asked Peter

"Can you see there is a well in your neighbour's garden? Imagine a line from that one to yours in the corner of the farmyard. If you carry that line more or less straight you come to that patch of brambles. It is my guess that is the line of an underground river. The second well would be to irrigate the vegetable garden."

"You think there are underground rivers here?"

"I know so, the water from Saint Etienne's well flows for less than a hundred meters before disappearing."

"So there may be caves like in Villars?" asked Peter.

"Who knows? The Dordogne is full of caves"

"Can I show you inside?" Irrationally John was bringing Francine's attention back to him.

"I am sorry John but my lunch break finished twenty minutes ago. I really have to get back to work."

"Another time. One way or another I am going to buy this house. When I do I would like to invite you back to look at it properly."

"That would be wonderful. Thank you so much. It was a pleasure to meet you and your son. I am sorry I have to go."

"I quite understand. Thank you for your help. Good bye"

"Au revoir"

Chapter 6
Homecoming

After Francine left Peter and John went into the house. "She seems nice." John looked at his son. He was not fishing, nor stirring. He was still in that age of innocence when 'She seems nice' means exactly that, no more, no less.

"Yes." The response was intended in the same spirit.

"Cool car."

"Yes."

"Is that all you've got to say for yourself?" Sometimes Peter sounded exactly like his mother.

John focussed. "Sorry, I was thinking about the house.

"That's cool too, in an old kind of way."

They had mounted the stone steps and were in another kitchen. It was much bigger than the first. In the eighteenth century this would have been an entire dwelling, although not some poor peasant hovel. The animals were lodged separately. The tenants boasted their own well, four cows, two pigs and a dozen chickens, not to mention a substantial vegetable plot. Even shared with the neighbour it would have ranked, by today's standards, as middle class. Opposite the church, next to the baker it would have been seen as a desirable residence.

Over the past century even more amenities were added: electricity, running water and, thanks to Monsieur Leclerc, drains. The mayor made it his mission to put Saint Etienne on the sewage map. He built a septic tank big enough for twenty houses. He then ran pipes from every house. Now was there were over thirty houses connected, with predictable consequences. His tenant occupied the tiny kitchen they first entered. Her two up, two down dwelling was encased by her landlord's larger property. He constructed toilets for both dwellings borrowing space from the largely redundant barn. His own even boasted a wash basin and rudimentary shower. Thus it was that in their dotage both of them were spared the inconvenience of trekking outside to the privy built on the end of the pig sty. In his latter years the landlord spared himself the inconvenience of going outside at all. He moved his bed into the kitchen and the chickens into the shower cubicle. Thus he ended his days much as his ancestors had done over two hundred years previously, in the single room in which John and Peter now stood.

Originally two farm dwellings the adjacent room became an enormous living room over the workshop.

From here you passed through original external walls almost a metre thick to an equally large bedroom over the garage. "You and mummy can have that bedroom; I can have one in the little house." This made sense, except to get to the rest of the house Peter would have to go down the tiny staircase, out the front door, round the barn, up the back steps and into the kitchen. Clearly there were alterations needed.

"There's another door there" said Peter pointing to the end of the living room. Behind it was an unlit staircase that went to the loft. The extent of the roof damage was now clear. In two places you could see daylight. Watermarks stained the floorboards below, some of which were starting to rot. If it was re-tiled they would save the building from irreparable damage. In the loft the entire history of the family was stored. Magazines from the twenties; school exercise books filled with immaculate copper plate handwriting.

"If only Francine had more time, she would have a field day up here." John almost said 'orgasm' but remembered who he was talking to. He looked at his watch. "It's late; we need to get the keys back before the office closes. Come on Peter." His son was having almost as much fun as Francine would have had. So far he had found a stuffed hawk, a ceremonial spear, a tricolor, and an ancient rifle. "Peter, put that down NOW!"

"Can I keep it?"

"Certainly not!" Reluctantly Peter returned to the car. Tomorrow they would be going back to England.

On the return journey John's mobile rang. "Can you get that Peter?"

"Cartwight residence, gentleman of the house speaking" said Peter in his best Hyacinth Bouquet voice.

"Tell them to hold there is a lay by here, I'll pull in."

"Putting you through now..."

"Sorry about that... really? That is good news... No, the roof definitely will need replacing, I was up in the loft yesterday... Monday? No, that's not possible, I'm on the way to the ferry now...Next weekend will be the earliest but it is rather inconvenient...Well if it is a condition of acceptance I suppose I will have to...Both of us? I need to speak to my wife...Why does it have to be a Monday?...The solicitor? I don't have one yet...His solicitor will act for both of us? Shouldn't we have our own?... Yes I know this is France...What will we be signing?... Hang on, let me right that down. Peter, there's a pen in the glove compartment... compromis de vente. Do we have to pay a deposit?... 10% on signing, balance in six months ... I'm not intending to change my mind...Ok, but then it would be 10%... Can he change his mind?... Only if we don't pay in full within the six months...No that is not a problem...Not in the bank as we speak. It's an inheritance, it is with probate at the moment... No I'm sure it will be through before then. Can we start work straight away, the roof is urgent?...Yes I know it is at my own risk...As long as you are sure he can't pull out. I wouldn't want to put a new roof on his house so he could put the price up and sell it to someone else…Ok that's reassuring. What about access?... Ok, I'll speak to him about it, but you don't think it will be a problem?... No of course… Well thank you, and thank you for letting me know. Goodbye."

"What was that about?"

"We've just bought a house."

"Does mummy know?"

"Not yet."

"I'll call her."

"No, let me do that." The rest of the journey passed without incident. He didn't call, preferring to wait and talk face to face where he could gauge the temperature of the water. They pulled in to the drive and Cathy came to the door. Peter rushed up to her. "Mummy, daddy bought a house!"

Cathy shot John a look. "I heard he found one he liked."

"No, he bought it. The man phoned on the way back."

Cathy again looked at John. "Put the kettle on darling," he replied "I'm shattered"

Peter was happily reunited with his games console; his parents sat on the settee, mugs of tea in hand. She had considered opening the conversation with 'I can't believe you bought a house without me seeing it.' Instead she simply said "Tell me about the house". Despite John's suspicions she genuinely wanted this experiment to work. She knew being confrontational would send the opposite message. He went on endlessly about the region, the village, the house. She found her attention wandering. Did she genuinely want this experiment to work? Sometimes with Stuart she wondered. 'God it's a mess' was how she described it to Julie from HR when they were playing 'women wot lunch'. She had come full circle to the 'make it work' spot. 'Do I love him?' was not a question she could answer whether she applied it to John or Stuart. The answer was 'yes' in both cases. Nearly a week ago Stuart was still in the shower when Peter came on the phone and blurted out about the car accident. Her stomach churned at the thought that they might have been killed. She was wrestling with the idea of living without Stuart. She couldn't conceive of living without John and Peter. "There's your answer" said Julie. And there it was. The answer was that the only certainty was that she loved Peter. He and John were inseparable. She could no more tear him away from his father than she could countenance living without her son. She said as much to Stuart.

"He wouldn't be without a father, he would have me."

"It wouldn't be the same." She replied. So there it was, they were that clichéd couple staying together for the sake of the children. All this time John had been babbling about the house. She looked at him. He was like her favourite vinyl record that she kept a deck especially so she could play. Old, scratched, familiar. 'Yes you old bugger, I do love you' she thought. "Hang on, next Monday?" She realised that she had been listening all along.

"I'm afraid so. It's a condition of acceptance."

"But I'm working."

"Don't you have any holidays you could take?"

"Well yes, but that's not the point."

"What is the point?"

"I feel rushed. Yes I know I said we would do it, we don't need to go over all that again. It's not you, although I've never seen you like this before."

"Like what?"

"Like this. You've talked non-stop for half an hour. I couldn't get a word in edgeways. But like I said, it's not you, it's the seller. The place has been empty for years, why is he suddenly in such a rush?"

"I don't know, he has been trying to sell for years. Maybe he thinks now he has a bite it needs to be reeled in quickly."

"That made me think you offered too much."

"Not at all. He had already knocked a big chunk off to get it moving. I offered much less than that, and lowered the offer again to take in the cost of a new roof."

"Something happened."

"What do you mean?"

"Something happened to make him desperate to sell now. He didn't get to be as rich as he seems by making poor financial judgements. We need to find out what it is."

"We may never know."

"We will know, or we don't sign." Cathy had stopped dithering. She was going to go for this. She still had no idea why John wanted this house and no other. She was going to find out why the seller was in such a hurry. "When is the appointment with the Notary?"

"10 am. The agency just texted me."

"On a Sunday? They must want their commission. Change it to 4"

"Why?"

"I want to speak to the current Mayor first"

"Why do you want to speak to the Mayor?"

"Because he will know what's going on. French Mayors know everything."

"So do you it seems."

"I do, it's part of the job description." Cathy was PA to the MD of a FT100 company. That was not the job to which she was referring. She meant the job of being married to John.

"Then you will know that there is no point in phoning either the Mayor's office or the solicitor on a Sunday. Why don't we swap these teas for a glass of bubbly to celebrate our new life?"

"Over supper. Do you have any ideas?"

One of the many strange things about their relationship was that Cathy never cooked. 'Her turn' meant picking up a take away on the way home.

"I'll think of something. I bought a bottle on the boat. What have you got in the cupboard?"

"Not much."
"I'll have a look and pop down to the supermarket" This was something he would have to get used to when they moved. No more 24 hour out-of-town superstores.

"Aren't we forgetting something?"

"What?"

"Peter. He will be at school."

"We will just have to keep him out"

"We can't. I had a letter from the school. New government policy, they are cracking down on truancy. No days off without a doctor's certificate."

"Bloody Tony Blair, he's worse than the Tories."

"It'll be Brown soon. He's just trying to help. Anyway, let's not start on politics. We need someone to look after Peter. I don't need to remind you we have recently run out of grannies. That is how you got this money to buy a house in France."

"What about your sister?"

"She lives in Stratford John. The whole point is that Peter has to go to school."

"Couldn't she take time off?"

"I'm not even going to ask. She has just started a new job, besides she has a new girlfriend" The relevance of this was left unanswered. "I could ask Stuart."

"What?"

"He said if ever we needed to spend time together he would look after Peter. Stuart could sleep here, get Peter to school, and still get to work. He works flexi-time so could pick him up too." The irony of her lover helping John and his wife spend time together was not lost on John. Cathy also seemed to know a lot about Stuart's ability to get time off at odd times.

"I'm not sure…"

"I'll give him a call."

John got up. "I'll see what's in the cupboard for supper." He didn't want to be within earshot while she talked to him. She was right. There was bugger all in the fridge. He waited awkwardly then went back to the living room. "There's not much in the way of food, I'll pop to the supermarket."

"OK pet, Stuart said yes to the babysitting."

"I'm not a baby" Peter piped in proving he had been listening. It was a parental control thing that the games console stayed in the living room. If it was in his bedroom Peter was quite capable of borrowing an adult game from a friend who had a big brother.

Cathy corrected herself. "Stuart said yes to looking after Peter"

"I want to come with you"

"I'm sorry darling but you can't, you have school."

"I don't want to go to school."

"It's football on Mondays"

"Oh yes, have you washed my kit?"

"It's on the bed"

"Thanks mum"

"You're welcome. Speaking of bed it is time to go up."

"I'm hungry." Standard delaying tactic.

"Go and get ready and I'll make you a sandwich" Standard riposte.

"Chocolate spread."

"Cheese."

"Triangles"

"We don't have any, I'll do cheddar."

"Don't like cheddar."

"I'll toast it."

"Thanks mum."

John was putting his coat on. "See, you do cook."

"Yeah right. I even managed spaghetti once."

"In a tin."

"Cheeky bugger." Cathy went over and kissed him.

"Eugh! Get a room!"

"You, bath. I want you in your pyjamas by the time I get back or there's no story."

"It's not bath night."

"It most certainly is, there was no bath in the gite"

Cathy joined in. "I thought he was a bit smelly."

"Hormones are kicking in. See you later".

Peter was in bed. The meal was finished and the Cleremont almost empty. John looked at his wife. "I missed you."

"I missed you too. No, don't look like that, I honestly did."

"I'm glad. Well, you know what I mean."

"I know exactly what you mean. I'll go and wash." That was code, and John knew exactly what that meant too. They were definitely going to need a room. The dishes could wait till morning.

Chapter 7
The Mayor

Stuart arrived exactly on time, impeccably dressed, charm personified. Everything was carefully crafted to inspire confidence. At university John found it difficult not to like him. Tree and Horse had no problem.

"I can't stand the bloke" affirmed Horse, replacing bloke with a vulgarity reserved by forwards for the backs.

"Too right" chipped in Tree "Typical wendyball player" a disparaging reference to soccer.

"Nah he'd never get his kit off in front of the lads," continued Horse "he's more interested in them getting their kit off in front of him."

"Oo-er missus. Don't drop the soap!"

There was a knock at the door. As usual Peter got there first "Hello Peter. I've got a present for you."

Peter's natural dislike of the man was overruled by the bribe. "What is it?"

"Guess" Stuart handed him a small parcel.

"CD?"

"No"

"Video game?" He asked, more in hope than expectation.

"Open it."

"Wow! Mario in space! Thank you!"

Cathy took John on one side "That was going to be my present."

"Have you already bought it?"

"No, it's not out yet, I pre-ordered it."

"So how did he get it now?"

"God knows, probably a knock-off"

"Stu, I've asked you not to buy him presents"

"Think of it as an early Easter present"

"Well thank you, it is very kind." Cathy felt as if the gratitude had been wrested from her.

John looked at his watch. "Cathy we need to go."

"Ok. Stu, you know the routine?"

"8 O'clock bath, then story and bed."

"9 O'Clock" Peter tried to correct him

"School nights are 8. Tomorrow school for 9 and pick up at 3.30"

"Yes. If you drop him Tuesday we will be back to pick him up."

"Understood. You concentrate on having a lovely time and don't worry about Peter."

Stuart was apparently cooperating in the rapprochement of his mistress and her husband. John would didn't know he was being cuckolded until his wife hadn't confessed. They left, John feeling like he was watching a magician. He'd seen the trick but couldn't work out how it worked. Cathy had not even understood it was a trick.

The plan was to stay at the airport hotel, take the first flight out, pick up a hire car and drive straight to the appointment with the mayor. After they would then see the Solicitor, stay overnight and take a late morning flight back Tuesday in time to pick up Peter from school. "We'd better get an early night" said John having run through the itinery with her. Cathy was not happy having to get two days off at short notice but something else was bothering her. She slid into bed. "It's the first time he's had to sleep without one of us being there."

"That's not true. He stayed with mum our anniversary weekend."

"That's different, she was family. I hope Peter can cope with staying with a stranger."

"Stuart is hardly a stranger." He knew instantly he had said the wrong thing.

"Please don't start."

"Cathy, I'm sorry, I didn't mean it like that."

"I know." In a rare moment of reconciliation she added "It must be hard for you too."

John moved closer. She allowed him to spoon her. He slid his hand over her breast. "Sorry, John, I'm not in the mood."

Dordogne

They were late for their appointment with the Mayor. She did not seem in the least bothered. Nor was she anything other than welcoming. A retired teacher of English she had no problems communicating and appreciated their attempts to speak French. She regarded it as a great compliment that the wanted to move to her village. "I always find foreigners much more enterprising than the locals" John said later this was more to do with the locals staying close to their place of birth than any superiority of the immigrants.

Cathy cut to the chase. "We were wondering why Mr Leclerc is suddenly so anxious to sell. Is there a problem we don't know about?"

"I don't know what you don't know. There are problems, certainly." Cathy shot John her 'told you so' look. "The main problem is the roof."

"It is starting to leak, yes we know. I made allowances for that when I made my offer."

"May I ask how much?" John looked at Cathy who gave the slightest of nods before turning to the Mayor. When she heard, she inclined her head slightly. "Quand même. It is much more than our offer."

John could not conceal his astonishment. "So there was another buyer! I thought the agent was bluffing."

"Bluffing?"

"Pretending there was someone else to get us to make up our minds."

"Ah I see. But the commune is not, how should I say, in a fight with you. We are delighted you are buying Mr Leclerc's house."

"So why did you make an offer?"

"It was not, as you say, an offer. It was more like an order."

Cathy worked it out before John. "You were making a compulsory purchase order?"

The mayor paused. "Yes, I think that is how you say it in English"

John still hadn't understood. "Why would you want to knock it down?" In his experience council compulsory purchases were when the building was in the way of something, like a bypass.

"We do not want to knock it down. We want to save it from falling down."

"Like the church steeple." He had lost Cathy again.

"Ah you heard about the steeple." John wanted to ask about this but he let it pass. "Once the roof falls in a house quickly becomes derelict. Monsieur Leclerc's house is not a *monument historique* but it is important to our village. The commune decided to purchase the property and convert it into apartments to rent."

"Like gites?"

"No, these would be for local people to rent."

"That sounds like a good idea. Why did Mr Leclerc not agree?"

"Shall we just say that our offer as you call it is considerably less than yours?"

"So we are paying too much?"

The mayor thought for a while. "I would say that your offer is fair. It is almost but not quite a bargain. Mr Leclerc does not give bargains, he receives them."

Cathy worked it out long before John. "That means the offer from the commune is not fair?"

"Fair? We are the government. If what we did was fair your taxes would be much higher."

John touched Cathy's knee to stop her getting into a political argument. "Thank you. I take it that you are happy if we buy the house."

"Delighted."

"And you do not think we are paying too much."

"Exact."

John was convinced, Cathy not quite. "Is there anything else about the house we should know?"

"As I said I do not know what you know. I can say that there are a great many things about the house that you don't know. None of them are I think things that should stop you from buying it." She paused before adding: "Let me say this as a friend and future neighbour, not as the mayor. I am delighted you have chosen to live here. I think you will be happy. Now, you must excuse me." She stood up signalling that the meeting had ended.

"Thank you very much Madame?"

"Guichot"

"Madame Guichot. You have been most helpful."

"Je vous en prie. Bonne journée."

John took Cathy's hand as they left. "Are you feeling happier about buying it now?"

"Financially yes, although it is not my call, it is your mother's money. Don't forget I haven't even seen it yet."

"It's right in front of you."

"What that?"

"Yes."

"All of it?

"Yep, from the barn, all the way to that letter box."

"Bloody hell! Our whole house in Reading would fit inside the barn alone and cost four times as much. How many bedrooms are there?"

"One.

"You have to be joking."

"Nope. See the balcony? The French window there is the bedroom."

"What about the other one?"

"That's in a separate dwelling that comes with the house. We could make it into Peter's room but we would need to knock through to connect it up. The window near the barn is another room we could make into a bathroom."

"Doesn't it have a bathroom?"

"Not really. There is a toilet and shower off the kitchen at the back. We could make that the utility room."

They didn't have the keys so Cathy had to make do with looking from the outside. She was having difficulty picturing herself living there but she hoped his enthusiasm would rub off. It was so totally different to their current life. The area was beautiful, that's why they came here on holiday. She wanted to have his good feeling about the move. It was after all she who was giving up the most. "We have a bit of time before the solicitor. Shall we go into Thiviers and find a hotel?"

"We could, or we could try and stay in the village. That house on the end says Chambres d'hôte". They knocked. There was no reply. John phoned the number on the sign. He was about to give up when there was a reply. John explained.

"J'arrive."

Cathy did her 'what's going on?' face. "I think she is coming to the door" he explained. They waited. Eventually an old lady answered.

"Je suis désolé, j'étais dans le jardin" Translation was unnecessary as she was holding secateurs and gardening gloves. Her lack of English was matched by an almost total lack of hearing, but they managed to explain that they wanted a room for one night. She ushered them in with expansive gestures. If the house they were buying was high on room size and low on number, this house was the opposite. She led her guests through a labyrinth with bobbing gestures reminiscent of Gollum at his most obsequious. Every available inch of wall space was covered with paintings, all the same artist. "Did you do these? Vous avez faites…" John shouted, gesturing brush strokes. She smiled and nodded. "Very good. Très bon." He lied, jerking his thumb upwards. Each room she showed them was identified by a colour, the word hand painted on the door. The room was faithful to the warning on the door. Walls, carpet, ceiling, furniture, accessories and of course, paintings were all the same colour.

After four or five viewings Cathy had had enough. "We will take the green room" she shouted hoping it would be the least likely to trigger a migraine.

"Nous prendrons le vert" John explained. He hoped that was right as he couldn't think of a mime. Cathy pushed past him back up the corridor and patted the door to make sure. Another series of mimes ensued. "We come back…" (circular motion with arm) "Supper" (eating gesture) "What time?" (pointing to his watch). Her face lit in comprehension before she started to shake her head vigorously and wave her arms.

"I'm guessing she doesn't do supper" observed Cathy.

Chapter 8
The notaire

They made sure they were on time for the solicitor.
She however shared the same relaxed attitude to
timekeeping as her compatriots. By leaving the waiting
room door open they could see her office. From her
occasional sorties they could see that she had no client
with her. The secretary clearly disapproving of such
underhand surveillance tactics closed the door. Cathy got
up and opened it again making fanning motions with her
hand to suggest it was for ventilation purposes. The
secretary gave up and went back to doing whatever
secretaries do when they have nothing to do. Eventually
they were shown in. After the exchange of formalities
the Notaire pointed out that she practiced French law,
not common law. She emphasised the word "common".
It was clear that she regarded Napoleonic law as far
superior. John wondered whether she would express
regret about the outcome of the battle of Waterloo. "I
represent Monsieur Leclerc."

Cathy objected. "We were told you would represent us." John had forgotten to explain this idiosyncrasy of French law.

"I will represent both parties, that is how it works in France."

"But how do we know you will represent our best interests?"

"Because I am a notaire, and I am fair."

"And if there is a dispute?"

"I will resolve it to the satisfaction of both my clients." Already there was a tone of 'don't tell me how to do my job' in her voice.

Cathy was about to launch into a defence of the British adversarial system when John touched her knee. "Do you have the documents?" John hoped he sounded conciliatory

The notaire moved them to the centre of her desk. "Of course. Monsieur Leclerc has already signed them. I understand this is a cash purchase." John nodded. "And the money derives from an inheritance? In that case I will need an attestation from the tribunal de succession. I am sorry I do not know how that is called in English."

"Probate court. Why do you need that?"

"It is to prevent money laundering." She hesitated and coughed; glancing up to check she had closed the door. "Speaking of funds, you will notice that the figure on the forms you are about to sign are not those which I understand you agreed with Monsieur Leclerc." Cathy sat up and craned her neck, trying to read the document upside down. The notaire turned the document for them to see.

"No, it is less, a lot less. What's going on, and what is that figure underneath?" John pointed at figure beside a note saying *'Taxe provinciale sur le transfert de propriété'*.

"You do not have to worry about that. Monsieur Leclerc must pay that from the figure above."

The penny dropped for Cathy. "He is declaring the lowest price he thinks he can get away with so he pays less tax! The wily old buzzard"

"Correct, but I do not understand the word buzzard."

"It's a kind of bird. I think in French it is chouette"

"Ah une chouette. Ok. That is not a word the French use when paying their taxes."

Cathy was lost again. "So how exactly will it work?"

The notaire coughed again. "On the day the funds are transferred Monsieur Cartwright must come here again. Monsieur Leclerc must be here too. After you have both signed I leave the room."

"Why?"

Cathy whispered "God John, you are so naïve"

"I will be fetching some wine to celebrate the transaction. I am sure you will have a 'gift' for Monsieur

Leclerc to thank him for selling his house to you. While I am looking for the wine it is customary for the vendor to verify that the gift, ahem, meets his expectations."

John looked at Cathy. She mouthed "I'll explain later."

"For now it is only necessary for you to add your signature below that of Monsieur Leclerc. You have three weeks to pay 10% and six months to pay the balance. As soon as I have received the deposit Monsieur Leclerc must take the house off the market."

"I will transfer when I get home, I do not have a bank account in Euros yet."

"I expected as much. Here are my firm's bank details and your own holding account number. Make sure you quote that in your transfer." John signed. The notaire was about to take the document back to witness.

"Don't I sign too?" asked Cathy

"If you wish, but it has no legal status except as a witness."

"What if I want to buy a house?"

"You can, if you are célibataire, or your husband is dead."

"And if not?"

"Then your husband buys the house and signs a document to say he gives you the legal right to live in it even if he dies."

"Jesus, who thought of that?"

"Napoleon. He was a good general, and he made good laws, but I think he was un peu misogyne."

"Do you have such a document?" John asked

"Yes, but it is not necessary as it is you who buys the house."

"I would like to give my wife the legal right to live in our house"

"As you wish. I will prepare it to sign when you return with Monsieur Leclerc. Is there anything else I can help you with?"

"Yes, the roof. We need to start work immediately as it already leaks."

"I am sure Monsieur Leclerc will have no objection once the deposit is paid. Madame?"

Cathy had raised a hand. "Can Monsieur Leclerc change is mind?"

"Not for six months. If you do not pay the balance in that time he can keep the deposit and look for another buyer."

"Can we change our minds?"

"Yes, but you lose the deposit."

"That seems fair to both sides" John always liked things to be fair.

"We aim to be fair to both sides, in fact we do not think of it as sides, maybe just a problem to which we must find a solution to suit all."

John stood up. "Thank you very much for your time"

"Je vous en pris. Au revoir" They shook hands and were escorted to the door where they were offered another hand shake.

Outside they were glad to be in the early spring air, although the sun was already dipping. John took his wife's arm. "Well, we have done it! What did you think?"

"I didn't like the bits about Napoleon, positively mediaeval. Are you sure women are allowed to vote?"

John ignored this historical inconsistency. "Yes it does seem a bit unfair on the woman, that's why I asked for that other document."

"Very generous. Did you get the bit about the brown paper envelope?"

"I do now. What if we don't produce the balance in cash?"

"I'm guessing the solicitor won't give us the deeds. She acts for both sides remember."

"Yes, odd that, seems to work though."

They were suddenly both hungry. Discovering that in rural France restaurants do not open Mondays in February they looked for a supermarket. It was about to close. Supper was bread, cheese, chocolate and crisps eaten on a green bed with a green bedcover surrounded by green paintings on green walls. Cathy was starting to regret her choice. The next morning they realised they had no idea when breakfast would be served. They had a fairly early flight and Limoges was a good hour away so they went looking for a dining room. Eventually they found a conservatory with a dining table set for two. It was clear they were the only guests. They were tempted to skip breakfast to make sure they were in time for the flight, however no lunch and a bread and cheese supper left them very hungry. There was no sign of their hostess; they had no idea what the bill would be. Eventually a car drew up and Nadine got out carrying bread and croissants. Seeing them in the conservatory she accelerated to a kind of amble and flustered in. She turned over the cups with one hand whilst waving a coffee carafe in the other.

"Tea please" said Cathy. Nadine poured coffee for John, and then almost poured it over Cathy's hand covering the cup. "Tea. Christ John, what is tea in French?"

"Thé I think." Nadine disappeared into the garden, returning with two sprigs of mint. Cathy looked aghast as the leaves were plunged into her cup and covered with warm water. They pointed to the bread. Their hostess nodded and cut two thick slices before fetching the butter. John remembered a phrase from his croissant expeditions. "Et avec ca?" Nadine first looked offended, and then forgave them their lack of manners, putting it down to their limited French. She gestured expansively to shelves that lined the conservatory. They were full with row upon row of home made jam. John resisted the temptation to joke about it being the conserve-atory. Aware of the time, but unsure when they would next eat, they hurried through a bewildering range of fruits. John regretted choosing cherry the moment he found out the stones had not been removed. Standing up and gulping the last of his coffee he spluttered "Christ, we have to go."

Cathy grabbed her credit card and went in search of Nadine who was loitering in the kitchen. She wrote a number on a piece of paper. Cathy offered her credit card. Nadine looked horrified and started waving her hands. "She doesn't take cards, do you have any cash?"

"No, I used it up in the supermarket last night." Nadine waved an illustrative bank note then a cheque. Cathy made jabbing motions with the credit card simulating a cash point.

Nadine looked relived. "Thiviers"

John looked at his watch, they would barely make the flight. "Cat, get the bags packed and outside, there is nothing else we can do." Eventually his car squealed back into the square.

Cathy grabbed the proffered 50€ note, thrust it into Nadine's hand and jumped into the car. "We're not going to make it."

"We have to make it" snapped John, adding a breathless hour later "go to the gate with tickets and passports. I'll drop the car and meet you there." An agonising ten minutes later John rushed into the terminal. Cathy was standing by the closed gate. The plane was already taxiing. She was crying.

John held her. "Don't panic we will sort out something."

"I'm not panicking, I'm crying. Help me John." Cathy was always in control, until she ran out of options. Then she became a child. They went to the information desk. There were no more flights to UK today. "Can we go from another airport?"

"The nearest is Bordeaux, do you have a car?"

"No, we have just returned it."

"Then you cannot get to Bordeaux today. Even by car it is nearly three hours."

Cathy was on the phone. "Stuart? We've missed our flight. Can you pick up Peter?...No, I've no idea at the moment. John is trying to sort something, but it's not looking good...Thank you so much...Love you. Bye" She instantly regretted the 'love you' bit. To be fair this was not John's fault. She acknowledged that the whole France thing was for her, because he loved her. She tried to love him, she really did. "I'm such a bitch. I don't deserve him. Then there is Stu, looking after our kid knowing that he is helping me dump him. I don't deserve him either. Oh Christ!"

John turned to see her crying. Misinterpreting the reasons he put his arms round her. "Don't worry my love, I've had an idea. Go to the cafeteria and get something to eat. I'll be back in a minute." A child once more she did as she was told. Exhausted she didn't even have the energy to ask John what his idea was.

John was back at the car hire desk. "Hello, I just returned a car. Can I hire it again?...Good. I would like to hire it for twenty four hours and leave it in Reading...Why can't I do that?... I know they drive on the left in England...Ok I suppose it makes sense...Can I leave it in Calais?... I'll do that then, but then I only need it till midnight...If that is the minimum 24 hours then." He went to look for Cathy. She was staring at an untouched Panini. "Grab the bag, where going."

"Where?"

"Home. Don't forget the sandwich"

"I can't eat it."

"Then I will. I'm starving." She followed him like a zombie. He explained his plan.

"What happens when we get to Calais?"

"We cross as foot passengers then get the train from Dover to Reading"

"Trains don't go to Reading from Dover."

"Via London."

"Oh, sorry, I'm not thinking straight. I love you."

"I love you too."

"John, I'm sorry about what I said to Stuart, it just slipped out."

"Can you just stop saying sorry?"

The combination of exhaustion and motorway driving meant that Cathy was soon fast asleep. John was wide awake. Alone with his thoughts he was aware that despite the crisis he was happy. Cathy had gone to pieces; he was her knight in shining armour. He was happy that she needed him. Without him fishing she had said she loved him. Just as important, they had bought the house.

Chapter 9
Home again

In Calais French lorry drivers had found something
new to complain about. Traffic was backed up onto the
motorway. They inched forward. Emotions were running
high; there were only two more sailings that night. The
cars in the holding area would fill at least three. Finally
they reached a gendarme directing traffic. Every other
driver paused to argue the case for special treatment. The
officer listened, shrugged and waved them on. John only
wanted to know if he was in the right queue. The
policeman moved a traffic cone and waved him into an
empty lane. Once rid of the car they trekked on foot
through car parks full of desperate looking people.
Emergency services were distributing space blankets and
coffee. Most were unpacking their cars in search of
warm clothes and rations of their own. Finally John and
Cathy reached a ticket office. They explained their
predicament and were directed elsewhere. Finally they
found someone to issue the tickets, but missed the ferry.
The next one was the last. On board John headed to

information to ask about their onward journey. There was no train or coach service after midnight. He relayed the information to Cathy. "Maybe we could hitch." Dutifully he took her suggestion and toured the tables. He returned empty handed.

"Why don't you try? The damsel in distress angle might work." Cathy wasn't so sure but felt she ought to do something. Anyway it was her turn. She returned two minutes later spitting feathers. "What happened?"

"Your damsel in distress idea worked too well. Second bloke I asked said yes. When I said I'd tell my husband he swore at me calling me a cock tease." John got up angrily. "John please don't. Enough has happened already today. I couldn't cope with you being beaten up by a sex starved trucker". John sat down. There was nothing to do but find a corner and get what rest they could. They finally reached London in broad daylight with the rush hour in full swing. Going against the flow they took the train to Reading and a taxi home. It was nine thirty when they let themselves in.

Peter rushed up to John and hugged him, then remembered he was angry. Cathy never quite coped with the hurt she felt when Peter, given the choice, picked his dad. "Why aren't you at school?"

Stuart emerged from the kitchen and answered for him. "I think he's a bit upset you didn't pick him up yesterday."

Cathy had done everything she could but guilt still washed over her. "Didn't you explain?

"Of course, I told him I would stay with him until you came back."

"I'm so sorry to put you out Stu" said Cathy "it was very kind of you."

"You're welcome, but I really need to get to work."

"Of course, and Peter you must go to school."

"I'll write you a note." Added John.

"I can drop him, it's on my way." Said Stuart.

"NO!"

They all turned to the boy. "Peter, that is very rude, say sorry." He glowered at them and said nothing.

"It's alright" said John softly. "I'll take him" That was when he remembered the car was still at the airport.

"I can do it." Insisted Stuart. Peter, banned from saying no, crossed his arms and glowered.

John struggled to find a compromise. "How about if Uncle Stuart takes both of us? It'll save me writing a note. I can pop into the office instead." Reluctantly Peter agreed, but not before pointing out he was not his real uncle. Cathy was just grateful he didn't say his mummy's boyfriend. She had enough to cope with them all in the same room. She wished her stomach didn't flip whenever she saw Stuart.

"How will you getting back darling?" The endearment was for Stuart's benefit, and an instruction to her stomach to get the right man if it wanted to flip.

It was easy to slip back into normal routines and forget they now owned a house in France. For Cathy these included Stuart. Whilst the French project was taking on a life of its own, John never lost sight of the fact that it was his way of removing Cathy from the influence of Stuart. To that end he insisted the three of them go back in the Easter holidays. He said it was so Cathy could have a proper look at the house. This time they rented a gîte in the next village having no desire renew his acquaintance with stone jam. At the Library John introduced Cathy to Francine.

"Watch her" Warned Cathy. "She fancies you."

John was genuinely surprised. "I'm old enough to be her father."

"Not quite, but she is a lot younger than you. Or me." She added. This annoyed John. Cathy of all people had no right to be jealous, especially as there was nothing to be jealous about.

John kept his promise to show Francine the inside of the house He invented an excuse about wanting her advice on the beams. Peter was more interested in canoeing so his mother took him to Brantôme. John and Francine were in the living room. "Yes, these beams are original. They would have been installed new."

John tried to look at the beams rather than Francine. "How do you know that?"

Older recycled timbers were shaped with an axe; the chop marks are clearly visible. By 1763 timber was sawn"

"Why 1763?"

"It's carved into the stone staircase outside."

John looked sheepish. He was finding it hard to concentrate. "Were there no derelict buildings to provide timber?"

"There are always derelict buildings in this part if France. During the 100 year war the English kept destroying them!" She had not meant to importune his ancestors so continued in a more conciliatory manner. "This room is too big. To find mediaeval beams this long you would have to go to Jumilhac." She noticed his blank look. "You have never been to Jumilhac? You must! It changed owners many times in the war."

"Hands." He corrected her

"Excuse me?"

"It changed hands many times"

"Oh, I see, thank you. My English is not good. You must correct me."

"Au contraire, it is excellent. But tell me about the beams." After Cathy's warning John was wary about straying from the strictly professional. He loved her accent. That was ok wasn't it?

"This beam was hand sawn. The tree was placed over a pit. One person was on the tree, the other downstairs. If the beam needed to be long as this one, they would swing it round. When they got to the middle they would start cutting from the other end. When they got almost to the middle again the two parts would split

apart. This left small triangle that was split not sawn"
Francine was looking carefully to find the tell-tale mark.
The ceilings were high and it was difficult for her. John
could easily have lifted her but Cathy's warning rang in
his ears. John with his height advantage found it. "Yes,
that's it, the very middle of the original beam. They did
not need to cut off much, this room is so wide."

In the loft there were even more beams for her to
get excited about. The personal items had been removed
so for now the most recent history remained hidden.
Francine pointed out that the beams were more modern.
They used metal bolts as well as the traditional wooden
pins for the joints.

"Does that mean the roof has been replaced?" John
asked.

"No, this roof is the same age as the front of the
house." They both fell silent. Francine gazed about her
as if trying to see through the superficial and unlock the
secrets of the past.

"Is everything ok?" Asked John

She looked up and smiled. "I think you will be
very happy here." In the silence that followed they both
realised they were alone. The house, happy to allow
these two to peek under her petticoats shyly retreated
allowing its two occupants some privacy.

"Cathy and Peter will be back soon. Thank you so
much for your time."

"It was a pleasure." Briefly the awkwardness returned hovering over the frail bridge between friends and strangers.

*

Finally in May probate released the funds and John went back to finalise the sale. This required a substantial cash payment. He felt like a criminal maxing out his daily cash withdrawal allowance and stashing the money in a suitcase. The bank froze his card because of 'unusual activity'. John called and said he was buying a car for cash. As they were near Blackburn market the bank accepted this perfectly reasonable explanation. Blackburn had regular auctions for the trade; John had even bought his last car there. Stuart had the idea then insisted on accompanying him. The regulars spotted a stranger immediately. At first they thought he was a narc. Stuart explained John was with him and was a rookie learning the ropes. "Don't let 'im bid, he'll push the prices up." They guessed Stuart had brought a punter along as a favour. John was fascinated by the collection of spivs and Dell boys. Stu was definitely the former. He was also amazed by the rolls of bank notes each was carrying. He whispered to Stuart. "Aren't they worried someone will rob them?"

"It would only happen once. Most of them are travellers - proper Romany, not your New Age hippy. They have their own way of dealing with stuff like that."

In early June John returned to complete the purchase. The roof had not even been started. One problem was not being on site. The other was actually finding tradesmen. After several attempts on the phone he gave up. He called in at the library to ask Francine. He almost imagined she was waiting for him. Greetings exchanged John got to the point. "I need your help."

"That is why I am here" for a second the silence that had engulfed them in the loft returned. I need to find a local roofer. Someone I can trust to do a good job without me being there to check. It is hard to organise these things from a distance."

"If he is local he will do a good job". This was not some form of civic pride. It was simply that a local tradesman had to do a good job if he wanted to work in the village again. "I will ask someone I know to give you a quote. But he will need to get inside the house to check the timbers." John said that was no problem. He explained about the Wellington boot. It was behind a watering can by the back door and was custodian of the keys when John was not there.

Next was the visit to the notary. Mr Leclerc was already there. In the chit chat before business he explained that there were still some items in the house He had not yet removed, but would do so over the coming weeks. He hoped John did not mind. John found he did mind. From today this was his house. He did not like the idea of the previous owner treating it otherwise. He said of course that it would be no problem. The formalities were quickly concluded. The notary did not leave the room. This made it difficult for John to judge when to present the briefcase. Eventually the notaire stood to offer an aperitif, the essential facilitator of all things in France. John produced the briefcase. Monsieur

Leclerc was far too polite to count the contents or even open it. He simply raised his glass. John had not intended his leather briefcase to be included in the 'gift'. He said nothing. He could buy another when he got home.

Chapter 10
School

Back in Berkshire it was parents evening. "Mrs Cartwright, please sir down. Peter isn't it?" The form teacher had her spreadsheet in front of her and a pile of folders to one side neatly arranged so the pupil name was visible on each. Since the change of head parents evening were run like secondary school events. No more popping in to see the class teacher after school, everything now had to be done by the book. The teacher looked over Cathy's shoulder. "Mr Cartwright?"

"He couldn't be here, business meeting." Mrs George smiled. The colourful palette of friendliness, sympathy, and disbelief smudged into a mask of indeterminate hue. Both parties wished they were elsewhere. Mr George, unsure when she would be home was cooking his wife a casserole. Stuart was babysitting at Cathy's house. She felt the need to be more specific. "John has gone to France to sign some documents. We are buying a house."

"Lovely, I wish I could afford a holiday home."

"Oh it's not, ... that is to say yes, ... for the moment, ... It needs a lot of work, ... we may relocate, ... I haven't decided yet." This was why parents' evenings always overran. Mrs George made a note before getting back to the matter in hand.

"Peter." Mrs George opened his file. "There is no doubting his ability, but lately he seems not to be trying his best." The end of year report contained lots of A+ for attainment and B's for effort. The art teacher's comment summed it up: Basically lazy. Cathy was not too bothered, bright children were often seen as lazy; they didn't need to work so hard. "The art teacher would like to have a word."

"The one who thinks my son is basically lazy?"

Mrs George blushed vicariously. "He has to write a report for every child in the school, that is why he keeps them short." She moved her papers nervously. "The school counsellor as well".

"Counsellor? What has he been saying?" Cathy's first thought was that Peter had been talking about her affair with Stuart. Mrs George understood it as 'what has the counsellor been saying'. "The counsellor is a lady. I'll let her explain."

"Mrs Cartwright, it is so good of you to spare the time. As practitioners we care about our service users. We understand the importance of the team around the child. This of course includes the birth family." Cathy stopped listening until the counsellor finally got round to "I have here a picture painted by Peter." For someone whose job was to listen she certainly liked the sound of her own voice. As part of the France project Peter had been asked to paint a picture of Les Miserables. It owed more to Munch than the French impressionists. Cathy was impressed. He had captured the helplessness of the peasant class depicted in Hugo's classic novel. "Mr Toni showed me the picture because he was concerned Peter may be trying to express some inner frustration or anger. Forgive me for asking, but is everything alright at home?"

Cathy snapped. "Fine. Perfect. Peter is gifted. The teacher asked him to paint a picture portraying the angst and hopelessness of the peasant class in revolutionary France and that is what he produced. If it looks like a horse and sounds like a horse that does not make it a fucking zebra. Stop looking for stuff that's not there just to justify your existence."

The therapist sat unmoved. They had been trained to deal with such situations. "We find it difficult to deal with your anger."

'We'? Is that the royal 'we'? Cathy stood up. "Really? That is strange because you haven't seen me angry." She stormed out.

She found Peter much as she had when they missed their flight. "Why does he have to be here?"

"Because you didn't want to come to parents evening and you are too young to be home alone."

"I could have gone to Greg's."

"They were at parents evening too, anyway Stuart offered first."

"He always offers first"

It was true. "Well he is going now so you can get ready for bed." Reluctantly Peter complied.

In a reflex reaction that characterises clandestine affairs Stuart moved to kiss Cathy as soon as they were alone. "Am I?"

"Are you what?"

"Going now? It's just that I didn't know when you would be back so I ordered a takeaway"

"Christ Stu, you don't miss a trick do you?"

"It was for me. If I was pulling a trick I would have ordered vegetarian."

Cathy sighed. "Where from?"

"The Raj."

She picked up her phone and added to the order, then turned to Stuart. "Ok we eat, and then you go ok? Honestly I'm not in the mood tonight."

Stuart held his hands up "Deal. Something is obviously bothering you, you can tell me while I eat my prawn vindaloo."

"That's it; you are definitely not staying the night!" In spite of her argument with the counsellor she felt better, and was actually glad he was staying, at least for a while. This was the problem, Stuart made her feel better. He was a good salesman; he knew how to sell himself. She had picked up a bottle of cheap wine on the way home, intending to get Peter in bed and get drunk. There's some plonk in the car, I'll go get it."

"Christ Cat, you don't miss a trick do you?" he mimicked her earlier barb. She stuck out her tongue and went to the car. Whilst she was out he fished out "their" song that she kept hidden at the back of her vinyl collection. When she returned, Olivia Newton John was declaring that she honestly loved him.

"Stu, please, I can't take it. I said I wasn't in the mood." She started crying. He stopped the record and came over to hug her."

"What do you want?" he whispered.

"I want to go to live in France with my son and husband. I want you to be happy for me, and to be happy yourself."

"That's a big ask"

"I know."

"Can we still be friends?"

The doorbell rang. Cathy answered it and returned with the takeaway. "You know we will always be friends. Open the wine while I put these on plates."

Over the meal she poured out her frustration about the counsellor. "She kept going on about 'caring' and 'being professional' what about love? They are not allowed to love these kids, that would be showing emotional commitment we can't have that can we? I'm his mother, I love him, doesn't that count for more than her social work degree?"

"I love him."

"I know you do, but he has a father, I can't take that away from him" instinctively she avoided saying 'you are not his dad'. These were treacherous waters.

"I could be his father."

Cathy looked hard at him making sure she understood him. "He would never accept you. You've seen how he has reacted recently, he didn't used to be like that."

"Has he said anything?" Stuart was studying her closely as he waited for her answer.

"You have heard. He doesn't like you babysitting."

"Has he said why?" Stuart's eyes never left her.

"No. I think he is being unreasonable. After all, you are only trying to help."

"Exactly." His eyes moved to her glass and the bottle. "More wine?" She nodded. As she drank he leant back. "It's not my place to say, but for what it's worth I don't like the idea of this counsellor."

She swallowed. "Why, apart from my pathological hatred of her?"

"Counsellors mess with your head. I don't think you should spout personal information about Peter. Especially to someone who is being professional and caring when they don't actually love him."

"Thank you Stu. I love you. I'm sorry about knocking you back earlier. You can stay the night if you want. It's the least I can do to thank you."

"That's very kind but I'll take the answer you gave me when you were sober. I've eaten prawn vindaloo remember." He stood to go.

Cathy giggled. "OK if you are sure." She stood unsteadily, leant to give him a kiss and stumbled on the coffee table. She fell into his arms.

He helped her up and kissed her on the forehead. "Goodnight Cathy. See you soon."

*

Peter was sitting in the counsellor's office. It had been rendered child friendly by the addition of a teddy bear and a game of connect 4 on the coffee table. The counsellor had just been on a bereavement course. Reading that Peter had recently lost his granny she was anxious to try out her knew found skills. She had provided them both with pencil and paper. On hers she drew a rough outline of a brain. "Your brain is like a box. You keep memories in it. It is also where you feel things like happiness sadness and even pain." This was where her 'service user' was supposed to say something helpful like "When I bang my elbow I feel the pain there not on my head". Peter was determined to say nothing. When his teacher made the appointment he asked if he had to go. He was told he did. Well he might have to go, but they couldn't make him talk. The counsellor chose a red crayon and drew a blob on the wall of the brain box.

"When you bang yourself this is where you feel pain. When someone bullies you that is where you feel pain too." Silence. She ploughed on. She drew circles inside the brain. "These are memories; they float around inside your head. Sometimes they hit the happy button, sometimes the sad button, sometimes even the pain button." She started again, drawing this time just one memory bubble, filling the whole brain. "When something really sad happens like granny dying the memory bubble is huge so it hits the pain button all the time." No reaction so she drew it again. This time the bubble was smaller. "Over time the memory bubble gets smaller. This means it hits the pain button less often. It still hurts when it does but the times when it doesn't get longer. Your memory of your granny will always be there but eventually you will find it is so small it hardly ever hits the pain button."

Peter could not keep up the silence. "That's rubbish. Granny was the best person in the world. She would never hit my pain button."

The counsellor wrote down: engaged after 20 minutes but confrontational. "I am sure she was the best granny ever. That means her not being here any more hits your pain button."

"Have you got kids?"

Golden rule: never talk about your own family. She hesitated. "What if I do?"

"They're not here are they? Is that hitting your pain button? No, because they are happy at home playing video games."

"But granny is not at home is she?"

"No she is in Heaven."

"That is lovely for her, but sad for you because you will not see her again."

"Yes I will because she will come back. She will be a kid in this school and you will have to teach her. Maybe then you will learn something." In the silence the counsellor wrote "reincarnation?" in her notes. Peter meanwhile was drawing his own brain. He divided into two sections. The bigger part had the pain button. The memory circles were different colours. He pointed to a green one. "That's a memory I tell people about." He pointed to a red one. "That's a secret, but I still remember it."

The smaller section at the back was filled with one big red ball. She asked him about it. "That is a secret that I know is there but even I don't know what it is. When it is locked in there it cannot reach the pain button so it can't hurt me."

Chapter 11
Holidays
Summer 2007

Choosing a holiday was no longer an issue now they had bought the house. John wanted to spend the entire school holidays in Saint Etienne. He was a systems analyst, an occupation he now referred to as his day job. With clients on holiday work slowed in the summer. He preferred to cut his losses and restart in September when everyone was in work mode. Francine had found local tradesmen; at the very least he must get the roofer started. The spring had been very wet. The roofer had put up scaffolding and small tarpaulins over the leaks but no remedial work had begun.

Peter jumped at the chance of spending the whole summer in France. "Anything to get away from this dump." These types of reaction were getting more frequent. At first his parents challenged him. This changed nothing and only made him clam up.

"We need to cut him some slack Cathy. He is on the edge of puberty, hormones will be raging. He needs to feel he can come to us with his problems."

Cathy felt it was about her and Stuart. Peter was old enough to know what was going on. They had even stopped trying to hide it. "He needs boundaries John. If you cut him some slack he will not know where they are and it will get worse."

Stuart had his own ideas but he kept silent. He was there during one conversation so Cathy asked him. "Not my circus, not my monkeys" was all he would say. She thought back to the evening she got back from parents evening. Then it certainly felt like he considered it his circus. Was that because John was not there? She wanted him to allow her and John to go to France with his blessing. Barely a week later she was making love to Stuart declaring she couldn't bear to live without him. On both occasions she had been telling the truth. She couldn't blame him if he started to wonder if she was worth it.

France

Peter wanted Greg to come with them for the whole holiday. Greg's parents of course had other plans. Cathy agreed to go to France for two weeks and bring Greg with her. She said it was to accumulate holiday allowance to cash in when she left work for good. With the restoration barely started living at the house would be what Peter called indoor camping. This was not Cathy's cup of tea, but she said she looked forward to spending more time there when a bit more had been done. For two weeks Peter explored caves and castles with Greg and Cathy, but mostly they went canoeing. When Peter was alone with his dad they worked on the house. It was hot so they allowed themselves to stop at four and go to the lake. The next village had dammed the river. There were trees and grass where people could picnic or sunbathe. There was also a ginguette, a wooden snack bar that kept Peter tanked up on fizzy drinks, crisps and ice cream. To earn these treats they busied themselves in the house and garden. The most obvious job when they arrived was the grass which was as tall as Peter. John had borrowed a trailer in England to transport some of his tools and equipment such as the lawn mower. He soon found them hopelessly inadequate for country living.

Lee came to their rescue. The mayor introduced him as 'the other English in the village' Lee lived on his own. He sold his business and retired to France fifteen years ago. He must have got a good price for it as he did not seem short of a bob or two. This was not reflected in the house which was in the same state of repair as John's. Lee was a 'diamond geezer' and only too happy to help a fellow Brit. The outhouses were filled with every conceivable type of garden machinery. He selected one which he thought would tackle the grass. Eventually the garden was tamed to the point where the ride on lawn mower could take over. Lee showed Peter how to work it. This for the young boy this was real life Super Mario Cart. He spent his days waiting for the grass to grow just enough to give him the excuse to take the mower out again. When John asked if he could buy it Lee gave it to him, declaring that he had three others and this one was 'just sitting there'.

The other place John needed Peter's help was in the loft. The loft of the small house and the main one were separated by a partition wall. A hefty shove revealed that this was not as stable as the rest of the house. Although brick, these were barely a centimetre thick and laid on edge. John gave Peter the task of demolishing it and handed him a sledge hammer. It was a task his son took to with surprising vigour. The school counsellor had been on another course. After it a punch bag and boxing gloves appeared in her room. Peter spent his entire therapy sessions punching; demolishing the wall was much more fun. Knocking it down was the easy part. Clearing the rubble from the loft, stacking the reusable bricks and taking the rest to the tip was hard work and time consuming. He was pleased when his mum arrived with Greg and offered to take them canoeing.

Eventually the school holidays ended. Peter started his final year of primary school. John turned his attention to his neglected clients. Cathy continued juggling work lover and family. In France work continued sporadically. John would phone Francine who would chivvy the tradesmen. The biggest job was knocking a new door to connect Peter's bedroom to the kitchen. It meant breaking through an original external wall.

The next family trip to Dordogne was at Christmas. The house had been rewired and essential plumbing work done. There was a working loo and, they were assured, a shower. To get hot water they would need to fire up the huge red boiler in the cellar. Francine arranged for the fuel tank to be filled. Even after completion Mr Leclerc had continued to take anything he considered may be remotely useful, including the central heating oil.

Cathy vetoed the overnight Caen route. She got sea sick easily and a storm was brewing Instead they took car and trailer through the tunnel. By getting up at 4 and getting the first shuttle they calculated they could still get to the house around six. At Folkestone everyone seemed equally keen to avoid stormy sea crossings and the queues for the shuttle were huge. Once in France John was desperate to avoid Paris so he set a course that looped west via Chartres. Not driving towards Paris proved surprisingly difficult. Road signs to anywhere else were either obscured by driving rain or non existent. John tried to rely on the sat nav. Every time they got to road works it decided they were in the middle of a field and gave up. Cathy's contribution to navigating was restricted to "Why didn't you download the updates?"

Meanwhile Lee was having problems of his own. He had met Cathy briefly in the summer. Now he wanted to make an impression. He fancied a bit of skirt and this one spoke English. It mattered not that she was married and was visiting with her husband. It was nothing a bottle of Dom Perignon would not overcome. He had driven over in the driving rain to light the fire. When he tried to leave his car became hopelessly stuck. It was not Sunday so there were no huntsmen to come to his rescue as had happened with John. The old biddy next door had closed her shutters and refused to answer the door. In any event she was incapable of helping him even if she possessed a car and tow rope. Lee walked home to fetch his tractor. Having liberated his car and driven it back he walked back to John's house to recover the tractor. He was stripping off his sodden clothes when the phone rang. It was Cathy. "Mr Smith? Cathy Cartwright here. John told me you might pop over to our house to light the fire. Please don't bother, we have only just reached Chartres. John is seeing if we can get a room for the night. We will probably been down late morning now."

Finally John let his family into the kitchen. The welcoming fire had long since gone out. In front of him was the new doorway. He looked more carefully. It was not a new door at all. An old lintel supported the opening. The architrave was stone and clearly also part of the original structure. John could not get over it. A stone step compensated the difference in levels. It was the only new part of the alteration. He sensed a presence. It looked like a child or a petite woman, the step raising her to John's height. "What you looking at dad?"

"The door, you can get to your room now." Peter pushed past him scattering the presence.

"They've done a lot since we were last here, but there is still a mass to do" said Cathy. She was still having trouble visualising living there. The difficult journey emphasised for her how far they were from England, and from Stuart. John had no such doubts. The house was welcoming him. The presence in the doorway was not Cathy, she was behind him and very real. Maybe it was a former inhabitant, or simply the house.

"I'll light the boiler" John turned to go to the cellar. He didn't mention the presence. He did not want Cathy to change her mind about moving to France.

After several attempts the boiler finally came to life. Peter was less impressed than his parents by the presence of hot water. He was offered the chance to be the first to try the new shower but declined. Cathy fetched a towel from the suitcase. "Then I will, it will warm me up."

The boiler, nicknamed Lazarus by Peter did not live up to its name. John's attempt to raise it from the dead whilst successful was temporary. Subsequent reincarnations were progressively shorter. Eventually they called the plumber. He put them on to the boiler agent. A young man arrived. He fiddled about as successfully as John before admitting that he wasn't familiar with this model as it was old. He would send his dad out. Dad recognised the boiler. He installed it when still an apprentice. Lazarus it seems was not the spring chicken he seemed. A new boiler was beyond their budget. With the money they saved by not having to cut a new door they bought a heat pump to provide hot water and a wood burner for the living room.

Cathy finally got into the Christmas spirit and started dragging greenery from the surrounding woodland. John managed a passable curry for Christmas dinner although none were sure about curried sprouts. The meal was cooked on camping stoves set on a table bought at the local troc. Francine explained that trocking was the popular French form of bartering. Unwanted furniture and other household items could be found in warehouses who sold them on behalf of previous owners. She had also arranged for a shipment of logs so John could keep the home fires burning. "She is being very helpful." There was something in the way Cathy said the words.

John refused to accept the implication. "Lee is being very helpful too."

"I had noticed John. There is no way I am going to show my appreciation, at least not in the way he would like!"

"Nor I with Francine."

"Glad to hear it!" Cathy came over and gave him a kiss.

It was New Year's Eve. They had finally finished the game of monopoly and Peter was in bed. The game had lasted all evening. Cathy was determined to win. She would have done so if John had not kept pointing out when Cathy had landed on property John had given Peter 'to get him started'. Alone they refilled their glasses of champagne and stared into the flames. Together they ticked off the planned milestones for 2008. The house would finally be finished. Peter would finish primary school. They would move to France permanently. The house in England would be rented to provide an income to offset Cathy leaving work. John planned to continue to service his existing client base remotely and look for new ones in France. Peter would start secondary school in France. Eventually Cathy leaned in to John and let him put his arm round her. "You've got it all worked out haven't you?"

"It won't work if we don't have the finances in place." John was well aware that he had started to lose Cathy when Peter was small. Money problems contributed. She gave up work to be a full time mum. John went freelance to provide the flexibility and share parenting duties. He would happily have been a full time dad to allow Cathy to stay at work.

"You can't, you don't have boobs. I'm not bottle feeding him. Anyway I've waited so long I want to be a proper mum." They took a big drop in income just as they had another mouth to feed. John did not mind being poor. Cathy did. Stuart had just started as a salesman in the local garage. John the computer geek was into beards baggy jumpers and sandals. Stuart was smart suits and smarter cars. He didn't own one of his own, he simply drove the ones he was selling. He adopted a similar strategy with women. It worked. Cathy was fed up with being poor; the reality of motherhood had hit her. Stuart made her feel young single and attractive. John concentrated on making her feel loved. He believed that was enough.

That was over ten years ago. They had weathered the storm, he thought. Now they were about to start a new life together.

Chapter 12
The meal, June 2008

We think we build our lives on solid foundations but even bedrock is just the outer skin of a tectonic plate. John built his life upon certainties. Cathy challenged them. The plates were shifting. He would not be able to stand against the movement of the earth. For now he could not feel it and was unprepared for the earthquake that was to come. He picked up the library books. He had been too busy to read any of them. He had not yet installed Wi-Fi at home. A year ago he asked Francine if he could use the library connection. She apologised profusely saying that their Wi-Fi was for staff use only. On the other hand for the princely sum of 9€ a year for the whole family he could become reacquainted with the pleasure of the printed page. Usually Peter went with his father to the library. This time he was back at school revising for end of year exams. Restoration work on the house was taking longer than predicted. He and Peter were fine with "indoor camping" but for Cathy nothing short of a fully functioning house would compensate for giving up Stuart. The plan was to move in the summer when Peter was between primary and secondary school. To achieve this John cleared a two month window in his work schedule and went to France for the final push.

For reasons he was reluctant to admit, today John was grateful not to have his son in tow. He found himself thinking about Francine more than he expected. More often than he should for a married man doing all he could to rekindle his marriage. He hotly denied his own accusation there was anything improper in his frequent visits. He was returning books to the library for goodness sake!

"Bonjour Francine, tout va bien?" He thought that by choosing this greeting he had avoided the tu/vous trap. He still struggled with this particular piece of French etiquette. Also he was not sure what their relationship was. Francine had no such problem. She jumped up, unable to disguise the light in her eyes. "coucou Jean, comment va tu?" She brushed each cheek in the traditional French greeting. Each touch was a millisecond longer than necessary, as was the briefest of eye contacts. "What can I do for you?"

"I have come to bring these books back"

"Ah, did you enjoy?"

"No. Er, that is to say I don't know."

"You don't know if you enjoyed zem?" Just when he fooled himself he was in control of his emotions, her inability to pronounce the English digraph floored him. "Of course, I mean, that is to say, er I haven't read them." He finished lamely.

"So why return zem?"

"The library is closed tomorrow, and I have finished my kitchen." She inclined her head questioningly which only added to his confusion. "As it is your day off I was wondering if you would help me christen my new kitchen." Now it was her turn to be confused.

"You want to make your kitchen Catholic?"

"What? No, I will be making my first meal in the kitchen and I'd like you to come and eat it with me."

"Ah bien sûr, but the library is not closed tomorrow" John was crestfallen. It was important that she did not refuse him. Why was that? He felt like a boy asking a girl out for their first date. He told himself to grow up. "Quand même I would love to join you." Suddenly the sun shone again.

"Brilliant, thank you. About seven?"

"Dix-neuf heures, parfait. A demain." He turned to leave. "Et Jean," he turned back. "Merci" Her look melted his heart. He left hurriedly before his legs gave way.

All the next day he poured over his extensive collection of cookery books. He wanted to impress, but not go overboard and scare her off. Off what? What would Cathy think? Given her repeated failures when it came to keeping her underwear on, Cathy was in no position to take the moral high ground. That was not the point. John was working his socks off building a new life for them all. He told himself he was simply thanking a friend who had helped him with the house by making her a meal. Tree was standing in the doorway. John told him to bugger off. The house had enough ghosts of its own without importing old rugby mates from England.

"Cooking for Francine?" Tree asked.

"Yes. Now piss off."

"Does Cathy know?"

"Of course not, now piss off"

"You old dog" said Tree with a grin. He ducked to avoid the incoming oven glove and disappeared.

Starter and dessert were in the fridge. Table was laid. No candles, this was a simple meal between friends.

"Yeah right"

"Tree, I said piss off." John collected his thoughts. Wine glasses, she would probably bring wine, if not he had some in the cellar. Main course was cooked so he turned off the oven. He looked at the clock. 6.50. Perfect. He went to get changed. Glancing out of the window he saw a car pull up. He hurriedly finished dressing. He resisted the urge to go out to the car to greet her. He feigned nonchalance wandering back to the kitchen to check all the things that didn't need checking because he had checked them a thousand times. He waited for the door bell to ring. It didn't. He started pacing. This was silly. All day he wondered if she would cancel. Maybe she simply wouldn't turn up. Now she was here but not getting out of her car. The door bell rang. He jumped, despite expecting it for the last twenty minutes.

John would never forget opening the door. She had spent as much time choosing what to wear as he had choosing the menu. Neither 'I'm on a date' nor 'I've just got home from work'. She didn't need to make an impression, she knew she already had. The dress was not 'I want to make you fancy me' it was 'I want you to understand that I fancy you'. It had the desired effect. He bent down to greet her. The French know which cheek comes first as instinctively as the gender of every noun. Not the English. As John stooped he hesitated, got it wrong, and their lips met. "I'm so sorry!"

"Don't say sorry." John blushed. "It was nice" she added with a smile. Not knowing where to put the smile, he invited her in. She proffered a bottle of wine. "I have brought a Pecharmant." It was a Chateaux Corbiac deux milles cinq. Had John known more about wine he would have known how much this evening meant to Francine.

If John should have known from the wine and her dress how important this meal was to Francine, she was left in no doubt as to the effort he had made trying to make it look like he hadn't made too much effort with the meal. John was full of surprises. She had no idea he was a good cook. Round here the only men that ever cooked were trained chefs. To find a man, and an Englishman to boot, that could cook blew her away.

As the evening passed so did the awkwardness, helped in no small measure by the wine. Francine stood. "I need to use your bathroom." Instinctively John stood too. This small act of chivalry did not go unnoticed. "Up that step and to your left". Momentarily alone John remained standing. He needed to clear his head. It was not just the wine. Francine was intoxicating. This had not been the plan.

"Really?"

"Tree, I said piss off!" If it was not the plan, what was? John didn't know. All he knew was that he was married was working to repair that relationship and now he needed Francine more than he ever remembered needing Cathy.

She returned and stood on the step before him. Like this they were almost the same hight. She smiled and put her arms round his neck. "Thank you for a wonderful evening." She was saying goodbye! Had he misread the mood so much? Was he simply too overwhelmed by his own emotions to read hers? She lent into him and kissed him slowly, deliberately, waiting for a response. If this had been the movies the response would have been a full blown tongue-penetrating snog accompanied by ripping off of clothes. The detritus of the meal would have been swept to the floor and they would have made wild passionate love on the dining room table. This was not the movies. He mirrored her kiss willing it not to end. When she drew away she looked at him as if recording every detail of his face lest one day it would be a memory. "Thank you" she repeated.

"Do you have to go?"

"No,"

"Then stay"

"I would like that very much indeed"

"I am married."

"So am I." His look of horror made Francine burst out laughing. "Don't worry, we do not live together. I do not even love him. You can be my gigolo, you say that in English? And I will be your mistress. This is France remember!" She ran a finger down his cheek. She had managed to make what would have been heavy guilt-ridden English sex into light, joyful French sex. In doing so, far from devaluing the experience she had raised it up to another level. Sensing that John was lost she continued to take the lead. "First we must get to know each other much better. Are you going to show me what you have done to the rest of the house?" She held his hand, lifting hers in an invitation to lead her.

John felt like a young guillemot. One moment he was sitting in his nest begging to be fed. He walked to the edge of the cliff. With that kiss Francine had pushed him off. He flapped frantically as she led him across the living room towards the bedroom. She was the wind beneath his wings. Before they reached the door he found the updraft. He scooped her in his arms and carried her over the threshold. She was so light. Like a sparrow. Who was that French singer they called the sparrow? Edith Piaf. "Non," he whispered to himself, "je ne regrette rien." Gently he placed her on the bed. She smiled up at him. He pushed her hair away from her face. Finally he could stare at her. He drank in every detail, plunging into her deep brown eyes, swimming in her soul. She held his gaze, returning it with a smile. It did not waver, nor was it fixed. It blazed like the sun, constant, yet ever changing, infinite energy that burned with love. Energy so powerful it could destroy mere human flesh. He was not destroyed. He was consumed. Finally she broke the spell. Effortlessly she sat up, bouncing slightly to pull the hem of her dress from under her. She crossed her arms grabbing two handfuls of frock before raising her arms above her head to let the light material float down on to the pillow. She lay back, arms still raised. Soft tufts of hair nestled at the base of her arms. It was the same soft gold as that which tumbled about her face. John bent towards her. She opened her mouth slightly to accept the kiss. Instead he moved his mouth to her armpit and kissed her there. The soft down caressed his cheek releasing her fragrance. He listened to her breathing. Every sense was assaulted by her presence. His own body could not resist such an onslaught. His organ strained against the restriction of his undergarments. As Johns lips moved from her armpit and up to the side of her breast she lowered her arms. Raising her buttocks she removed the last remaining piece of clothing. It was already damp. Eventually he stood taking in her nakedness. "Your turn" she whispered, placing a finger on his belt buckle. He unbuttoned his shirt and let it fall to the floor. His trousers followed, revealing the full extent of the effect she had on his body. Now it was her turn to search him with her eyes. She sat up, swinging her legs over the side of the bed. Holding his buttocks she kissed him lightly just below the navel. She felt the indentations under her fingertips deepen as his muscles clenched beneath her touch. She inclined her head downwards. Gently he pushed her away. He was not ready for that. Maybe he was too ready. He did not know. What he did know was that he was not ready for it to end. He pushed again. This time she fell back, her legs still bent over the side of the bed. He knelt between them. He mirrored her last kiss, exploring her navel with his tongue. He knelt between her knees. She allowed him to do what he had prevented her from doing.

Finally she lay with her head on his chest, breathing the heady scent of his bare skin. John now understood why he had never "remembered" being here with Cathy in the future. He also remembered that he would be happy here. He did not know what the future would bring. Was the house telling him false stories? Did the house tell him what he wanted to hear? Were there two futures and like Schrödinger's cat he would be simultaneously dead with Cathy and alive with Francine? He gave up on such thoughts; they were making him waste the experience of holding her in his arms. "I thought you would not come." She lifted her head and looked at him. "For the meal" he added realising that the remark could be taken quite differently.

"Why did you think that?"

"You sat in the car for nearly 20 minutes"

Francine laughed. "I was early"

"Only a couple of minutes, I saw you arrive."

"C'est le quart d'heure Perigordoin. In the Dordogne, if someone says arrive at seven, you must not arrive before seven fifteen."

"That's silly"

"Not at all. Suppose I had arrived at seven and you were not quite ready, I would have embarrassed you. That is not polite"

"If I know you are not going to arrive until seven fifteen then I would try to be ready for seven fifteen. You of course know this so you cannot arrive until seven thirty in case I am not ready for seven fifteen which is the time you should arrive if I say seven."

"Now you are being silly"

"I know, I am very silly, you should know that"

"I do know, I like it."

John was serious again. "Why did you kiss me?"

"When?"

"In the kitchen, I thought you were leaving."

"To see what would happen."

"Did you like what happened?"

"What do you think? You know. You just want to hear me say it."

"True"

"Well John Cartwright, I did like it. I liked it very much. Your turn."

"Francine Lefevre I liked it too. I like you too. So much it scares me."

Even in the post coital glow where only truths are uttered he could not say, even to himself, that which deep down he knew. Somewhere deep in the cosmos where such unions as theirs are recorded there was an echo.

"I love you Francine."

Francine was standing in the newly opened doorway where John had sensed her six months ago "I love you John" she whispered.

Part 2
The Mistress

Chapter 13
Love songs

Francine woke. She gazed at the man sleeping beside her and smiled. Silently she slipped out of bed sliding her dress over her naked body. Pushing her feet into sandals she went in search of her car keys. They were on the table with the remains of last night's meal. She picked them up and crept out of the door. The curtain in the next house twitched. There would be gossip. There was always gossip. She did not care. Whatever the neighbours fabricated it would be less than the reality. She smiled again as she turned the key in the ignition.

John woke. He was alone. Briefly this confirmed that he had been dreaming. He could still smell her. The sensation instantly stirred his loins. As wakefulness crept upon him he realised that the smell came from the pillow beside him. He held it to his face and re-lived every moment from the door bell to sleep. A low pitched purr invaded his reverie. A car door closed. A stair creaked.

"Good morning! Breakfast is served!" She held out a brown paper bag. "Coffee is brewing." John patted the bed. "I cannot stay. I am a working girl remember." She scooped up her knickers from the floor. "Better take these; I wouldn't want your wife to find them!" With that she was gone. Eventually she would have to wash but today at least she wanted to be reminded of him.

John listened to the car leave and tried to feel guilty. He could not. Eventually there was the sound of another motor, this time at the back of the house. Shit! The carpenter! He jumped out of bed and into shorts and T shirt before hurrying barefoot into the kitchen. The Carpenter looked up and instinctively held out a hand in greeting. He noticed the remains of the repas a deux but said nothing. The work was finished and he wanted to be paid. What his client did when his wife was away was none of his business. John had a snagging list but for the life of him he could not remember where it was. He went through the list from memory. This mostly consisted of him pointing and the carpenter nodding. John remembered the skirting board in the bedroom. He led the way and was met by Francine's fragrance. Almost imperceptible it still overwhelmed him. He wondered whether the carpenter had noticed. If he did he said nothing. He saw Francine in her car as he entered the village. She waved to him. It was Francine who found him the work.

Like Francine John had no desire to shower. He offered the carpenter the coffee Francine had brewed and made some more. Unable to answer the big question turned to the snagging list. It could not keep out

Francine. On the principle that girls appreciate a bunch of flowers the next day more than a necklace the next week he drove to Thiviers to visit the florist by the church. When he was last there with Peter and Cathy, Peter asked why they always had florists near churches. "For the same reason they have undertakers near hospitals."
Cathy was horrified by John's remark and told him so. "You will give him nightmares!" Today John had other things on his mind. Bouquet in hand he strode up the hill to the library. It was not the exercise that made his heart race. At the library desk he produced the flowers from behind his back.

Francine let out a little cry of surprise. "Why have you brought me these?"

"Because I love you." There. He had said what he could not last night

She lowered her voice. "I know you do, and now the whole town knows. You might as well have taken a full page advert in Sud Ouest."

She was right; he had not given it any thought. "I don't care" he said defensively.

"Are you sure? I don't mind. I knew as soon as my car was parked overnight at your house the whole village would have me marked as the other woman. I am French, I have lived here all my life. It is normal here." She touched his hand. "Cathy might not see it the same way." A customer had entered. Francine smiled at her then turned back to John. "Let's talk later, half twelve at the ice cream parlour. They do galettes for the commercants."

"Galettes?"

"Savoury pancakes."

"I thought you were worried people would talk. Worried for me that is."

"Ariane will not spread gossip. She may not be French but being Belgian is the next best thing!"

They ate surrounded by people but inside their private bubble. Francine was fifteen years younger, and half his size but she had the measure of the situation. "I will start by saying that I love you John, last night must have proved that. I have loved you for longer than you know."

"How long?"

Francine thought. "From the day you first showed me the house and we talked of Cyrano de Bergerac." John nodded engulfed by his own emotions. Francine continued. "I do not have to ask whether you feel as I do, I felt that last night too." John was thankful that he didn't need to talk, he did not trust his voice. "Remember those two things when I say this: Why did you come to Perigord?" She put a finger to his lips. "You came because you love your wife and you wish to save her from this, sorry I do not remember his name."

"Stuart."

She nodded. "Before you say that now you love me I will remind you that I know. It changes nothing."

134

"It changes everything." He could barely speak the words.

"You think that because you think that you cannot love two women. Why? Before we met you loved Peter and Cathy. You still do? It is possible to love two people."

"One is my wife, one is my son. They are completely different kinds of love. It is normal."

"And now you love Cathy and you love me. One is your wife and one is your mistress. They too are completely different kinds of love."

"And you are ok with that?"

"Absolutely. I would not want to be your wife!"

"Thanks very much!"

She put her hand on his knee. Softly she began to sing

« J'ai l'honneur de ne pas te demander ta main. Ne gravons pas nos noms au bas d'un parchemin. Laissons le champ libre à l'oiseau, nous serons tous les deux prisonniers sur parole. Au diable les maîtresses queux qui attachent les coeurs aux queu's des casseroles ! »

"That is beautiful, but I do not understand it"

"It is a man singing to his lover. It is as if he is proposing to her. Instead he asks for the honour *not* to marry her, not to put their names at the bottom of a parchment. Instead of being free like the birds in the fields he and his lover would be two prisoners. The devil wants to tie their hearts to the handle of a saucepan."

"Now I understand, it is even more beautiful."

"This is what you are going to do John. You are going to go back to England, and you will bring your wife and your son to the home you have prepared for them."

"And you?"

"You have granted me the honour not to marry you. Our love will be on the wing with the free birds in the field"

Now it was Johns turn to hum. Eventually the words came.

"... *where once we watched the small free birds fly. Our love was on the wing, we had dreams and songs to sing. It's so lonely round the fields of Athenry.*"

"Why is it lonely?"

"It is an Irish lament. During the famine her husband stole to feed his family. He was caught and deported to Australia. She is remembering him."

"It is beautiful. Would you say it is a love song?"

"Of course."

"And sad?"

"Undoubtedly"

"Ha! you said Cyrano de Bergerac could not be a love story because it is sad, now you sing me a sad love song."

He looked into her eyes. "Francine, what am I going to do without you?"

"I am not going to answer that question. You will not be without me. Now, answer that phone."

The ringing had broken the spell. After a brief conversation he turned back to Francine. "I'm sorry that was the plumber, he is at the house. I completely forgot. I have to go."

Ariane was at the table. The lunchtime rush was finished so she was clearing. "Another coffee?"

"Not for me, I have to dash." John put some money on the table.

"Yes please" said Francine.

Ariane returned with an espresso and a tea for herself. She generally had an hour between the last of the lunches and the tea time rush."

"He seems nice."

"He is, but he is messed up."

"Why?"

"We made love."

Francine and Ariane were close friends. Francine's family had worked the Périgord soil for generations. Ariane had arrived with her English husband less than five years ago. Nevertheless Ariane made friends easily. It was the key to the success of the business. That and the quality of Chris' home made ice cream. Ariane nodded but said nothing. She waited for Francine to continue.

"I do not understand English men. You are married to one. Did I do the right thing?"

"You, did not do anything you both did."

"I took the lead; he is quite shy."

"But it was he who invited you to supper when his wife and son were not here."

"You knew that, it was only yesterday!"

"This is rural France, news like that travels fast."

Francine gave a Gallic shrug. "Oui, mains quand meme." She did not ask if they had done the right thing. Instead they talked about John. "How can I help him? I have made life hard for him."

"He has made life hard for himself. You can help him by always being there. I know you are not taking him away from his wife."

"How do you know that, were you eavesdropping?"

"Of course not, but I heard you sing. The non demand a marriage made it pretty clear."
Francine blushed. "c'est vrai."

Ariane put her hand on Francine's. "He must do this on his own. You must let him. I know that is hard. I suspect in the end it will not be his decision." Francine looked puzzled. "His wife, sorry I forget her name..."

"Cathy."

"Yes, Cathy. I think it will be her who decides. You told me she has a boyfriend in England. Let's see whether she leaves him."

Francine looked worried. "She must! Look at the mountains John has moved!"

"I do not know her; she has only been in the shop a couple of times. If she changes her mind it will leave him free to marry you." Ariane had a way of getting to be nub of the matter.

"But I do not want to marry him! Look how unhappy being married has made him!"

"Then don't. But life will be much simpler for him. My experience of Englishmen is that they are not very good at infidelity. If his wife joins him he will have to learn to be French, if she doesn't he is going to need you to guide him through some very troubled waters"

"Thank you."

"You are always welcome to talk. Now you have to excuse me, I have a customer."

John had now seen all the tradesmen and given them final instructions. It still needed decorating but that they could do themselves. He hoped Cathy's flair for interior design would give her some ownership of the house. There was one problem. It would mean giving up Francine. For the first time he understood what he was asking of Cathy. Now at least he could make the same sacrifice. He hitched the empty trailer to the car, ready to return to England. He stopped outside the library. When he came back with Cathy and Peter there would be no more John and Francine. How could he say that? It would make that night together a one night stand. He could not bear to cheapen it so. Tears running down his face he turned the key in the ignition. Francine looked up from her desk. She had seen his car pull up. She watched it leave.

Chapter 14
Letter writing

John drove through his tears. The N21 unrolled pitilessly before him. The climb towards haute Perigord and Limousin was imperceptible. It marked the end of Dordogne's micro climate. The summer thunderstorm bypassed Thiviers. Here it was telling him to go back. Rain mottled the oncoming headlights, an endless stream of lorries heading from England to Spain. Another returning blared aggressively as John slowed to pull into a lay by. He listened to the storm outside and in his head. Again John saw things from the other person's viewpoint. What if Francine had seen him pull up outside the library and leave again? She would know he had left without saying goodbye. She would think the meal and what followed meant nothing to him. He even asked himself if this might not be for the best. He reasoned that if she thought he did not love her she would cease to love him. This was the only way he could make his new life with Cathy work. Her talk of loving two people was very French. She could be a mistress.

Cathy could take a lover. He could not. He ignored the inescapable fact that he just had. He made up his mind. He could not bear to think of Francine watching him leave without saying goodbye. He wanted her to know that last Friday was not just a one night stand. Again he ignored the truth that it was now his intention that it would become just that. He would decline her offer to be his mistress. He told himself it's the least he could do if she left Stuart. He pulled out of the lay by to the vociferous annoyance of another approaching lorry. At the first roundabout he turned back to Thiviers.

He jumped out of the car at the library not waiting to rehearse what he was going to say. Francine was not there. The man behind the computer looked up. "Good afternoon, I am looking for Francine."

"Good afternoon, she is not here."

"When will she be back?"

"I don't know. Not today I think. She went home early saying she was unwell."

John felt responsible. "When you see her please tell her that John called to say goodbye." The man nodded, never taking his eyes from the computer. John could not see the screen but whatever was on it was clearly far more important than John's message. On the way home John decided that he would write to her.

England

Cathy greeted John casually. "I've not made supper; I didn't know what time you would be back. Shall I order a takeaway?"

"Not for me, I stopped at the services. Get one for yourself if you like."

"I'm not eating, Stu says I'm getting fat."

"Cheeky bugger." He wanted to say more but refuting it would lead him into a minefield. He resented Stuart making these types of remark.

"Drinks then and you can tell me about the trip. Beer?"

"Thanks" He wittered on through all the trivia before trailing off. The news seemed inconsequential compared to what he could not say.

"Is everything ok?"

"What? Sorry, yes, I am fine, just very tired. Was your boss OK about your resignation?"

"Yes. That is, I haven't done it."

"What? You promised you would do it while I was away."

"Please John. I looked at the contract, it is a month's notice."

"Peter breaks up in less than a month. We could have gone then."

"But we don't need to be there before September. We have to get this house ready to let."

John sighed. "Hand it in on Monday and we will move beginning of August." He looked at his wife; she was not making eye contact. Now it was his turn to say "Is everything OK"

She looked up and smiled. "Now you're back. It is hard when you are not here." Memories of last Friday filled him with guilt. He wondered if she felt like that after she had been with Stuart.

Cathy had her own private thoughts. Stuart was starting to act strangely. He had always been a bit unpredictable, that was what she liked about him. Wasn't that what affairs were about? A counterpoint to the predictability of married life? They had become a ménage a trois. This hurt John terribly. He had to either accept Stuart or lose Cathy. He chose the former. He picked up her train of thought, comparing it with his own infidelity. At the start Cathy had seemed genuinely happy. That was why he did not put his foot down straight away. He also hoped it would be an affair that would burn out. It was also the line of least resistance.

Once John bought a ticket for Twickenham for Stuart's birthday. In the bar pre-match Horse and Tree took an instant dislike to him. The thinning of the crowd told them it was near to kick off. Stuart was nowhere to be seen. They found him after the match. "I met a mate and blagged my way into a box. Bloody brilliant. Free drinks!" It annoyed John but he put it down to Stuart being Stuart. Horse was less forgiving "I would have tried to get us all in. That's what mates do."

It was the same with Cathy. After a date Stuart left her to get the bus because a mate had offered him a lift home. "You are on the bus route; I was hardly going to deliver you to your front door with your husband at home." Instead of putting her off Cathy found herself trying harder to please him. Sandy confided in John when she split from Al. "He is gaslighting me." John had not heard of this before so he looked it up. He recognised many of the signs, not just with Stuart and Cathy, but the way Stuart behaved towards him too. He would lie, and then deny he had said it. He played John and Cathy off against each other. His charming exterior concealed snide remarks that made both of them doubt themselves. Cathy never realised he was wearing her down because the pill was always coated with "but you are doing really well considering...".

Once John had recognised the signs he found it easier to remain unaffected. The spell had been broken. He wondered if Stuart embracing Buddhism was not part of the trick. It allowed him to coat his dark inner self with a benign, almost saintly covering. Stuart didn't bother with vegetarianism. The first time John caught him he passed it off with "vegeburger" and a grin. John could smell it was a lie but Stuart didn't care.

John tried pointing these things out to Cathy. It only prompted a vehement defence of her lover. He even tried confronting Stuart. "John, we are best mates, I would never do that to you. You take all this meditation stuff far too seriously. Lighten up Om, it's driving you nuts." John was ok with the nickname when Tree and Horse used it. From Stuart it rankled.

Having failed to confront Stuart John decided to remove Cathy from his influence. Falling in love with Francine had not been part of the plan. It now threatened everything. He rolled it over and over in his head that night. Finally he got up and slipped down to his study to write to Francine. He flipped open the laptop, then closed it again. They shared this computer; he did not want to risk Cathy finding the letter. He opened the draw and pulled out a pad of his mother's pale blue Basildon Bond writing paper. It was what she used all her life. He picked up her broad-nibbed fountain pen. He missed her simple words of wisdom. These, combined with her unconditional love had made him the person he was today. He still felt her love. He hoped by using her pen some of her wisdom would find its way to the notepaper. Page after page he wrote before screwing them up and throwing them in the bin. Eventually he produced this.

"Dear Francine,

"I will start as you did at the ice cream parlour by saying that I love you. It grieves me more than you can imagine that I have given you cause to doubt it. It is completely my fault. To leave without saying goodbye is unforgivable. I returned but you had gone.

"Perhaps writing to you I will be able to express myself better. When I am with you I am overwhelmed by your presence. With a smile you render me incapable of speech. Your beauty flows from deep inside you. It makes me feel unworthy of your love. The song you sang, le non demand de marriage, was beautiful. It could not have been written by an Englishman. I realise now how different we are. No English girl would talk as you do. Peter could not believe his ears when you talked of priests, spires, and penises! For my part I struggle with your attitude to being a mistress. That may seem strange coming from a man whose wife is mistress to someone else. It seems that for you a wife and a mistress existing side by side is the natural order. In the world I inhabit, the 'other woman' is a transient state. Either the affair runs its course and the man returns to his wife or he divorces so he can marry his mistress.

"I have waited too long for the former. The affair is now the status quo. Neither of them have anything to gain from changing. It is therefore up to me. The simple thing would be to divorce. I cannot do that so I proposed we move to France and start again. The plan was all but executed. Until a week ago I loved her with all my heart. Now a part of that heart belongs to you. And yet I love her still. It seems you are right and I am wrong. It is possible to love two people. I am still not sure. My love for you has changed my love for Cathy. It is now a recognition of our shared history; a concern for her welfare. You will no doubt say that is how a husband loves his wife, and last Friday is how a husband loves his mistress.

"Why can't I leave her to be happy in England with her lover? I could then accept your non demande de marriage. The truth is that I know see Stuart for what he is. I cannot leave the woman I once loved in the clutches of such a man." John did not even notice he had slipped into the past tense when talking of his love for Cathy

"I do not know if the word exists in French but there is a phenomenon called gaslighting. One person, usually a man, completely controls another person. The victim is unaware they are being manipulated. Eventually they are under the total control of the other person. Until they recognise this is happening to them they cannot escape. I have to bring Cathy to France to break this spell. When I do it will require all my love to rebuild her self esteem. What we shared will be held in the most secret part of my heart for all eternity. It will be a testament to what might have been. It will be unsullied by the banalities that must accompany any long term relationship. It will not, as you said, become tied to the handle of a saucepan. Rather it will be a shooting star that shone briefly and brilliantly for two lovers.

"I remain forever your friend, John."

He addressed the matching blue envelope inserted the letter and carefully placed it in the inside pocket of his jacket. He crept back upstairs and slid into bed beside his wife, finding sleep as dawn was breaking.

Cathy was up first. She and Peter were running late. She had bundled her son out of the door when he came back "Dinner money." Cathy went to fetch John's wallet and spotted the letter in the same pocket. She handed her son a banknote and ushered him back out the door. Back in the study she pulled out the letter.

"We're out of shower gel" John had finally woken and made his way to the bathroom.

"There's more under the washbasin" Cathy's first instinct was to rip open the letter. For the moment she had the upper hand as John was unaware she had found it. This was useless without knowing what he had written. She wondered how she could open and reseal the letter without him noticing. She really should read less spy novels. The bathroom door opened. Quickly Cathy returned the letter to his pocket. She noticed the waste paper basket full of pieces of screwed blue notepaper. Thinking on her feet she called up "Can you bring the waste paper baskets down, it's bin day." She picked up the waste bin from the study. Instead of emptying it in the main dustbin she put the contents in a carrier bag and hid it behind the bushes. "We need to go or I'll miss my train"

John clattered down the stairs. "Do you have the keys?" Cathy waved them at him. "I'll get a coffee and croissant at the station" He grabbed his jacket feeling for the letter as he put it on. At the station John saw Cathy on to the Paddington train before heading to another platform to get the local train to Bracknell. He paused as he passed a letter box. He drew out the letter and looked at it before dropping it into the box.

Chapter 15
Letter reading
Thiviers

Pascal carefully spread the butter to the very edge of the bread. He liked English white sliced. Every slice was identical with square corners. If you put it in the toaster for 2 minutes 50 seconds it was just the right shade of brown. There was a rumble beneath his feet. The house he shared with his elderly mother was built just above the railway tunnel. The 7:37 from Perigeux to Limoges was a minute early. That was why he had not finished his third slice of toast. He left the house. It was 273 paces to the library. He counted a pace as every time he placed his right foot on the ground. A pace was 1.75 metres. If he lengthened his stride to 1.86 meters he could get to work in 256 paces. This was important because at 64 he was a quarter of the way there (drainpipe) at 128 halfway (fire hydrant) and at 192 (rubbish bin) three quarters. This morning he arrived on the left foot not the right. A car had passed as he was about to cross the road causing him to break step. He unlocked and went inside. Francine should arrive in seven minutes. Sometimes it was five, sometimes ten. That bothered him. It also bothered him that the post lady used the book return deposit for letters. There was a green box outside for letters. Francine pointed out that it saved him the trouble of taking out the books then going outside to empty the letterbox. That was not the point. The book box was for books, the letterbox was for letters. Today there was a blue envelope handwritten and addressed to Francine. She came in. She knew better than to touch Pascal. She waved vigorously and smiled.

"There is a letter for you from England. The stamp has a picture of an insect. They were issued on 15th April. Since then there have been stamps on St Paul's Cathedral, British films and the 1908 Olympics..." Pascal was staring into space as he spoke.

Francine moved into his field of view and waved. "Pascal!" She put her finger to her lips. He stopped. "May I have the letter?" She put it in her pocket.

"Aren't you going to open it?"

"In my coffee break, we should have started work." Mortified Pascal picked up the books to return them to their proper places.

As soon as he had gone Francine ripped open the letter. Pascal had of course relayed John's message. She knew he had returned; she did not know why. Since meeting John, Francine worked every spare moment to improve her English. She did not tell him, just hoped he had noticed. She could read well enough now but handwritten texts left her struggling. She would ask for Ariane's help.

Ariane took the letter. "Are you sure you want me to read it? It might be very personal."

"Please. We have no secrets. Besides I cannot read his handwriting so how do I know if it is personal?"

"He starts by saying he loves you. He is very sad that he has done something to make you think the opposite. He says that is his fault." Ariane looked up. "What did he do?"

"He stopped outside the library. I think he was going back to England because he had the trailer. Then he drove off without getting out of the car."

Ariane nodded. "He says he came back but you had gone."

"I know. Pascal told me."

"He hopes he can explain better in a letter." Ariane read on. "Gosh, he is head over heals in love with you. He talks about the song you sang, saying it could not have been written by an Englishman. He says you and he are very different. Apparently you were talking to Peter about priests' penises!"

Francine giggled. "I said that priests liked to have churches with large steeples in the same way that men like to have large penises."

"I am not even going to ask how you came to have that conversation!" Ariane read on. "He doesn't understand how you can be ok with being a mistress even though his wife is mistress to another man."

"I know."

"He says for you wives and mistresses existing side by side is normal. For him being a mistress is temporary. Either they get fed up with each other and end the affair, or the man leaves his wife and marries his mistress."

Francine pulled a face. "All men are the same! What about the woman leaving her husband and marrying her lover?"

"He says the affair between Cathy and Stuart has been going on too long. If Cathy was going to do that she would have done so by now. Reading between the lines I think he is saying because he didn't make a fuss at the beginning she doesn't have to leave him. She can have the best of both worlds."

"But that is exactly what I was offering him. It is clear he still loves her. I can't change that. Nor can I stop loving him. I just want him to love me too." The strong confident woman had gone. She was a small girl asking to be loved.

"I think you're right. He still loves her. That was not changed by her affair with Stuart. I think it has started to change since he met you" Ariane looked back at the letter. "He says that when he bought the house he loved Cathy with all his heart. Now he says that he has given part of his heart to you. He admits that you are right and he is wrong, it is possible to love two people."

Ariane looked at Francine. "He talks about his love for Cathy. Are you ok for me to read it?"

"Please. I need to know everything."

"His love for Cathy is recognition of the life they shared and concern for her welfare. He says that is the way a husband loves his wife. He says the night you spent with him is the way a man loves his mistress."

Francine looked hopeful. "So he will come here and we can still be lovers?"

Ariane read on. "I'm afraid not. He tries to explain why he cannot leave Cathy in England with Stuart and come to France and live with you." Ariane looked up. "That is the English way to do it. Convince yourself that your ex is happy so you can move on to your next partner." She returned to the letter. "This is really interesting. He says 'I cannot leave the woman I once loved'. That is a Freudian slip. He has not yet admitted to himself that he no longer loves her. Maybe he pretends out of duty, or he is clinging to the past when they did love each other. In that phrase the mask slips."

"Does he say why he cannot leave her?" Turning back to the letter Ariane was silent for some time. Involuntarily she put her hand to her mouth. Francine could not wait. "What is it?"

"Stuart is controlling Cathy. John can see it, but Cathy does not realise. John thinks if he leaves it will get much worse. By the time Cathy knows what a monster he is she will be completely under his spell."

It was Francine's turn to look shocked. "Mon Dieu!"

"He finishes by saying that has to bring Cathy to France to break the spell. He will have to give all his love to her. He says the love you and he shared he will hold for all eternity. As a memory it will not become sullied by the ordinary things of everyday life together. He calls it a testament to what might have been."

"He loves me."

"Most certainly"

"He doesn't love her."

"No. He feels a duty towards her as a doctor might to a patient." Francine wept silently. "Francine, I am so, so sorry."

England

Cathy recovered the plastic bag from behind the bush. She had not handed in her notice that day as they had agreed. She needed to find out what John had been doing behind her back. She felt no sense of irony. Far from it, she intended to get to the bottom of it and then discuss with Stuart what they should do. She unscrewed random scraps of paper. The story was disjointed, the final draft absent. Her emotions boiled before settling into cold anger. She carefully ironed each sheet and tried to place them in order, not easy as there were several drafts. It did not matter, he had declared his love for another woman. Even in their first flush she could not remember him writing to her so eloquently. That hurt. It also hurt that Francine was so much younger than him. She folded the letters carefully and hid them inside the cover of the Olivia Newton John record at the back of the cabinet.

Insecurities crept in. She was being traded in for a newer model. Would Stuart do the same? She picked up the phone. "Stu? Missing you already" They had lunched together only a few hours ago. "I've been thinking about that cottage you said your mate would lend us. Yes I know I said I had too much to do before leaving but like I said, I've been thinking. I don't know how many more chances we will get." She heard footsteps. "Got to go, his Lordship's back."

The front door opened. "You could have told me you had taken the car. I thought it had been stolen."

"Sorry, I managed to get an earlier train."

"That's not a problem, I just wish you had said that's all." Cathy found herself thinking 'I bet he never talks to her like that.' "Did you do it?"

"What?"

"Hand in the letter?"

She instantly thought of the letter she had just hidden. "What letter?"

"Christ Cat, your resignation letter!" He sounded just like Stuart.

"No, Evelyn was not in today."

"You don't have to hand it to him in person. You could have handed it in to HR"

"You don't know him. He'd go ballistic if he learned from HR that his PA had resigned without talking to him first."

As usual John was losing the argument. "Tomorrow then."

"Fine. Oh and he is going away on a business trip, he needs me to go with him."

"I thought you said he wasn't there today."

"He wasn't. He sent me a text."

"Where are you going?"

Cathy plucked somewhere out of the air. "Dubai"

"In July? Good luck with that! What about the letting agent? We need to get that second meeting sorted."

"You don't need me there for that. Anyway I don't have exact dates yet. It's just a heads up"

A few days later and she had gone. She did not take her passport. He had never believed the Dubai story.

Cathy was watching the sunset over the Dart, champagne in hand. She was wearing the red lace knickers Stuart had bought her for Valentines. She had already told him that John had been playing away from home. "I'll show that French midget who is the better lover." She gave Stuart her best come hither look.

"If you really want to do that you should be making love to your husband, not me. You really say some daft things sometimes."

This only made Cathy more determined than ever to please Stuart. "But you're the one that I want" She sidled up to him.

"You are bloody obsessed with that Olivia Neutron Bomb. So come on, prove it!"

Over breakfast Cathy produced the ironed blue notepaper. Stuart browsed through them. "The old dog! I never thought he had it in him" He sounded almost complimentary.

It was not the reaction Cathy had expected. "What do you think I should do?"

"Do? Isn't it obvious you stupid cow? Now you can divorce him!"

Was she really stupid not to think of this? "What about Peter?"

"Christ Cat, do I have to spell it out? You're his mother, you keep him, you keep the house and screw John for maintenance."

It seemed harsh words from someone who claimed to be John's best mate. She bridled to her husband's defence. "With friends like you he doesn't need enemies."

"Don't you start going soft on me. Now is our chance. You always said that you couldn't live without Peter. If you asked him for a divorce based on our affair some bleeding heart liberal judge might grant him custody and you would lose your son." As an afterthought he added "They would probably say I would have to support you. You wouldn't get any maintenance either."

"You see things much clearer than me. What do you want me to do?"

"That's my girl! Sit tight. He doesn't know you know about the letter. That was a smart move pretending to put out the trash Clever girl! Say you've handed in your notice or he'll just keep banging on about it. Then say the boss is insisting on up to six months if he can't find a replacement. That will buy us some time."

"Time for what?"

"It will take us past the beginning of school. Peter will have to start secondary school here. That will give us more leverage with the judge."

"But then he will have to change schools again when he goes to France."

"Bloody hell Cat, don't you listen to anything I say? He won't go to France. He'll stay here and I'll have him."

"What do you mean you will have him?"

"I'll have to look after him with you. That will look good in front of the judge. Try and get John to go back to France to organise the school."

"He's already done that."

"Well buy school uniform or something."

"They don't have school uniform"

"For fucks sake Cat! Stop being so bloody awkward! You can say you are sending him back to screw his French tart for all I care, just get rid of him!"

"Why?"

"It will be abandonment. He will have left the jurisdiction of the English courts, he will never get Peter."

Cathy felt crushed. Stuart had got it all worked out. It was as if he had been planning this for years and suddenly sprung the trap.

Chapter 16
Growth and evolution.

Of the three only John still meditated. He set aside time each day while Cathy went to the gym. She joined when Stuart started making snide remarks about her weight. It was her thinking time. While John emptied his mind to allow peace to enter she filled hers. Doubts were always at the head of the queue. Things Stuart or her boss Evelyn said made her doubt herself. She decided self doubt was positive; she reasoned it made her strive to be a better person. With that she redoubled her efforts to achieve some arbitrary target set by the bike. While John tried to reassure her with comments like "You are lovely as you are." Stuart, along with every magazine she read pulled her in the other direction.

John was unused to self doubt. As a child he received nothing but support and praise from his mother. "You can achieve whatever you want" she would say. He grew up confident in his own abilities. These included an ability to see things from other people's point of view. Both these qualities attracted the young girl who bounced up to him at the Buddhist society stand. Her goal was to stick two fingers up to Christianity and meet boys. What's not to like?

Today whilst Cathy sweated at the gym John emptied his mind curious to know what enlightenment would come. Today it was growth and evolution. All life grows continuously. At certain times that life can no longer be contained by the structure it builds around itself. The snake sheds its skin; the hermit crab leaves its shell in search of a more accommodating home. John reasoned that these are times of evolution. Peter had grown in recent years. He had outgrown the shell of primary school and cast it off. Soon he would enter another that would allow him to grow towards Adulthood. Like the hermit crab he was vulnerable waiting to occupy a new place defined less by his parents and more by his own personality.

Cathy was not a bad person despite the things Stuart said. She did think for herself. Her opinion of John was that he was a genuinely good person whom she loved. Stuart excited her. John was her nacho, Stuart her salsa dip. Stuart challenged the 'you're wonderful' sentiment expressed by John. This was good she told herself. Everyone can improve. If she only had John she would never get better. She would live a life suffocated by his 'I love you just as you are.' Even so, 'What would John do without you?' was a genuine question that bothered her for years. Francine changed that. Cathy's first reaction was jealousy. John did things to Francine that previously he only ever did to her. At Uni John believed Cathy was The One and remained faithful.

Cathy was like a one eyed cat peeping in a seafood store. John was blind to the multiple sources of inspiration Cathy brought to the bedroom. Years moved on, and with the exception of Stuart, so did her lovers. At first Cathy was livid that Francine benefited from what she taught John. Later it became a way to salve her guilt. Deep down she was sorry she could not be the girl John thought she was. Perhaps Francine was The One. If so it freed her to a guilt free life with Stuart, maybe others. "Never say never" she smiled to herself. Then she realised she was forgetting Peter. When he eventually arrived John wanted Cathy to breast feed. It did its job of bonding despite her lack of mothering instinct. She was determined to keep Peter. Stuart seemed to have no problem with that. Quite the opposite, he seemed to positively relish the idea of a ready made family. When Cathy showed him the letters he saw an opportunity. Cathy thought he would want to shift Peter to France with John and have Cathy all to himself. Instead he insisted Peter stayed with his mother.

For Stuart it was all coming together. Peter taking a dislike to him was a bore, but nothing he couldn't handle, especially after he had got rid of John and moved in with Cathy. John had almost sussed him. That didn't matter, he was expendable. There was nothing to be gained from controlling him once Stuart had neutered John's influence on Cathy. Stuart doubted even he could make Peter turn against his father. Now that didn't matter. The stupid French tart had unwittingly done it for him. "Daddy doesn't love you anymore. He left you and mummy to go and live with another woman."

Peter saw more and understood more than he said. There were thoughts bouncing round in his head he would not share. Sometimes they hit the pain button, but nothing he couldn't handle. The one hidden behind the wall couldn't reach his pain button. Like his best friend Greg had said, what you don't know can't hurt you.

Back in France Francine was lost. Plenty of men had been drawn to her. Some she found sufficiently attractive to respond in varying levels of intimacy. John was different. Never had she given herself so completely, never had she felt such a response. She was sure she had made him an offer he could not refuse. He had. How could she have got it so wrong?

Under Stuart's careful direction Cathy put their plan into action. "I know John; I'm as gutted as you are. The contract does say one month's notice, but there is a get out clause. Apparently for key staff the employer can extend that to six to give them time to find a replacement."

John couldn't believe it. "Why didn't they make that clear when the signed you? It must have been in the contract. It's your job to spot things like that."

Stuart warned Cathy John might say something along those lines. She was prepared. "Of course I spotted it. I queried it at the time. 'key staff' seemed a bit vague. I was assured that personal assistants were classified as secretarial and support. They were not considered key. I remember it because I was miffed at not being regarded as important."

"So the six months doesn't apply to you."

"It does now. My role was redefined as key."

"They can't do that."

"Evelyn can. It's his company."

"What about Peter? He is due to start school in France 3rd September."

"We'll put him into Little Heath until Christmas."

"I don't want to go there; Greg is going to Langtree"

Cathy turned to her son. "I know you want to go to the same school as Greg sweetheart, I asked but they are full"

John was not at all sure. "Is there much point in putting him there for one term? He will have to make friends all over again a few months later"

"He's got to adjust to secondary school and a new country; this way he can get used to one at a time."

"Hey, will you two stop talking about me as if I am not here!" They both turned to look at their son. "Mum, you are not making sense. Yes it will be hard making friends in a new country, especially as I don't speak French. If I don't turn up until after Christmas they will have made friends. That will make it harder for me to fit in."

Cathy had to say something to turn this round. "Sweetheart I know it's hard for you to understand. You need to let the grown-ups decide what's best". John said nothing. Peter was doing pretty well on his own.

"It's not hard to understand at all. Daddy wants us all to move to France so you stop seeing Stuart."

Cathy was shocked. "John, what have you been saying to him?"

"Nothing. Scout's honour." They had both promised that whatever problems they had neither would bring Peter into it.

"He hasn't said anything. He doesn't have to. Daddy I want to go to France with you as soon as we break up. Mummy I want you to quit your job like you promised and follow us as soon as you can."

Cathy tried once more. "Sweetheart, it's not as simple as that."

Peter could not sustain the grown up facade. "YES IT IS!" He stormed out, ran upstairs and slammed his bedroom door. The bubble he kept imprisoned in the back of his brain was threatening to break out and hit his pain button. He wasn't going to live with mum if dad left because he knew Stuart would move in.

John stood. "I'll go and talk to him. Cathy I swear, none of this has come from me." Cathy knew she had lost. What she feared most was not that. It was what Stu would say. John sat on the bed. He put his hand on his son's shoulder. "Story?"

"Yes please."

"Which one?"

"The one where Christopher Robin says goodbye because he is growing up." When John went downstairs there was a note. "Gone out, don't wait up"

Stuart stared at Cathy in disbelief. "What? You stupid fucking bitch! You had one job!" Cathy sobbed. Stuart was pacing. "Are you sure he doesn't know we know about the French tart?"

"No. I mean yes, I am sure he doesn't know."

"Good. We can still do this. Let him go. Let him take Peter. We will give it a month or two then you can file for divorce. We will throw the book at him: desertion, infidelity, child abduction. There is no way a judge will not give you custody. Has he ever hit you?

"Of course not."

"Pity."

Cathy hated Stuart when he was like this. Perhaps after all a slow death from suffocation beneath John's love was better than being mauled by the tiger that was pacing in front of her. "I should go. John will wonder where I am."

Stuart nearly said 'if he wonders that he's even more stupid than I thought.' but bit his lip. He had gone too far calling her a stupid bitch. "Don't go yet. Please. I'm sorry I shouted. I'm scared of losing you."

Cathy looked at him. She had got used to Stuart having two sides but this was too much. He needs help. So did she. She took it badly when John suggested marriage guidance. Maybe he was right. Maybe the three of them should go. Did people actually do that? Stuart had stopped pacing. She stood and put his arms round him. "Just a quickie, but I'm not staying the night."

John did not hear the front door but was woken by the shower. Cathy always showered before and after making love. This was both. It was a first even for her. She slipped into bed and moved close to John.

Chapter 17
Summer

For more than two years John's sole objective had been to reach this point. The house was ready. Peter had finished primary school. A new life waited for them in Périgord. The house in Saint Etienne had gone over budget. They did not given the house in Reading much thought beyond renting to supplement their income. The letting agent was confident he could get a good price. Cross rail was announced last year and construction would start in 2009. Demand for commuter accommodation was already starting to boom. Houses such as theirs could command good rents as soon as they were brought up to spec. John had not given his much thought. Now there was no money left. Taking out a loan was problematic; he had switched to freelance to allow him to work from France whilst Cathy was quitting her job. Her salary would eventually to be replaced by a rental income but that did not help them getting the house ready to let. Instead of leaving at the start of the holiday John found himself redecorating the house in

Reading. Then there was the packing. John packed and Cathy unpacked declaring "I'm going to need that". He finally managed to get together a vanload but was now hesitating about making an advance trip. There was still a lot to do to in Reading. Peter, usually keen to go back to France, decided one day in Saint Etienne did not justify of a 12 hour road trip each way. John was torn between desperately wanting to see Francine again and having no idea what to say to her when he did. The other problem was they simply had too much stuff. Professional international movers were outside their budget. Tree knew a Polish bloke with a van. It seemed that whatever problem you had, Tree knew a bloke with a piece of equipment that would solve it. "Why are they always Polish?"

"Lena has a large family" he showed John a photo of his latest girlfriend. The van turned out to be a Luton. Not as big as they hoped, but John would follow him down with the trailer.

Since they intended to let the Reading house furnished only a minimum of furniture was going to France. The rest they could buy from second hand locally. Normally John let Cathy take the lead on interior decorating. She had quirky ideas that somehow worked. The letting agent was unsure. "Tenants want a neutral canvas their own stuff will fit into."

"I like it." Said Cathy.

"I'm sure you do Mrs Cartwright, but you will not be living here." Silence. John was studying his wife's expression. "I'll let you have a think about it." The agent continued, trying to move the conversation on. "The garage is very full; I take it all that is going with you. There was Peter's drum kit. The school counsellor suggested it around the time the punch bag arrived in her consulting room.

"I'm keeping that, and the trampoline. You said we could take that."

"What about your spinning and weaving stuff Cathy? You haven't used it for years."

"Take it. I won't have time to use it before the move. In France I will be a lady of leisure." Cathy said it simply to reassure John that she intended to follow him. Painting the hall dark red was a mistake. She had done it for her African mask collection. It was clearly not the action of someone intending to let. She would send Stuart to get the loom back later. She imagined his approval. "Smart move" he would say. Much of her life now was focused on gaining Stuart's approval. When she didn't get it she just tried harder. "What about your brewing stuff?" Cathy asked. Everyone it seemed had something they could not bear to part with.

"Of course, but we cannot get everything in the trailer. It will need two trips."

"Or another van. I'll drive the car and trailer, Lena's brother will take the Luton, you can hire a transit."

"You are not coming down in August remember?"

Cathy had forgotten. She agreed with Stuart that she would never go to France. She had to convince John that she would follow him. Without that they risked him sitting tight until she worked her notice. She couldn't go at Christmas for the simple reason she had not resigned. In her eagerness to cover up her real intentions she became confused. "Of course, I'm not thinking straight."

"You certainly aren't. Even if you were able to come with me in August how will we get the transit back to England?" If it had been Stuart speaking he would have mocked her stupidity. Not John. "Don't worry pet. It's a stressful time for us all. Everything will be fine once we are all down there. I'll have a think. We've solved more difficult problems than this." Both had missed the obvious, which was that Cathy could have come with them, taken the van back to England and returned to work to serve out her notice.

Stuart spotted it of course but said nothing. He had his own plan. He wanted an excuse to meet Francine and deal a death blow to John and Cathy's marriage. He offered to drive the extra van and take it back to the UK. Tree was as mystified as John about Stuart's motivation. "What's his game?"

"Maybe he just wants to help a mate."

"I'm sorry to break this to you Om, but Stupid is not a mate." The last time John and Tree had this type of conversation John made the mistake of asking Tree why he thought Stuart was not a mate. "Because he's shagging your missus." This was what Tree called tough love. John had not worked out Stuart's plan but was still uneasy. He suggested to Cathy they refused Stuart's offer and paid another of Tree's friends. She had been briefed by Stuart and was having none of it. "Why are you paying a Polski to do it when Stu will do it for nothing?" John had no answer so Stuart and Cathy got their way. Before he explained Cathy asked almost the same question of Stuart. "Why are you doing this, John has already said he'll get another Polski to do it."

"I want to meet the French tart. We might find out something we can use."

Thiviers

Francine was trying to move on. She found she couldn't. She was at Ariane's for her usual lunchtime galette. "I want to answer John's letter, will you help me?" Ariane was always ready to help a friend.

"Of course, in what way?"

"Your English is perfect, if I write it in French could you translate it for me?"

"I'll do my best. What do you want to say?"

"That's the problem, I don't know. Can you help with that too?"

"That might be a bit more difficult. Why don't you come for supper on Sunday?"

"Thank you. Are you sure Chris won't mind?"

"Of course not. Have a think about what to say. It needs to come from you and come from the heart"

They sat in the garden with drinks. Chris stayed a while but then excused himself. This was girl talk and in French. He had learned enough French to follow most conversations. On this occasion, while both insisted they were happy for him to stay he preferred to let them get on with it. By the time supper was ready Francine had decided what she wanted to say and Ariane had written it in English. They all sat down to eat. "I have written a letter to my English boyfriend. Ariane has translated it. I would like you to read it. You are a man and you are English. Maybe you can tell me if it is a good letter."

"I will do my best."

Francine read the letter aloud.

"Dear John,

"How are things going in England? Are you selling your house there? You must be very busy. If there is anything I can do too help here please say. I do not know when you are planning to come down again. Ludo has more wood. I asked him to put 4 stair on one side for you. You can have more if you want. Peter's new teacher was in the library yesterday. The school is expecting him on September 3rd so I guess you will be here before then. As you missed the open day for new parents she would like to see you. Can you call in at the library when you arrive?"

Now Francine was stuck. The general chit-chat about daily life was easy. She lived in a small town; he would be in a small village a few kilometres away. They would meet. What then? Ariane urged Francine to bite the bullet. "You need to sort this out face to face; you can't do it in a letter." She said.

Francine continued the letter. "There are other things we need to sort out too. The library my not be the best place. I would like to talk to you alone. I know that will be difficult to arrange. We must. We will be neighbours and for my part, friends." Now they were coming to it. Francine looked at Ariane. "I love him. I always will. Nothing can change that. I will never apologise for that evening, or for the part I played in making it happen."

"Then you must say that. Do not say it in the letter. It has to be face to face."

"You are right. I will finish the letter there. How do I sign it?"

"With love, Francine"

"Should I say love?

"Of course, like the French it can mean many things.

Francine whispered in French "I love him so much."

"I know you do. You have to tell him."

There was one final problem: how to get the letter to him without Cathy seeing it.

"Does it matter, the letter says nothing."

"It says you want to talk to him without his son or wife being there. That is enough."

"True."

"Leave it with me. I'll get it to him.

England

Tree and John were in the clubhouse. Pre-season training had started. They no longer played of course but Tree coached the U13s. "Bring Peter along, he's a natural"

"He's only into soccer."

"I feel your shame. Your secret's safe with me."

John laughed. "One for the road?" He held up his glass.

"Go on then. Speaking of secrets, I have a letter for you."

"Bloody hell Tree, when did you learn to write?"

"Not me mate. Lena gave it to me."

"Lena? Hope it's not in Polish!"

"No, but it might be in French. Look at the stamp." John took the letter. His name was in a hand he instantly recognised. His stomach flipped. Lena's address had been written by someone else. "Open it then." Tree was intrigued. He was itching to know what was inside, and how it came to be delivered to his girlfriend. John could help him with the first; the second was a complete mystery.

"It's from Francine."

"John, I may be ex Gloucester, and a forward but I had worked that out." It was traditional when they played Gloucester for Irish supporters to mock the Kingsholm crowd. It was only banter. John let it pass.

He read the letter. "Blah blah blah, when do we arrive, missed school open day, Peter's teacher wants to see me. Blah blah, do we want more wood..."

"Christ John, sounds like a letter from the wife."

"No such luck." The unconsidered response hung between them. Tree stared into his beer. John was a good mate; he was going to miss him. As men always do Tree steered the ship to less dangerous waters.

"Why send it via Lena?"

"Francine wants to talk."

"Yea women are like that. It scares the shit out of me when Lena says we need to talk."

John laughed. "Francine is right, we do need to talk, I was a real Bastard. I'll write back."

"What you going to say?"

John tapped his nose. "That's for me to know and you to wonder! I'll just say when we will arrive. Cathy is staying here to work her notice. I'll invite Francine over when Peter's not about."

"Careful, look what happened last time." John did not need reminding. "I still want to know how the letter got to Lena."

"I have absolutely no idea."

Chapter 18
The move.

The day in August finally came. Peter got his way and joined the advance party. The trailer was filled with the garage contents. Brewing equipment, loom, trampoline, drum kit. Most of the garden stuff had already found its way to France. What gaps there were left in the trailer were filled with small stuff like forks and spades. The bikes were on the rack on the tailgate.

"Put those on last or you won't be able to load the boot." Stuart had arrived and was taking charge of operations. He liked to pretend he was ex military. In reality he was a corporal in the cadets when he was at school. With only John and Peter in the car they had put the seats down and filled the back with suitcases and bedding. "Last in first out" said Stuart. "Equipment needed to make the bridge head as soon as we arrive."

"For fucks sake! Leave out the military jargon!" John was on edge and had run out of patience. He was starting to regret accepting Stuart's offer of help. Lena's brothers Jakub and Filip arrived with the Luton. John marked stuff with coloured labels. These identified each item as staying or going, if so in which vehicle. They did a quick tour of the house. Much nodding, some sucking of teeth and the brothers set to work. There was a spare armchair and a wardrobe that just wouldn't fit. "Leave them" Said Cathy. "It will make the place look less empty when we rent it." Stuart smiled and slipped Cathy a conspiratorial wink. She shot him a warning look. John was in the room.

The Polish brothers left to take the night crossing. John calculated that he and Stuart could take the first morning one and catch them up. Eventually the car and transit were loaded. A strange family sat in the half empty house. Supper was courtesy of the Raj, wine supplied by Stuart. Cathy sat awkwardly between her lover and her husband. She was feeling guilty and hoped it didn't show. John was silent, lost in his own thoughts. Stuart was playing the endgame of a chess match he was winning. "Well this is cosy" he said.

"Can I eat in my room?"

"No sweetheart. Eat with the grownups then bath and bed."

"I'm not a baby."

"I know darling, you are growing up fast. You still need an early night. It is a long day tomorrow."

In a break with tradition Cathy decided she would read the story. "I want daddy to read" It was the one part of his childhood to which Peter clung.

"It is my turn. It might be the last time." Stuart shot her a look. "For a long time" she added. All Peter's books had been packed. The exception of course was Winnie the Pooh which was in the overnight bag. His own Pooh was on the pillow. "When do you think Peter will stop taking a teddy bear to bed?" Cathy asked John once.

"When he takes his first girlfriend to bed." John answered. He was not far out.

Tonight it was Pooh or nothing. The one thing the three of them agreed on was that mummy did not read Pooh. She could not do the voices. Peter was sitting up in bed. His mother sat awkwardly beside him. "Just a hug then."

"Just a hug mummy." They embraced. Neither wanted to let go, both were unsure when they would be together again.

Cathy eventually came downstairs to an awkward silence. Neither John nor Stuart had anything to say to the other. "Early night?" She asked. It was not immediately obvious to whom she was speaking.

John looked up "Yes, we need to be up at 4. "Stu, the bed in the spare room is made. I left a towel there too." There was no way John was going to give Cathy any say in this. As soon as he got back Stuart would be over but tonight at least this was John's wife, his house, his rules.

John and Cathy were undressing, stepping awkwardly over open suitcases. As Cathy slipped off her knickers John patted her bare cheek. "Not tonight John.

Not with Stuart next door." To be honest sex was not on John's mind at that moment. He did not know why he had done it, probably out of habit. They usually love the night before one of them went away, and when they returned. If it was Cathy going away it was generally to be with Stuart. Nacho then salsa. John tried unsuccessfully to feel guilty about the night he spent with Francine. Now when he made love to his wife felt as if he was being unfaithful. Ariane was right. English men are not very good at infidelity. John slipped into bed and turned away from Cathy. Both fell asleep wondering what the future would bring.

The journey passed without incident. Stuart wanted Peter to take turns doing one leg in his dad's car and one leg in the transit. Peter put his foot down. He didn't make a fuss, he didn't argue, he just made sure it was non negotiable. "You coming in the van for the next leg?"

"No." Peter got in his dad's car without another word. John knew his son well enough not to quiz him. If he wanted to talk he would. They arrived as planned around tea time. Jakub and Filip had come and gone. According to the neighbour they had got there 8 hours ago, unloaded everything into the garage and left. They had put in a full day yesterday and driven through the night. Now they were off to Poland for a return load. John and Stuart decided to leave the unpacking until the morning and headed to the local auberge for supper. Stuart turned on the car salesman charm. He filled the gaps left by John's reluctance to talk. So what made you choose this part of the world? Will you start supporting Brive or Bordeaux now? The wine started to kick in. He moved on to asking about Peter's school. Going to be tough doing lessons in a foreign language, do you think he will cope? At each new tack John kept his replies brief and non committal. Stuart ordered another bottle of wine and pressed on regardless. He hoped Cathy would not miss her job too much. Was she really cut out to be a lady of leisure? At every new turn he carefully planted another seed of doubt. John ignored him. Once he had seen through him he ceased to be affected. John asked for the bill. He wanted to get Peter to bed. Stuart ostentatiously declared that he would get this. He also left a generous tip. "You don't need to do that."

"What?"

"They don't tip in France."

"Why not?"

"Dunno. Maybe they pay better so they don't need them." Stuart ignored him. He got up to leave and shouted 'merci beaucoup' to the waitress pointing to the money on the table.

Peter hardly said a word the whole time. Stuart feigned sympathy. "He must be tired, pool lamb."

"Yes I'll get him to bed. If you help me get a couple of mattresses up from the garage we can sort the rest out in the morning." If he was honest Stuart was shattered too. John had done the journey often enough and was getting used to it. For Stuart, deprived of company in the van, the road stretched endlessly before him. He had not needed to research he route as John was leading the way. The names of each town were meaningless to him so he could not mentally tick off his progress. He sat on the floor watching John read his son a bedtime story. Winnie the Pooh was secure in Peter's arms listening to a story about himself that he had heard a thousand times. He wondered if the man listening had ever been read a bedtime story. Piglet did not think he had. Pooh was sad. Stuart was sad too. France was alien to him. He had never learned the language. This added to his sense of isolation. He was dependent on John's translations. John was working on his French as hard as Francine was with English. The locals struggled to understand but appreciated his effort. To Stuart he seemed fluent. Stories finished John turned to Stuart. "Nightcap?" Stuart was fast asleep. John took his whiskey to bed. He too was asleep before finishing it. Even the thought that he would see Francine tomorrow could not stave off the exhaustion.

"Pooh, are you awake?"

"Yes Piglit"

"You know when I said Eeyore was alright really, and you said everyone was alright really?"

"Of course."

"Do you think Stuart is alright really?"

Pooh rubbed his nose. "I don't know. He's not from the Hundred Acre Wood, and he is a grown up."

"Christopher Robin is a grown up. He's alright."

"Of course, and so is John"

Piglit snuggled closer to Peter. "Peter is growing up just like Christopher Robin. He will be alright too."

"They will all be alright"

"So why are you not sure about Stuart Pooh?"

"Nobody read him bedtime stories when he was little"

"That is really sad"

"Yes it is. Goodnight Piglit"

"Goodnight Pooh."

John woke. The morning sun had cleared the church roof and was full on his face. He slipped out of bed. Leaving the others sleeping he crept out to fetch croissants. He thought back, as he did almost every day, to the time Francine had done the same. Back in the village and back in the bed where they had made love he could think of nothing else. He returned with a breakfast courtesy of the local baker. "Where have you been?" Peter was awake. Stuart was not.

"Getting breakfast."

"I wanted to come with you."

"You were asleep."

"Next time wake me ok?"

"Entendu."

"What does that mean?"

"It means I heard you." John busied himself with coffee and setting the table. Stuart stirred.

Eventually they were all sat round the table planning the day. The van needed to be unpacked. There were some bigger pieces of furniture Jakub and Filip left down in the garage. John could do with some help getting those up to the living room. Stuart only had one thing he needed to do, that was meet Francine. He was not sure how to work it without showing his hand. John solved the problem for him. "Can we do the unloading this afternoon? The Library closes at midday and I need to speak to Francine?"

"Sure thing buddy, I am at your disposal."

"You can stay here if you like" John was talking to Stuart. Peter shot his dad a warning look. "Peter, you will need to come with me, it is about school."

"Sure dad, I like Francine, she's hot!" The little boy who liked bedtime stories was gone, the proto-teenager was very much awake.

"Well if she is hot, I need to meet her!" Stuart joked. Like taking candy from a baby he thought.

They climbed the hill to the library. Peter thought about running ahead. In his own way he too was excited to see Francine again. That would spoil the surprise he thought. He was at school the last time she and dad were together so he had not witnessed the seismic shift in their relationship. It was obvious to him that there was a relationship. It was obvious to everyone except John. Typical of the repressed Englishman he had hidden his feelings, first from himself, and then he hoped from Francine. It had finally dawned on him that the man beside him was not his mate. Tree had tried to warn him. Peter was already at the library door. John quickened his pace. He grabbed the door as Peter opened it but Stuart was only one step behind. Francine had her back to them, arranging books on their shelf. Hearing the door she turned, let out a little cry and rushed to John. "Hello Francine, I'd like you to meet..." The name was knocked out of him as their bodies collided. "Stuart."

She stepped back to be able to see John's face. Her expression was saying "*The* Stuart?" His warning expression answered her question. "He's..."

Peter interrupted. "What about my hug?"

Francine turned. She and Peter got on really well but he had never asked that before. "Peter! It's so lovely to see you again." She leaned in to brush his cheek in the traditional French manner. As soon as she was within range he put his arms round her and gave her a hug. Astonished and pleased in equal measure she responded.

Peter drew away and turned to Stuart. "Everyone says hello like that in France, that's why I want to live here. He shot his dad a conspiratorial wink.

Francine, overwhelmed by the sight of John was struggling to make sense of it all. She had played countless scenarios in her head for their next meeting. This was none of them. She turned to Stuart, hand outstretched. "Pleased to meet you" The Lefevres and the Cartwrights were forging a Franco-British alliance in the face of a common enemy.

"Stuart is helping us move" John explained. "We had to hire an extra van. Stuart kindly drove it for us. He is going back tomorrow." They had not discussed a return date. Announcing it now before witnesses put

John in control. It was the first time and represented a significant shift in the balance of power.

"Then you must come to my house tonight for apero. Say dix-neuf heures?"

Chapter 19
School

Stuart was lost, the master magician beaten by the three card trick. He looked from Peter to Francine to John. He had no idea which one held the ace. It certainly was not him. It started well. The unscripted greeting had been just what he wanted. Then Peter's actions set alarm bells ringing. That of course was Peter's intention. He wanted to portray the greeting Francine's had given John as normal. Stuart and Francine were impostors in the relationship between John and Cathy. Peter, as the fruit of that relationship was the key. Whoever controlled Peter controlled the war. Stuart saw it as that, something to win, something that would suffer collateral damage, something that would ultimately result in him owning Peter and Cathy. He had done everything to make Peter like him. The harder he tried the more Peter seemed to hate him. When Cathy and John went down to sign for the house Stuart saw an opportunity. He went too far. He realised that now. He often went too far with Cathy. He could recover that by sending in the good cop. Now no matter what he did Peter shunned him. Francine however did not seem to need to do anything. Peter was literally throwing himself at her.

Peter had long conversations with Pooh and Piglit. He loved his mum of course. He loved his dad too. Not more, just differently. He could not remember a time when Stuart was not part of the dynamic. He understood the threat Stuart posed to his parent's marriage. He applauded his father's attempt to reconstruct the family away from Stuart. Pooh had warned him that Stuart was not 'alright really'. Just like Christopher Robin leaving the Hundred Acre Wood changes were happening that Peter could not stop. He helped with John's nest building in France because it was where he wanted to be. One day he would of course leave, just as Christopher Robin had done. Until then he was staying with dad. It upset him no end that it was now clear that meant losing his mother. He looked at Francine. You are not my mother but you are a good person. You make dad happy. He was not sure mummy made daddy happy any more. He looked at Stuart. You are an arsehole. I hate you.

They stayed at the library long enough for John to make an appointment to see Peter's new teacher, then they went back to the house to unpack. Francine finished off at the library and headed to the ice cream parlour. It was very busy. "Ariane you must come to my place tonight at seven."

"Francine I would love to but I am rushed off my feet. Odette finishes at six, we are open until ten." Francine explained what had happened at the library. "I really need your support. Stuart scares me."

Ariane turned to Odette. "Could you come back at seven and finish off for me?" She turned back to Francine and smiled. "There, sorted. Do you want me to bring anything?" It was a silly question, Ariane arrived with a freezer bag full of pots of ice cream. Peter was delighted. Francine greeted Stuart with the smiles and courtesy the French reserve only for those they really loathe. Stuart was well used to playing such games. They were contests he invariably won. This time Francine had home advantage. More important the rules of engagement were completely different. Stuart's gaslighting simply did not work. He needed time, he needed someone susceptible to his non verbal communication. He needed someone who did not realise what he was doing. Francine was fighting for the man she loved. She looked at Peter picking out his favourite ice cream. She corrected herself. The men she loved.

"It is such a shame that Cathy could not be here for the beginning of term Mr, I am sorry I do not know your nom de famille..." Stuart was not about to help. Francine wondered if he was sulking. "Stuart then, if I may be so informal." She turned to Ariane and spoke in French. This was deliberate. It put Stuart at a disadvantage. He also had no way of knowing whether the translation was faithful. He had seen enough. Quite what useful information he hoped to garner by coming to France was not clear. Maybe it was no more than curiosity. To see the house, meet Francine. Now he had done both and wanted to go home. Back to a language he understood and people he could control. The confrontation Francine feared never materialised. Stuart was beaten. He poured himself another glass of wine, taking it into a corner where he could lick his wounds.

"Can I have some wine? Peter knew the answer his dad would give.

He was astonished therefore when Francine answered first. "Pourquoi pas ?" She picked up a glass; half filled it with wine and topped it up with water. She saw John's disapproving look. "If he is going to live in France he must learn to drink wine. It is how we teach our children." She looked across to Stuart who quickly looked away avoiding eye contact. "Maybe I should have put some water in my wine when I talked to Stuart." She picked up her glass and the bottle. Crossing the room she offered to top up Stuart's glass and made small talk.

John turned to Ariane. "What did she mean by that?"

"She thinks she spoke too harshly to Stuart. Un peu d'eau dans le vin means tone down your language."

"I didn't think she spoke harshly to him, she sounded very polite."

"She meant to sound polite. The French would understand it differently. How can I say? Sarcastic? Not quite, more like diplomatic speak. You know, they say full and frank discussions when the mean they argued the whole time." John realised that there was a lot more to learning French than grammar and vocabulary. He was desperate to talk to Francine. Stuart watched them like a hawk whenever they were together. Francine knew she had made a blunder at the library. She could wait. It was enough that they were in the same room.

Stuart made an early start the next day. He was getting into the van when an old lady came out of the house next door. She gestured to him that she wanted to talk. She had been babbling for some time before Stuart could get 'je ne parle pas Français' in edgeways. She switched to sign language. She pointed to John's car then shook her finger. John's car? Not John's car? Another car. She ran to the front door and mimed knocking. Someone came to visit John? "visiteur oui. Francine." Francine came to the house? She pointed to the balcony. Francine was on the balcony? The penny dropped. The French windows on the balcony led to John's bedroom. Francine stayed the night? She looked blank. Stuart mimed sleep by placing his hands together and placing them against his cheek. She nodded. You little beauty! "Merci!" He kissed her on the cheek before jumping in the van and driving off.

"Has he gone?" Peter asked.

"Yes"

"Good. When are we seeing my new teacher?"

John looked at the clock. "Now. We'd better go."

"Will she be cross that we are late?"

"Not if we get there in the next fifteen minutes."

The door was open. John knocked. Madame Blanchard motioned for them to come in. "Mr Cartwright, thank you for coming to see me. I understand you have just moved to Saint Etienne." She turned to Peter. "Are you looking forward to coming to our school?"

"Yes but it has a strange name"

"Leonce Bourliaguet? Yes many of our English students say that. It is named after a famous writer who was born in Thiviers over a hundred years ago."

"Do you have many English students?" With the new term so close Peter was starting to realise what a big deal it was to change country.

"Around ten I think. Most are mixed marriages so mum or dad is French. That helps of course."

John too was starting to realise how much he was asking of Peter. "Are there any who speak no French at all?"

"Not English, but there are some refugees. They are all with French foster families so they learn quickly."

"What about their parents?"

"We think they were either killed in the war or became separated on the journey."

"How did the get here?

"They walked." Peter was silent. Madame Blanchard turned to John. "The point I am making Mr Cartwright is that these young people are very resourceful. They are surrounded by French and yet they still struggle. I am sure Peter is very intelligent but he really needs to be immersed in the language. If he does not there is a risk of doubling."

"Excuse me?"

"If he does not pass his exams at the end of the year he will have to repeat the year. That means making a whole new set of friends."

Peter did not like the idea of that. "Could I have extra lessons outside school?" He turned to his dad. "Francine could teach me!"

"Francine Lefevre from the library?" The teacher asked. "Yes she would make an excellent teacher. I am not sure she would be able to spare enough time, she already has a full time job."

"I'll ask." Said Peter.

"I think your father should ask. Mr Cartwright let me know what you have arranged. Peter I look forward to seeing you on the 3rd" This signalled that the meeting was over. They both stood, leaving with the usual pleasantries.

Peter ran to the Library to get there before his dad. He managed to get himself ensconced with Francine behind the desk before John got to the door. "Francine is going to teach me to speak French!" Peter was clearly enjoying himself. "I left it to you to tell her the bit about moving in so we can do it every day."

"Peter, that is enough! Francine I am so sorry. His teacher was saying he needed extra French lessons. She suggested you might be able to help find someone."

"No she didn't, she said Francine would be a good teacher. She also said that I need to speak French at home."

"Peter, I am serious. There are lots of things Francine and I need to discuss." Peter opened his mouth to speak. "Alone" John added.

"Then invite her to supper and I will put myself to bed."

"We have just dumped three van loads of possession at home, I can hardly move let alone cook."

"We passed a pizza kiosk on the way from the school."

John realised he was not going to win this. If he put up any more objections Francine would think he didn't want to see her. He turned to Francine. "We do need to talk. Are you free tonight?"

"Of course. You go and sort out the house. I'll order the pizzas, vegetarian right?"

"Yes please. I'll give you some money."

"No you won't!" Francine realised she sounded bossy. "You can pay next time."

"I'll dig out some wine." John was unsure whether there was any left in the cellar. "Or beer. Are you ok with beer?"

"Of course, we French do drink other things besides wine."

"Good. I know we have beer. I brought my home brew with me."

"Home brew?"

"Home made beer. It is a hobby of mine."

"I am no longer surprised by you John, but I do wonder what else I will find out about you."

"Lots I hope." He was flirting? He couldn't help it. Francine came over and gave him a quick kiss on the cheek. Not the universal double kiss and not a lovers kiss, a familiar kiss between couples. "See you tonight"

Chapter 20
The storm

The three of them sat on boxes eating slices of pizza with their fingers and drinking homebrew from the bottle. If Peter thought the incident with the wine would get him a bottle of his dad's beer he was mistaken. This was almost as strong as wine but John would not countenance adding water to make it child friendly.

Francine came to the point. "Yes Peter, I would love to teach you. Your teacher is right; the quickest way to learn is to only speak French. It will be very hard not to speak English with your father. I am sorry John but he would learn your mistakes too. Now your father and I need to talk. You said at the library you would put yourself to bed. When you are in your pyjamas I have a little surprise for you."

"What?"

"Pyjamas first!"

Peter got up to go without another word. John pulled his 'I'm impressed' face. "Are you sure you don't have children? You are a natural. Were you teasing me that night when you said you were married too?"

"No I wasn't teasing. Like the song 'Mon père m'a mariée...'"

"I don't know the song. Are you saying it was an arranged marriage?"

"Sort of. I was the eldest, and a girl. He wanted me to marry his cousin to avoid the farm being split up. Then he worked out how to make boy babies so it wasn't necessary."

"How many brothers do you have?"

"Five. Mammy named the fifth Benjamin to make sure he didn't give her any more."

"Sorry I don't understand."

"The youngest son in France is always called Benjamin. A nickname I think you would say. My mother actually christened him Benjamin to make sure he was the last. He is two months younger than Peter. In many ways they are very similar."

"But you couldn't have been married when your mother was still having babies."

"It is possible you know! No, you are right. There is six years between my eldest brother and me and sixteen between me and Jean-Mark, my husband. My father promised me to him when I was old enough as part of a land settlement."

"What? Your father sold you for land? That's barbaric!"

"No, it's not like that at all. In France inheritances used to be split equally between the sons. When there are several sons the land becomes fragmented. Now that daughters inherit land too my father wanted to make sure my share stayed in the family and reunited land fragmented a generation ago."

"So what went wrong?"

"Let's just say other essential ingredients to marriage were not there."

"That's awful."

"Not really. It's like the song:

'Bonsoir Monsieur l'curé, j'ai trois mots à vous dire, Hier vous m'avez fait femme, aujourdhui faites-moi fille.' Monsieur Curé, yesterday you turned me into a woman, now turn me back into a girl. To which he replies 'De fille je fais femme, de femme je n'fais point fille,' I can turn girls into women, but I can't turn women back into girls. It is a very old song."

Peter came back in his pyjamas. "What is my surprise?"

Francine pulled a book from her handbag. "It's only a library book but if you work hard on your French I will buy you your own copy."

Peter looked at the title: Winnie l'Ourson "It's Winnie the Pooh in French! Wow, thank you Francine!"

Peter rushed up to her and gave her a hug and a kiss. "Are you going to read it to me?"

"No, daddy will. That is his job. I will listen and correct his pronunciation. He needs to learn French too!"

"OK Francine, but not tonight. You two need to talk." He kissed her again then went to kiss John. "Goodnight Francine, goodnight dad." With that he was gone.

"Is he matchmaking?" Francine asked.

"Yes"

"He is adorable." Francine could bear it no longer. She looked at John. "John, what is happening? Peter says he doesn't think his mother will come to France. Will she?"

John looked doubtful. "She said she would. I fear for her if she doesn't. She may think that Stuart makes her happy but the reality is the opposite. Also Peter deserves two parents." Francine looked hurt. "I'm sorry Francine you are wonderful. You are wonderful with Peter."

Francine finished the sentence for him. "But I am not his mother."

"Francine, I'm so sorry. Now I have made you unhappy."

"Please John, stop apologising. And stop trying to make other people happy."

"You are right, I shouldn't keep saying sorry, but what is wrong with making other people happy? Do I make you happy, apart from just now of course?"

"Yes you do. But you should think of yourself too. You make me happy but that is not your job. That is my job. Cathy too, it is her responsibility to look after herself."

"I am her husband. It is my job to look after her."

"No John, she is not a child, she must look after herself."

"What If she can't?"

"Then she must learn." Francine moved closer and took John's hand. "Do you think that she ever took responsibility for her own happiness?"

"Yes. She has always done whatever made her happy."

"And did that make you happy?"

"No. Sometimes it hurt. It hurt a lot."

She put her arm across his shoulder. "When did it hurt?"

"When she made love to other men."

"So it was not just Stuart?"

"No, there were others."

Francine kissed his cheek. It was wet and salty. "If it hurt you so much why did you let her do it?"

"Because I loved her." John could no longer hold back the tears.

Francine cradled him in her arms gently rocking him until peace returned. "Do you love her now?"

"No. Not any more"

"If she leaves Stuart and comes to France could you love her again?"

"I would have to."

"Why? Because she is your wife? Because you thought she was The One? Has she earned your love, your loyalty?

"No she hasn't. I wanted her to but she couldn't."

"I would like to earn your love. I want it because it makes me happy. You made selfless love a noble goal. When we made love you thought only of what would give me pleasure. I tried to do the same. Tonight I want you to only think of how I can give you pleasure and I will do the same. Take me. Ask for anything."

"And if I ask for something you don't want to give?"

"Then I will say no and I will have learned something new about you. It is just as likely I will ask you for something you don't want to give".

In the bedroom John was nervous. It did not help that the weather was closing in. Thunder clouds were gathering, waiting for the sun to set. Distant rumblings sounded like an orchestra tuning up. He felt as if something or someone was watching him. He put it down to guilt. The last time he was swept away on the tide of his emotions. It scared him when Francine said ask for anything. Love making had always been about the other person. He wanted to ask to be allowed to do what he did to her last time, the things that gave her so much pleasure. Something told him that she would not accept that. He had to ask for something. They had both undressed, studying the other's body. John was not yet aroused. That came from her arousal. She was waiting for him to tell her what to do. He had such a limited pool of experience. He thought back to Cathy. He could not help it; it was his only point of reference. She found him too compliant. "Whatever you want darling" sparked an outburst. He could not remember what they were arguing about. Cathy was a person who always wanted her own way. She was also a person who liked her men to be decisive. "The trick with Cathy" he once confided in Tree, "is to find out what she wants to do, then tell her she has to do it." Is that what Francine wanted? He did not know. Last time Francine made to take him in her mouth. He was so aroused he would not let her for fear of the consequences. Now, as before, she was sitting on the bed. This time he moved in front of her, guiding her head. When she finished she stood. John was about to whisper. She put her finger on his lips. "No, don't say thank you. Now it is my turn." She went to the kitchen and returned with a bottle of olive oil. "If you want to get me a present you can buy massage oil. For now this will do." She lay on her back on the bed. John sat behind her head holding it in his lightly oiled hands. He was still for a long time as if meditating. Eventually he started massaging her face. He pushed his fingers into her scalp then moved down her neck. He pulled her arms towards him, massaging each in turn. When he could reach no further from this position he moved, rolling her on to her stomach. Warning the oil in his hands before applying it he explored every inch of her with strong firm strokes. He rolled her back and moved down to her feet. From here he moved upwards. He had saved her most intimate parts until last. Her response was transmitted to his own body with predictable consequences. Again he felt as if he was being watched. The thunderstorm was closing in. The flickering of the lightning grew brighter, the thunderclaps louder. In the next room Peter clung to Pooh. He was determined not to disturb his father and Francine. He was old enough to know what they were doing. The presence was not Peter or Cathy. With an enormous bang a lightning bolt blew the main fuse. Francine was urging him on in the darkness.

1942

The presence that was watching them took form. Safe in the total darkness a small figure was pressed against the far wall. The young man was dressed in matching jacket, shorts and waistcoat. The brown material was thick and hardwearing. There were four pleated patch pockets. Two buttons were fastened hiding the waistcoat. The linen shirt was open at the neck. Francis looked at the couple making love. Francine was exactly as he wished he could be. If he was a woman Jean would love him. Now Jean was dead. Another lightning bolt illuminated a huge figure in the window. Francis was cornered. He was no longer afraid. He

204

turned to face his enemy. While they both lived Jean and Francis could not be a couple. They would be united in death. One day he told himself there would be no war. Beyond the veil he would find his love.

2008

In the darkness Francine lifted her hips further, pulling John towards her. "Do it" she whispered urgently. Grateful that he had been generous with the oil he complied. Afterwards thought how different she was to Cathy. Francine spoke softly. "J'aimerais lire dans tes pensees." He immediately felt guilty. Francine had just offered him a penny for his thoughts. She kissed him lightly on the temple. "It is ok. The more often we make love the less you will think of her."

John looked at her "How did you know?"

"Female intuition. It's ok. If you were using me to make love to her I would know."

"What happened?"

"You changed. She changed. I also suspect she was never the person you thought her to be."

"Will we change?"

"Yes. We will grow old together. We will know each other better. We will love each other more." John fell asleep unable to understand how it could be possible that one day he would love Francine more than he did at this precise moment.

Part 3
The Cad

Chapter 21
Two letters.

John woke first. The storm had passed. The light that crept across their pillows turned Francine's tangled mass of hair to burnished gold. She was the diametric opposite to Cathy. He had talked about his love for Cathy. How could he once have loved someone so different to Francine? A shaft of sunlight penetrated the tangled hair and woke her. "Good morning!" he said.

Francine squinted, blinded by the morning sun. John moved his head to block the light for her. Now all she could see was his silhouette. The sun behind him produced a halo giving him the appearance of a mediaeval saint. She remembered the things he had done to her last night. He was definitely not a saint! She could not say why she had asked that of him, it is not how they make love in France. Not men and women anyway. Instead she said! "Ah non! Aujourd'hui on dit bonjour. C'est que Français jusqu'à Vendredi." John asked (in French) why Friday. The agreement was that the three of them would speak only French Monday to Friday to help

John and Peter. At the weekends they all spoke English to help Francine. There was a bit of backsliding when John and Peter were alone but generally it worked well.

Peter did not start school until Monday. Francine told Pascal yesterday that she would be in late. It allowed her to take her time. "When I said I would learn something new about you I did not think it would be that." John was about to protest when there was a timid knock on the door. "Peter?"

"Are you awake Dad?"

"Yes, do you want to come in?" He looked at Francine to ask if she was ok. She nodded. Peter came in, still clutching Pooh and Piglit.

"That was quite a storm Dad, did you get wet?"

John was puzzled. "When?"

"After the big thunderclap. You must have gone to the bathroom. You came in to my room to see if I was OK, then went to your room via the balcony."

Francine's eyes were wide. She tried to catch John's eye. When she did she nodded, indicating that John should agree with his son's interpretation.

"Oh yes, I did. I wanted to close the shutters. It was getting windy." The shutters were still open. Peter did not argue the point. He had got what he wanted. He guessed his mother would not come to France. After last night Dad would not take him back to England. Peter was prepared to lose contact with his mother if it meant he did not have to see Stuart again.

Francine simply stayed. It was as if they had lived together for years. Peter never questioned it. His eyes nearly popped out of his head when Francine wandered about the house naked. It took a while for John to adjust too. For Cathy nudity served a purpose. For Francine it was natural. "Why should I have to put a towel round me to walk from the bathroom to the bedroom? I will only have to take it back after I dress. It is not as if you have not seen me naked before."

"What about Peter?"

"He needs to learn what women's bodies look like."

The weeks passed. John pushed Cathy to the back of his mind. Peter was probably right; she was not intending to leave Stuart. It niggled him was that if that was the case why she had agreed to Peter going to France? Their son had shown absolutely no enthusiasm for returning to England at half term. John broached the subject once. Peter simply said he didn't want to talk about it. John couldn't believe he had a problem with his mother so he concluded it must be Stuart. Then the letters arrived. Francine came in with the post. "Two letters from England, one for you and one for Peter"

"Did you go to the post like that?"

Francine was in her underwear. "Like what?" John gave up. He opened his letter.

Dear John,

It will come as no surprise to you to learn that I am not moving to France. I was shocked and hurt to hear from Stuart that you have been seeing someone behind my back. You have not even had the decency to hide it from our son. Stuart told me Francine kissed you in public in front of him when Peter was watching. She even had the nerve to make light of it by kissing Peter as well. She invited Stuart for drinks at her house with you and Peter as if you were already a couple. I was even more shocked to hear that she tried to get Peter drunk. He is barely twelve years old! The final straw came when a neighbour made a point of saying that this woman had moved in with you. Into our house! I do not need to remind you that only a few months ago you signed a document giving me the legal right to live there.

I have to protect our son from this corrupting influence. Please arrange for him to return to England. If you are too much of a coward to bring him yourself put him on a flight and I will meet him at the airport. You will hear from my solicitor regarding my sole custody and maintenance payments. I will have to switch to working part time now you have abandoned us. Raising Peter as a single mother will be expensive.

Cathy.

John read in stunned silence. "What is it?" Francine asked. John handed her the letter. She had only got half way through when she looked at John. "There was a letter to Peter too." They both rushed into Peter's bedroom. He was clutching Pooh to his chest and rocking. The secret he had locked in the back of his brain had broken free. It was crashing against his pain button.

None of them spoke. John and Francine sat either side of Peter. At first they rocked with him. The love they shared held Peter in its grip. The rocking gave way to anguish. This too fell away allowing the tears to flow. Still they held him. When Peter was finally able to speak he whispered "I'm not going."

"Nobody is going to make you do anything you don't want." It was Francine who spoke.

John started. "Why don't you tell us..."

"Not now John, he will tell us when he is ready."

Peter turned to her and buried his head into her bosom. "Stay" he whispered.

"I'm not going anywhere." Francine released John so she could put both arms round Peter.

John stood up. "I'll tell the school Peter won't be in today." He went to find his phone.

Francine was trying to second guess what was in Peter's letter. "Your mum must be missing you terribly."

"I miss her too."

"Then why don't you want to go back?"

"Stuart will be there"

Francine suddenly knew. The thought made her physically sick.

Francine trained as a social worker but never qualified. The field work was too upsetting. She applied for her library job instead. Her tutor's words came back to her "think the unthinkable". She had been watching

Stuart ever since John wrote to her from England. She likened him to a card sharp playing 'cherchez la femme' Francine turned the card. It was not Cathy, it was Peter. John came back in the room. She put her finger to her lips. "Do you like Stuart"

"I hate him!" Peter spat the words.

Francine remained calm. "Why?"

"He does stuff to me"

"Do you want to talk about it?"

"No. I am bad."

"Peter, you are not bad. What happened was not your fault."

"You don't know what happened."

"No, I don't. But I know when a grown up and a child do things it is the grown up who is responsible. If daddy takes you canoeing it is his job to make sure you stay safe."

"That's different. Daddy loves me." He thought for a moment. "Stuart said he loved me."

Francine looked up at John. Her tears would come later. Now she had to be strong. "Do you think he does?"

"No."

Francine squeezed him tighter. "I love you Peter." He snuggled into her accepting her love.

John sat beside them both. "I have phoned the school and told them Peter is not well. Francine, you need to get to work. Peter, are you ok to stay with me?"

"Of course."

"Are you sending me back to England?"

"I will never do that against your will, and certainly not if Stuart is there. If that changes you must choose."

"How will that change?"

"I don't know, but nothing is the same forever."

"You could kill him."

John could not deny the thought had crossed his mind. "That would not help. They would send me to prison"

Peter extracted his face from Francine so he could look at his father. "You could make it look like an accident." He smiled. John sat beside him and hugged him.

Francine stood up. "Are you both ok for me to go to work? I could phone in sick too."

John hesitated so Peter answered "I'll be ok with daddy. He can help me with my homework"

"Ok, but in French, it is still a school day remember."

"No it's not. I am not in school" The delightful Peter logic resurfaced. The squall had passed. The storm was far from over but they would weather it. They were family.

Francine was at work. The library was empty. Pascal was consolidating his love affair with Dewy classification. Francine picked up the phone "Thelma? It's Francine from the Library... Yes it has been a long time. How are you?... Good, and Paula?... I'm sorry to hear that, I hope she feels better soon. Thelma, I need you help. A young friend of mine... he's just turned 12. He was abused in England by his mother's boyfriend... Yes, he's English. He moved to France with his dad... No, his dad has only just found out. His son disclosed when his mother tried to get him back to England... Could you take him on?... I know you have retired but this lad really needs help... As far as I can gather it is type 1 trauma. The abuser made his move about 6 months ago. Since then the victim seems to have been successful in avoiding repeat incidents... No I haven't spoken to the police, I came to you first. He only disclosed this morning...You will? Thank you so much. Can you come to supper tonight?... Tomorrow then?... With Paula?... That's a shame, another time...A sitter? I did not know it had come to that. If ever you want me to stay with her so you can get out just say. Bring her to the library we can play cards...Not at all; it's the least I can do. Tomorrow about 6.30? You can chat to Peter while we make supper... Sorry yes, 'we'. Peter's father, John... at his place... St Etienne, place de l'eglise. The big house with the balcony... Yes we are. Thelma, you are completely unshockable, you should have been French... Ha, yes working in child protection would do that. Look, thank you so much, we'll see you tomorrow. Give my love to Paula."

Chapter 22
Therapy

Thelma completed her PhD in child psychology in 1973, the year Maria Cowell was murdered. Thelma's thesis predated the public enquiry which corroborated her research. Both the thesis and the enquiry were deeply critical of social work practices of the time. Thelma became the bête noir of her profession. Her methods and relentless exposure of poor practice won her many enemies. They attacked not only her methods but her private life. Her sexuality made her an easy target, especially as her chosen field was paedophilia. She was one of the few practitioners who undertook studies into to both victims and perpetrators. At an American conference on child abuse she was famously quoted as saying "How can you understand the fucked if you won't try to understand the fuckers?" She was often called as an expert witness in Judicial Reviews and court cases. She kept herself anchored by continuing to take on clients ranging from Fred West to grooming victims. When her long term partner started showing signs of

Alzheimer's she retired and moved to France. Within a year she was perfectly bilingual. She arrived for supper with a selection of fruit and vegetables she had grown herself.

"Bonsoir! What language are we speaking?"

Francine answered. "We try to only speak French on weekdays, but Peter still struggles so I thought tonight we could make an exception."

"Hey! I don't struggle; my teacher says I am making a lot of progress." He moved close to Francine for support. "Thanks to Francine," He added.

Thelma turned to him. "You must be Peter. I am Thelma, a friend of Francine." She held out her hand.

Peter took it. "That makes you English. The French are always kissing. Not that I mind" he added shooting Francine a mischievous look.

John came in wiping his hands on an apron. He had been making supper. "Hello, I'm John, Peter's dad."

"Pleased to meet you. To help me Peter has kindly agreed to forego speaking in French. Old people don't learn as quickly as the young."

"I'll second that, Peter is already better than me."

Usually when there are guests Peter could not wait to be excused and retreat to his bedroom. Tonight Thelma said very little but always drew Peter in. Nobody knew how it happened, but the conversation turned to Winnie the Pooh.. "Those are my favourite stories" said Thelma, "do you read them to your dad?"

Peter gave her his 'what a daft question' look. "Of course not. He reads to me."

"Why, you can read can't you?"

"You know I can. French and English."

"Then you can read your bedtime story to me. I'll let you choose the language."

"Ok, but it's bath night. I'll call you when I am ready." With that he was gone.

John looked in amazement first at Francine then Thelma. "That is the first time in his life he has ever allowed someone else to read him a Pooh story"

"I'm not reading it, he is. I suggested it because I'd like to spend some time alone with him if that is ok."

"That is why I asked you here."

"I never imagined he would agree to it the first time he met you." Added John.

"I told you she was good." Francine shot a look to Thelma.

"There's no need to butter me up, but it is kind of you to say so."

"Ready!" Peter called from his room. Thus was Thelma's cue. She smiled at her hosts and left.

"Beer?" Asked John.

"No thanks, I'll have another glass of wine." John put the bottle down and poured them both wine.. "I thought you were on beer?"

"I was but I'll join you. Beer then wine is fine, wine then beer, oh dear!"

"They have a similar saying in French. I am so pleased that Peter likes Thelma" Francine knew instinctively what John was thinking. It was the only thing she and Cathy had in common. In complete contrast none of them could read Stuart. That is except Thelma who had never met him. She had met too many Stuart's in her career. Thanks to her, abuse was being flushed out from the dark recesses of society. Boarding schools, children's homes, churches, were being thrown open to reveal the cancer in our society. Tonight she was doing what she did best. She watched every detail of Peter's behaviour. Every word, every movement happened for a reason. Thelma read every sign. She had no notebook. Alone tonight she would make meticulous notes, but with the child she gave no indication she was observing. Peter recited Pooh in English. He did not need to read. He knew every story by heart. Proudly he read the same story in French. They talked about the characters. Why Eeyore was gloomy, Rabbit bossy. They laughed at Owls pomposity. Above all they marvelled at Pooh's wisdom. And Piglit, Peter reminded her. Through the eyes of a child she penetrated his psyche. She understood his trauma. Given time she could heal it.

Thelma found John and Francine in the living room. She broke the silence. It was the quiet world that two perfectly attuned souls inhabit. Thelma remembered such times with Paula who was no longer capable of processing subtle non verbal communication. There were times when the woman Thelma loved did not even recognise her. The miracles she could perform on traumatised brains could not reverse degenerative conditions. She brushed the thought aside. "Peter would like you to say goodnight"

Francine had been sitting on the floor in front of John with her head on his lap. She got up in a single movement that denied the reality that even she would one day grow old. Next birthday she would be 34. She looked at least ten years younger. John rose too. "Coffee?"

"No thank you, but a herb tea if you have it."

"There's mint in the garden"

"Perfect"

John put the kettle on and followed Francine into Peter's bedroom. "Did Thelma like the story?"

"She loved it. She knows all the Pooh stories but had never heard one in French."

"Did you talk about anything else?"

Peter looked at his father and made the nose tapping gesture he had taught him. "She's my therapist, it's confidential. She will tell you."

Francine looked puzzled. "Then it is not confidential."

Peter put on the look of a teacher explaining something again to a slightly dumb student. "I tell her what she can say, and who she can say it to. I am in charge."

Now it was John's turn to be laid open to the exasperated teacher treatment. "I thought you didn't like therapists, you always moaned about the one at school."

"That was different Thelma gets it." Luckily John knew what Peter meant because that was all the explanation he was going to get. "She's coming again next week. She would like supper but will bring pudding. I said trifle because it is my favourite and they don't do it in France"

Thelma, John and Francine sat together mugs of tea in hand. Francine started. "Peter said he told you which parts of your session he was happy for you to share with us."

Thelma laughed. "I'm sure he did. You of course want to know everything. For me to help him he must be absolutely sure he remains in control of the process. The disclosure is a major event in his life. The trauma was too much for him. He locked it in a part of his brain that even he could not access."

John prodded the mint leaves in his tea in an effort to persuade them to release sufficient flavour to justify his cup of water being described as tea. "You mean he was in denial."

"Exactly. You said in three words what I said in ten. Lesson learned."

Francine touched Thelma's knee. "It was not a criticism, John is trying to understand. This is all new to him."

Thelma smiled. "It's ok; I did not take it as a criticism. John I have watched you with Peter. He is a very lucky young man to have a father like you."

John renewed his relationship with the mint. "Thank you."

Thelma continued. "There is not at present much he will not allow me to share. I hope that reassures you."

Francine remembered what she had learned as a trainee social worker. "It's on a need to know basis"

"Not exactly," Thelma continued. "There are often things you need to know that I cannot share because I do nor know either. We never have all the pieces of the jigsaw. We make guesses. Sometimes they are wrong."

"What has Peter said that you can share?" John asked.

"He was abused by Stuart when you came here with Cathy to sign documents. Francine you said it was six months ago. It was more, eighteen I would say. It doesn't matter. Peter has been careful to avoid situations where Stuart could repeat the abuse."

"Then I was right, it is type 1 trauma."

John interrupted. "Francine, slow down. This is all new to me. What is type 1 trauma?"

Thelma answered. "It is a single traumatic event. For example a jogger attacked and raped by a stranger. Type 2 is someone abused repeatedly because they are in an abusive relationship. It takes much longer to recover from the latter."

"That's good for Peter then?"

"John, there is no good, only shades of bad. His mother has been in a long term abusive relationship. He will have been affected by that. He was controlling you as well John."

"Yes I know. A friend told me about gaslighting. It clicked into place. After that I was not affected personally. I tried to help Cathy and failed. It never occurred to me he was doing it to Peter."

"More than that I would say Peter was his objective. What makes this case remarkable is that he started his relationship long before Peter was of an age that interested him. He was very patient."

Francine was finding she hated Stuart even more. "You make it sound like a virtue."

"Quite the opposite, when this comes to court, and I sincerely hope it does, such a sustained period of premeditation will enable the prosecution to press for the maximum sentence."

"Will it come to that?" John was starting to wonder what he had unleashed. He had not, of course unleashed anything. Peter had disclosed; Francine had contacted Thelma.

"I hope so" responded Thelma. "Does that sound harsh? It is to prevent him abusing again, and to help all the others like Peter he has abused."

John was shocked "How do you know he has done it before?"

"I have studied thousands of cases. Whilst every one is different, the patterns are very marked. If you want me to speculate, I would guess that not only is he part of a paedophile ring, he is probably their leader." Thelma let this sink in. She was charming and polite but when it came to safeguarding children she did not pull any punches. If people were shocked that was nothing compared to what was happening to innocent children.

Francine was trying to catch John's eye. When she did she mouthed "You ok?" Meanwhile Thelma was pulling something out of her pocket. She placed it on the coffee table. When Francine looked back she saw her favourite pair of knickers. Her first instinct was to laugh. "I've been looking for those for days, where did you find them?"

"In Peter's room, under his pillow." Thelma clearly did not find it funny. Francine, I can see how much you love Peter. I know too that your feelings towards him are entirely parental." She paused. "But Peter is entering adolescence. He has been introduced to inappropriate adult sexual activity. He is perfectly aware that you and his father have a sexual relationship." Both John and Francine opened their mouths to speak. Thelma silenced them with her hand. "Peter loves you as much as you love him. That too is perfectly obvious. What must not happen is for him to have any indication that a perfectly normal teenage crush on an older woman is in any way reciprocated."

Francine was shocked. What surprised her most was that she was shocked to be described as an older woman. "Thelma, I had absolutely no idea. I love him as my own son, I knew he had feelings for me too, but I assumed it was as his mother."

"It is. It is both. He oscillates between childhood and teenager. He sees you both as a mother figure and as someone upon whom he focuses his emerging sexual feelings. You must make sure his feelings are confined to the former. Does he try to see you naked?"

"I would not say he tries. We are a family. I do not try to hide from him. I am not bothered if he sees me naked, it is perfectly natural. I would rather he learned from me what a real female body looks like than he was misled by photo shopped images on the internet."

"Normally I would agree, however you are his de facto stepmother. You are young and attractive. We do not want him to feel he needs to challenge his father for your feelings. He has enough to cope with as it is."

Francine was shocked. "What should I do?"

"Be more careful about being naked in front of him. You do not need to hide your obvious feelings for his father. Quite the opposite, it will help his feelings of insecurity to see that your relationship with his father is strong and that this reconstructed family will not break apart. When you kiss John in front of Peter, give him a kiss too, but show him that the way you kiss him and the way you kiss John are quite different. It will help him feel loved, and learn the different types of love.

Francine said nothing. John eventually spoke. "You have given us a lot to think about. I cannot express my gratitude at the way you have helped Peter. Thank you so much"

Thelma finished her tea and stood. "All I have done is eat your excellent food and allow your charming son to read me a story. We have a long road ahead of us. It is a journey I look forward to sharing with you all. Now if you will excuse me I have my own family to think of. Paula will be wondering what has become of me."

John and Francine stood. This time it was Francine who spoke. "Do give Paula our love. I am sorry to take you away from her."

"That is quite alright. I need to think of myself too. It has done me good to get back in the saddle. Thank you for your hospitality and see you same time next week. With trifle!" She winked.

Chapter 23
John writes back

Francine looked at John "What now?"

"It's still early. There's an open bottle of wine on the table. I'll fetch it."

Francine sat on the floor waiting. She could then return to her usual position resting her head on his knee. She liked it when he fiddled with her hair. She pulled it over her left shoulder using it as a pillow. John cradled his wine glass studying her ear and neck. Francine stared into her glass swirling the wine, watching the way it clung to the sides. "My English is still not good."

John was astonished. "Why do you say that?"

"Because when I said 'what now' I meant what is going to happen to us, to Peter, to Stuart and Cathy. You clearly thought 'what now' meant shall we finish the wine or get an early night."

"First of all your English is excellent. 'What now' can mean both those things. I chose it to mean the latter because I don't have an answer to the former."

Francine nodded. "You do that a lot. At first I thought you were avoiding the issue. Now I see you are breaking the big question into small questions. You don't have an answer to the big question so you answered it by saying let's sit and talk about it."

John thought about it. "Did I do all that? Maybe I did. I am cleverer than I thought!"

Francine tilted her head back to look at John's face. You are. I would say wise rather than clever."

"So I am not clever?"

"Stop it John. You do that a lot too."

"What?"

"Twist people's words."

"Sorry."

Francine was about to pick him up on that other habit of always apologising. The last time she did that they learned a lot about each other but she was quite sore the next day. Tonight was definitely not the night for that. "I did the Compostelle once."

"The pilgrim's route that goes through Thiviers?"

"Yes. Not all the way. I set a target when I was really tired. I just concentrated on reaching the next crossroads, the next tree. Something I can see that is achievable. I think you do that with life problems."

"Yes I do."

"So what is the next tree?"

John thought, then answered. "I have to answer those letters. Cathy did not write them, Stuart did."

"Was it not her writing?"

"Yes, but he dictated it. She is a secretary remember."

Francine did not like the way he said it. In the past he had always referred to Cathy as a personal assistant, emphasising the importance of her job. Until the letter arrived Francine felt she and Cathy were competitors. John had rejected Francine's offer to be his mistress. If she was totally honest with herself she did not want to be his wife. At the beginning it was not an issue. He had a wife. That made her his lover. It did not matter whether he liked the term mistress or not, that is what she was. Why then did it not feel like that? First of all she had moved in. Then there was Peter. She looked at the pair of knickers on the coffee table. Thelma had raised the spectre of Peter and John becoming rivals for her affection. She adored Peter. It was part of her love for John. Father and son were inseparable. She could not love one without the other. She was being a mother to a boy who had lost his. It was so simple, so natural. She had never given birth. She had never placed a baby to her breast to feel that unique bond. When Francine was a teenager her mother, overwhelmed by the demands of five sons had pretty much handed parental responsibilities for Benjamin to her daughter. It was why Francine found parenting Peter so easy. So here she was.

She was wife to a man who already had one. She was mother to a boy who already had one. Her qualification was that as a teenager she had practiced motherhood on her baby brother.

John broke her train of thought. "You are very quiet."

"I was thinking about the knickers. Should I say something?"

"There is no need. He must know Thelma found them. He will be so embarrassed to think that you know. It's like your parents catching you masturbating."

"Do you think he has started?"

"Yes. We've had The Talk. He knows it is ok. He also knows that it is something private between him and his penis."

Francine frowned. "All the same I don't want him thinking about me when he does it. I think Ariane was shocked that I'd talked to Peter about penises when we first met."

"I don't remember that."

"Yes you do. We were talking about the old church steeple being replaced by a bigger one."

"I'd completely forgotten. Do you think I should get my steeple replaced by a bigger one?"

"Stop it John! You have had too much to drink! I was being serious. Beer then wine is clearly not fine in your case. To answer your question, no I do not think you need a bigger steeple. God, you men are all the same!"

John was suitably chastened. He wanted to say sorry but in her current mood use of the S word was probably not a good idea. "I'll give some thought to it and write to Cathy. We can't simply ignore her letter."

"No we can't. You are good at letter writing. I still have the one you sent me. I didn't like it but it was well written."

"You still have it? Why did you keep it?"

"Because it is part of you. You wrote from the heart."

"Shall I talk to Peter about writing? Mine will say I am not sending him back because he doesn't want to go. It would help if he said it too."

"Leave it to Thelma. If she thinks he should write to his mother she will help him."

"She is an amazing woman."

"Yes, we are very lucky."

John changed tack. "Do you think we should go to the police?"

Francine swung round to face him. He had found a stray lock of hair and was playing with it. When he brushed her neck it tickled. The knickers incident had put her off sex. She was sure it was temporary but just now she wanted to sort out their problems. "I spoke to Thelma whilst you were making the tea. She said the Gendarme will not be interested. No crime has been committed in France. Whilst Stuart is in UK they have no role. On the other hand she has a legal obligation to inform the police in the area where the offence was committed. That would be Thames Valley. She has contacts there." John was relieved to have this task taken away from him. His thought about what he should put in the letter. Francine picked up his thought. "I've just remembered, Thelma said it is very important that nobody says anything to Stuart. The police will want to raid his house to look for evidence. If he has been tipped off he will have destroyed it."

John felt he had stepped into a crime novel. Did those things happen in real life? He supposed they did. "Then I can't say anything to Cathy either. The first thing she will do is show it to Stuart."

The next day John sat down to write. He wanted to make it clear that he was not going to return Peter to England as she asked. He was now hampered by a possible criminal investigation. Eventually this is what he wrote.

Dear Cathy

I waited a few days before replying. With half term almost upon us my response has become urgent. Please forgive me therefore if what I say is poorly expressed or incomplete. I am writing in sorrow rather than anger.

Your letter came as a complete shock. I am not going to dignify the many allegations you make by responding. You make assertions based on the observations of your lover. He is hardly an impartial observer. We have both known him long enough to know that his respect for the truth is scant at best. It is obvious that the letter came from him. It matters not that it was written in your hand. I have tried to tell you many times that his is a puppet master but you refuse to see that you are being manipulated.

You promised to leave him and move to France with Peter and I. It is not we who have broken faith with that plan. I am here as we agreed. Peter is here. It is where he wants to stay. You have chosen to break faith. The manner in which you have done so makes it hard for me to see how our marriage can be salvaged.

I have made friends in France who have helped me to understand our relationship. All our married life I have taken responsibility for your happiness. At the same time you too have only thought of what makes you happy. The irony is that despite the best efforts of both of us it is clear that you are not happy whilst I am. I have found happiness in France. Do you begrudge me that? I have opened the door to a new life for both of us. You asked me to open that door, now you refuse to walk through it.

I can no longer take responsibility for your happiness. You must do this. This may be the last opportunity I have to give you advice. For your own sake please listen. If you want to divorce then so be it. Do not do so in order to fall further under the spell of Stuart. He is toxic. Find someone else to love. Best of all go to the bathroom and love the person you see in the mirror.

I will close by returning to the most important and urgent matter, Peter. I hope you never have to witness the anguish he expressed when he read your letter. I know you love him. The most generous response I can find is therefore that I do not believe you intended to inflict the hurt he felt. I cannot forgive you. One day I hope you will understand what you have done to him and be sorry. I hope then he will be able to find forgiveness. In both matters I am merely an observer.

You have opened Pandora's Box. The demons you have released will affect us all for the rest of our lives. If there is a path to redemption it is that along with the demons, hope too escaped. It took the form of a simple fact. Peter loves you. He was adamant that he did not want to return to England. He said too that he misses you. I leave it to you to reconcile those two truths.

I will offer one final olive branch. You are welcome to come to visit us at Christmas. If you have understood anything of this letter you will know that you will have to come alone. Peter will be delighted to see you. Francine and I will make you most welcome.

Your friend,

John.

John shared the letter with Thelma and Francine. They talked about Stuart. "I have reported the incident to Thames Valley Police. The last I heard they have not yet interviewed Stuart so we must assume he does not yet know he is being investigated. You have not said anything that would alert him so I think it is ok to send it. May I copy it to the police?"

John was not sure. "If it says nothing about what Stuart did to Peter why would they be interested?"

"It is to build up a picture. You said you were sure the letter from Cathy was more or less dictated by Stuart."

"I think so. It is so out of character for Cathy, but very typical of Stuart."

"They will want to see her letter too. You can of course say no."

Francine joined in. "Why would we do that?" They both looked at her. "Sorry, this has nothing to do with me. It is your letter John you must choose."

John touched her hand. "It is everything to do with you. I have nothing to hide." Thelma loved watching people interact particularly lovers or parents with their children. It vaccinated her against the toxicity of the dysfunctional relationships that were the daily diet of her professional life. John caught Francine's eye. "What's wrong?"

"It's the end if the letter. You said we would make Cathy welcome if she came on her own to see Peter."

"We would wouldn't we?" He held her gaze.

"Yes, of course. It is just that I had not thought about it."

"Is it a problem?"

"No, not at all, that is, I don't know. This is not how I imagined it."

"How did you imagine it?"

"The way we talked about it after our first time. You were going to be here being the dutiful husband, I was going to be the French mistress making you happy."

"You do make me happy. Happier than I ever thought possible"

"But I am no longer your mistress. Now Cathy is staying in England I have become your wife."

"You make it sound like a bad thing." John turned to Thelma. "I am sorry to have this conversation in front of you."

"Please don't mind me. It helps me understand Peter. It also helps me choose the most effective therapy. Keeping your love for each other strong is the best thing you can do to help him."

Francine turned to Thelma. "I am becoming too English. I am not even sure I want to be John's mistress. I feel like Julia Roberts at the end of Pretty Woman. I want the fairy tale."

"There is nothing wrong with that. In fact as Peter's therapist I would say that what he needs most is a conventional family with adults in monogamous relationships. He is too young to understand the wife/mistress dynamic. It is also one which led to his trauma."

Chapter 24
Peter's letter

"Ready!" Peter called from the bedroom.

"That's my cue. I'll leave you two lovebirds to talk about Christmas."

Thelma closed the door and sat on the bed. "What story have you chosen for me?" Peter was sitting up in bed beside Pooh and Piglit. Safe caring practice required her to leave the door open. As Thelma wrote the book she felt entitled to break the rules. They were there to protect the carer from malicious allegations. Thelma could identify that risk before the thought had entered the child's head. Her concern was for the child. Peter needed to know he was in control. That included knowing that what he said to Thelma was not overheard.

"The one where Tigger goes to live with Kanga and steals Roo's medicine."

"I love that one. Off you go." Peter recited from memory, breaking off every so often to comment on the story.

"Have you noticed Thelma, Kanga is the only female in the hundred acre wood?

"No, I never noticed that before. Why do you think that is?"

Peter had a think. "The author is a man. He is reading the stories to his son. They are real. The others are real too. They are Christopher's toys. They are only alive in his imagination." He picked up Pooh and gave him a kiss. "No offence Pooh"

"None taken Peter" said Pooh.

"Why do you think Kanga is the only female in the stories?" Asked Thelma.

"I don't know. Maybe A.A. Milne didn't think women were very important." Peter went back to the story.

When he had finished Thelma asked why he had chosen that particular story. "Because Tigger goes to live with Kanga and Roo. Kanga looks after him even though she is not his mummy.

"Do you think she makes a good mummy for Tigger?"

"It's hard to say. A.A. Milne doesn't write much about mothers. She's not bad. She is also about as different to Tigger as you can get."

"Is that important?"

"Yes. They are both wacky but in completely different ways."

Thelma was not sure where this was going but felt she was getting to understand this remarkable young man. She pressed him further. "Does that make it harder for them to get on?"

"Ooh no, quite the opposite."

"Why?"

"Think of a jigsaw. Imagine every piece was a perfect square. Every piece would fit every other piece."

"Does that make the jigsaw easier?"

"Just the opposite. You think they get on but they don't stay together. With a proper jigsaw you have to match a sticky-out piece to a sticky-in one. They are opposite but once they get together they stay together."

"What an interesting idea, I had never looked at it like that."

"Daddy and Francine are very different but they just fit together."

"Yes they do."

"I think mummy and daddy fitted together once."

"Do you think that has changed?"

"Yes. Stuart changed it."

"How did he do that?"

"He wanted mummy to fit with him. She didn't so he changed her until she did. Now she is broken but stuck with him."

"Why do you think she is stuck?"

"If you force two bits of jigsaw that don't really fit they get stuck." Thelma waited to see if he would carry on. "Daddy tried to pull them apart. He couldn't do it. Even if he did mummy has been broken and daddy would not fit any more."

"That is sad."

Thelma saw that he was crying. She gave him a hug. This too was not allowed. She didn't care. Withholding love is emotional abuse. Thelma once defended a social worker who had a troubled teenager in her case load. When everyone else gave up on him she turned his life round. In a review meeting he said it was all due to his social worker who spontaneously hugged him and hissed his forehead. She was reported. The young man filed a complaint against the local authority. Thelma led the prosecution quoting Section 8 of the Human Rights Act (the right to family life). Thelma argued that the local Authority had the same obligations as a conventional family. A normal family loves their children and demonstrates this with appropriate hugs and kisses. The judge accepted Thelma's evidence as an expert witness that it was insufficient to simply care for the child. He agreed that the Authority was under an obligation, not just to allow, but to encourage displays of affection. These were the only effective way for a child to feel loved. Thelma quoted her own Thesis:

Delinquents, the great unloved. How they are failed by society.

"Mummy wrote to me."

"I know, daddy told me"

"Do you want to see the letter?"

"Do you want to show it to me?"

"I think so. I think you would know what to do." Peter got out of bed and pulled a piece of paper from the bottom of his sock drawer. "Read it to yourself or I will cry again." He handed it to Thelma.

"My Darling Peter,

"I am missing you so much. It was very naughty of Daddy to make you go to France. It must be very hard going to school where nobody speaks English. I have been talking to the headmaster of Langtree. He is going to try and get you in so you can be with Greg. I know that is what you want.

"Stuart told me that daddy has a girlfriend in France. That explains why he wanted to move there so much. I am very upset that daddy has chosen to leave us both just so he can be with her. He clearly doesn't love you any more or he would not have done it. I have written to him to ask him to bring you home. Stuart and I love you very much and will look after you.

"Don't worry my darling; you will be home very soon. Stuart has a surprise for you. I am not supposed to say, but I will. It is a new games console. You are growing up so we both think you are ready. It has much better games than the baby ones on your old one.

"Looking forward to seeing you VERY soon.

"Lots of love,

"Mummy xxx"

When Thelma had read it she put it on the bed. "Thank you for sharing that with me. It was very brave."

"I haven't shown it to daddy or Francine, they would be upset."

"That was very thoughtful."

"I have written back. Do you want to see it?"

"If you want me to." Peter went back to the draw and pulled out another piece of paper. "Will you read it or shall I?"

"I'll try. Help me if my voice goes funny."

Dear Mummy

I miss you too. The things you said about daddy are not true. He does love me and so does Francine. Do you think I don't know why daddy wanted us all to move to France? It is because you and Stuart were having sex. Daddy would never have started seeing Francine if you had come to France with us. It is all your fault so don't blame daddy.

Actually no, it is not your fault, it is Stuart. He made you do it. He makes people do things they don't want to do. I don't know why you love him. He is horrible.

I have told daddy I do not want to go back to England. I want to see you but I can't because Stuart will be there. Come and see me, but come on your own. I never want to see Stuart again. All this is his fault.

Lots of love

Peter

P.S. Francine will be here. You will have to get used to it, just like daddy had to get used to Stuart being there in England. I don't know why he did. I would have just punched Stuart on the nose.

P.P.S. Bring the games console when you come.

Lots of love

Peter.

"That is a very good letter."

"I didn't say what Stuart did to me."

"I think you were right. Why did you choose not to?"

"It is hard to write about it. Stuart said not to. It would upset mummy."

"Yes it would upset her. How would she feel about Stuart if she knew?"

"She would hate him like I do. She would leave him."

"Do you want her to leave him?"

"Yes. I wanted her to leave him and come back to daddy"

"You said you wanted it. Do you still want it?"

"I don't know. Daddy is so happy now. I don't think he was happy like that with mummy."

"If you could wave a magic wand and have whatever you want what will it be?"

"A new games console."

"That's not what I meant. Would you live in England or France? Who would live with you? How would those people feel about each other?"

"That's easy. France. They have chocolatines. The chocolate croissants in England are rubbish."

"What about people?"

"Greg. He was my best friend in England."

"What about grownups?"

"Daddy obviously, and Francine, and mummy."

"Do you think that would work?"

"Not in a million years. Mummy would be jealous."

"What about Francine. Would she be jealous too?"

"I don't know. She's French they see things differently." Peter was quiet for a while. Thelma sensed there was more. She waited. "Francine would not be jealous because she knows daddy loves her more than he loves mummy. That is why mummy would be jealous."

"What makes you think daddy loves Francine more than he loves mummy?"

"Are you blind? Look at them! I knew daddy was in love with Francine before he did!" Peter sat up straight. "Thelma, you asked me what I want. Here it is. Stuart goes away and never comes back. Francine and daddy stay here and look after me. Mummy comes to France and lives somewhere else. Not Saint Etienne but near enough for me to visit on my own. Mummy stops having boyfriends."

"Do you think mummy would be lonely?"

"No, she would have me." He thought. "You mean what would she do for sex?" Even Thelma would not have put it quite like that. Peter was thinking the no sex bit would be a problem for his mother. Then he had an idea. "She could have a girlfriend. Auntie Jan has a girlfriend. They have sex. I know because they came for Christmas and slept together." Peter realised that Thelma did not know about Jan. "Auntie Jan is mummy's sister. She's a lesbian."

*

"You were a long time today" John was making Thelma her usual post-session mint tea.

"Yes, we got a lot done." John was fishing. Thelma had no intention of taking the bait. "Peter has written to his mother. I said I would post it for him.". She relented a bit more. "Don't worry, he said he wants to stay in France." Still John said nothing. Thelma wondered if these sessions were not harder for John than for Peter. "They also serve..."

"I'm sorry, I don't understand."

"They also serve who only stand and wait. I was quoting Milton. It must be hard for you being excluded from my talks with Peter. We are making great progress. I will suggest to Peter that our next session is family group therapy. He can bring you up to date with where he is. You can tell him what your plans are for Christmas." Gently Thelma was reminding them that they needed to make a decision on Cathy coming for Christmas. Privately she thought John should have discussed this with Francine before putting it in the letter. "Cathy needs to know that Peter is not coming back at half term. It is in two weeks so you can't really put the letter on hold until after the family group therapy next week. Can we talk about it now?"

Francine felt this was her cue. "I think John wrote a very good letter. The last paragraph caught me off guard because I hadn't thought about it."

"I'm sorry darling; I should have talked to you before writing. It was supposed to be a draft to discuss with you and Thelma. I was going to rewrite it after we all talked."

"You don't need to rewrite it. Cathy may not come of course but we must invite her."

"I agree." Said Thelma. "If she does not come please find another way for Peter to see her. Enough has happened to him without having to cope with losing contact with his mother."

"Surely as soon as they both know the Police are investigating that will be the end of their relationship?" John asked.

"You would think so wouldn't you? Stuart will of course deny anything happened. He will claim that you John have manipulated Peter into making a false allegation to divert attention from your affair with Francine."

Francine was shocked. "Will Cathy believe that?"

"I believe she will. Look at the letter Stuart made her send to John. He has almost total control over her."

Now it was John's turn to be shocked. "What will it take to make her see the truth?"

"I am afraid nothing short of a criminal conviction. Until then she will see it as Stuart's word against Peter's."

"Why would she not believe her own son?"

"She will think you have put the words in his mouth. Peter is a daddy's boy. She is jealous that he has picked you John over her. She senses manipulation is taking place. Stuart has deflected that and projected it to you. It is a very sophisticated gaslighting technique. Think of a magician who uses diversionary tactics so you do not see how the trick is done."

"So we wait until he is convicted."

"If you do that you could be waiting until Peter is an adult."

"But that is six years! I was thinking six months maximum."

"Sadly not. When the police start digging who knows what they will find. Other victims will come forward. Other paedophiles will be implicated. It is a nest of vipers. The police will want to destroy the whole nest."

Francine was crying. "This is why I never completed my social work diploma. I had this man in my library; I invited him to my house! There was something horrible about him but it was just a feeling. Now I know I couldn't face him. If I had become a social worker I would have to. I don't know how you do it Thelma."

"I do it for the children. Look, I am sorry, I must go. Will you post the letter?"

"Tomorrow John assured her."

"And I will post Peter's. Make a copy of the letter before you post it."

"Of course. Thank you again for what you are doing for Peter."

Thelma smiled and inclined her head accepting the gratitude. "See you next week."

Chapter 25
Holidays
Autumn half term 2008

Francine was cooking supper. She was determined not to become like Cathy who gave up trying to cook because John liked cooking and was good at it. She was getting used to making meat-free meals. Her mother and grandmother both kept geese. They made their own foie gras. Thiviers was famous for this delicacy. Neither could understand Francine's conversion to a diet as un-French as vegetarianism. "It's cruel" Francine declared. "Force feeding those poor geese to make their livers swell and then killing them."

Granny defended a centuries old tradition. "I don't force feed them, geese are so greedy they naturally overeat if they can." She also denied the geese felt pain when they were butchered. "They come to me for a cuddle. I slit their throats. They die so quickly they do not make a sound." All the same going to granny for a cuddle only to have your throat cut seemed unfair.

Tonight Francine was trying "faux gras" a vegetarian pâté made from cèpes and green lentils. She had found the wild mushrooms in the wood.

Peter came in. "what's for supper?" He asked. She told him. "How long?"

"Half an hour."

"I'll do a bit of homework. My rainforest project needs to be in before half term."

Over supper they discussed plans for the holiday. Peter was less than enthusiastic about Francine's suggestion that they do some decorating. John backed him up. "I looked at the forecast for next week. It is going to be warm and sunny. It would be nice to get away and soak up some vitamin D before winter."

"What about a cycling holiday? We could camp." Said Peter. John was not so sure. He was starting to feel his cycling and camping days were over.

Francine had no such doubts. "That's a great idea! I love cycling. We could take the green road. If we go for the full two weeks we could make it to the seaside. The only trouble is we would need to carry all our stuff. That makes it less fun."

John had a brainwave. "I could be your roadie! We can pack all the stuff in the car. You two set off after breakfast. I'll pack up and meet you for lunch. Then I'll go to the next camp site, pitch the tent and get supper ready."

Francine was half sold. "That sounds a good idea if you don't mind. We wouldn't be together much."

"It doesn't have to be every day. We could stay two nights at some sites and go sightseeing together on the day off."

Francine turned to Peter. "What do you think?"

"Great, if you think you can keep up with me!"

The next day while Peter was at school and Francine was at the library John dug out the tent and camping stuff. It had been a while but he soon remembered how to pitch the tent on his own. Peter came home to find him cooking supper on a camping stove in the garden. Peter went into the tent. "It's smaller than I remember, will there be enough room?"

"There's two bedrooms and a space in between. We managed fine when we went with mummy."

"I was smaller then."

"Francine is smaller than mummy so it balances out."

The side gate opened. Francine came in wheeling her bike. John greeted her. "Supper al fresco tonight. Practicing for the holiday."

Francine pulled some maps out of the panniers. "I brought these from the library. I thought we could plan the route."

"Good idea. New panniers?"

"Yes. I know you will take most of the stuff in the car but we will need to take stuff with us: waterproofs, energy bars, water, maps."

"You've got it all worked out haven't you?"

Francine nodded towards the tent. "So have you it seems. But yes, I am looking forward to it."

A couple of days later Francine and Peter set off on their bikes whilst John packed the car. They picnicked by a river before setting off for the first camp site. John was there well before them so he had plenty of time to put the tent up and start supper. This set the pattern for the next few days. Peter found he was not yet as fit as Francine, but as the days passed he got used to it. All the same he did not take much persuading when it came to bedtime. With zero sound insulation John and Francine found it hard to relax. Chatting was confined to whispers. Exchanging intimacies in total silence was frustrating. They were sensitive to Thelma's comments and did not want to make things difficult for Peter. Their son too was finding it hard to achieve his own intimacy. He waited until he thought John and Francine were asleep. Francine found herself concentrating on the tiny rhythmic sounds coming from Peter's half of the tent. "Peter!"

Stunned silence. Eventually he managed a "Yes?"

"Go and clean your teeth."

"I've done them."

"Do them again."

"Why?"

"It will help you sleep." Peter worked it out and left the tent heading for the darkness of the nearby bushes. His absence sparked a bustle of activity from

John and Francine's part of the tent. This stopped abruptly as they heard Peter return. "Goodnight Peter"

"Goodnight daddy." Pause. "Maybe you and Francine need to clean your teeth too."

There was a snort as Francine suppressed a giggle. "Maybe we should." Francine got up. Once out of the tent she poked her head back inside. "I'm not cleaning them on my own John." John got up too. Out of earshot of the tent they both collapsed in giggles. "Shall we?" She asked.

"What, here?"

"Why not? We can't in the tent."

"I can't remember the last time I made love out of doors."

"Then it is high time you did it again!" Nothing was said over breakfast. The only awkwardness was at bedtime now that cleaning your teeth had become a euphemism. Peter got round it by waving his toothbrush at them when he went to the toilet block to wash.

England.

Cathy was breakfasting alone. She assumed Stuart would move in once John had left. He had not. She was missing Peter terribly. She did not allow herself to miss John. She had made her choice; or rather Stuart had made it for her. She thought she would feel closure when she sent the letters he had dictated. She thought too that would be the point at which Stuart would move in. Bridges had been burned. It was time to move forward.

Stuart was nor letting her. The only thing they were united over was an urgency to get Peter back. Every time he visited he asked if there was news. Cathy stared at the two letters in front of her. She didn't want to open John's. She knew her letter had been unkind and unfair. He was entitled to defend himself. Over the years she had given him plenty of ammunition. She picked up Peter's letter. Her tears would not come. She could not feel anger. In any event, with whom should she be angry? John did not deserve it, Stuart would not accept it, she could not bear it. She needed comfort. Stuart fulfilled many need in her, comfort was not one of them. She had never asked for the simple reason that whenever she had needed it John had been there almost begging to be allowed to provide it. Now she had driven him away. Stuart was all she had left. She picked up the phone.

"I'm a bit tied up, I'll be round tonight." Why had he not dropped everything and come straight over? It had always seemed that getting Peter back was the most important thing for both of them. She phoned in sick. For once she did not have to fake the voice. Julie from HR took the call. "God, you sound terrible Cathy. Go back to bed. I'll tell Sir Evelyn not to expect you before Monday." Desperate for someone to tell her what to do she actually did go back to bed. It was where Stuart found her. Unable to think of any other reason why she would wait for him in bed he started to undress.

"What the fuck do you think you are doing?" Stuart was gobsmacked. The playground bully had just been kicked in the balls.

He quickly recovered. "What's up Cat?"

"Peter's not coming back."

"Like fuck he's not! How do you know?"

"He wrote. So did John." She pointed to the letters on the bedside table.

"You've not even opened this one."

"I didn't need to."

Stuart read Peter's letter then ripped open the other. He had played the end game. His opponent had already lost his queen. He expected them to concede. Instead they advanced a pawn placing Stuart's king in check. Mentally Stuart swept the pieces on to the floor. "Get your knickers on; we're going"

"Where?"

"To get Peter." Stuart stuffed the letter from John in his pocket. She had not read it. He would make sure it stayed that way. He had been downloading porn when Cathy phoned. There had been murmurings on the dark web about birdsong, a reference to canaries. It was code for saying that a child had talked to the police. With Peter in France Stuart was sure it was not him. All the same it was high time to get him away from John and under his control.

France

John and Francine made it to the coast. The plan was to cycle back as well. Peter had enjoyed the outbound journey but now was starting to feel unwell. Francine put her hand on his forehead. "He is running a bit of a temperature. What do you think we should do John?"

John touched Peter's cheek. "He's flushed too. How you feeling big fella?"

"I've got a sore throat but it's not too bad."

"The weather is starting to turn. Francine, are you ok if we put the bikes on the rack and head back?"

"Of course. Camping in the rain is no fun, especially if Peter is feeling poorly. Shall we stay here one more night and head back tomorrow?"

"Good idea. I'll see if the camp shop has paracetamol. How do you say that in French?"

"Paracétamol"

"Silly question. Keep an eye on the cassoulet, I'll go now." Five minutes later he was back. "They asked if it was for adults or children. I said he was 12. They gave me these."

Francine looked at the packet. "They are suppositories."

"Does that matter?"

"Think about it John."

He did. "Oh Christ!"

"Don't worry, I'll change them." Francine took the packet and was gone.

They got up early and struck camp under threatening clouds and rising winds. The outriders of the storm chased them east, finally overtaking them just before Angouleme. The final hour was in driving rain. Summer was over. It was time for the Dordogne to hunker down and wait for the cranes to return. John pulled up in front of the barn. "Keys are round the back. Leave everything in the car; we'll unpack when it stops raining."

Francine turned to Peter. He had made a nest on the back seat. He had hardly spoken the whole journey. "How you feeling darling?" Francine used the same terms of endearment with father and son.

"I'll be ok." Peter was rarely ill. Francine was unused to him being subdued like this. It brought out the mothering instinct in her. John had already made a dash down the side passage and up the steps to the back door. Peter grabbed Pooh and followed him. Francine collected a few essentials from the car and followed.

Chapter 26
Police

"You must have forgotten to lock up." John was by the back door. He was calling to Francine.

Peter caught him up. "I did it and put the keys in the boot."

John found them on the ground "Got them!" He went to unlock and found the door was open. He turned to Francine who had followed him in with an armful of stuff from the car. "It was already open."

"What, wide open?"

"No, just unlocked." There was a note on the kitchen table: YOU CAN RUN, BUT YOU CAN'T HIDE. I'LL BE BACK FOR PETER. John screwed up the paper and put it in his pocket.

"What is it?" Peter asked.

John said the first thing that came into his head. "The chimney sweep. I must have got the date wrong. He's done both chimneys."

"He should have locked up afterwards, I'll mention it when I see him." Francine looked at John. "You ok? You are very white."

"Yes, maybe I'm getting Peter's cold. I'll put the kettle on."

Peter had gone through to his bedroom. He came back with a parcel. "Mummy was here! She left me a birthday present!"

Francine shot John a look. She had seen him put the note in his pocket. "Are you sure Peter? She would have said if she was coming."

"Of course I'm sure, there's a card from her as well." The two adults formed a protective cordon round him wishing Thelma was there too. Peter read.

My darling Peter, I am so sorry I missed you. I came down with your birthday present to surprise you. You must have gone on holiday. I have to go but I will come back at Christmas. How are you getting on at school? Can you speak French now? I am really missing you, but daddy will look after you. All my love, Mummy xxx.

"She should have said she was coming, I would have stayed to see her."

"She wanted it to be a surprise." Francine could barely get the words out.

Peter looked at her. "She came with Stuart didn't she?"

Francine looked at John. She knew the chimney sweep story was a lie. "I don't know."

John answered for her. "Yes she did." He hoped he was doing the right thing. Lying to protect Peter now might make things worse later. "They've gone now. When she comes for Christmas she will be on her own."

"I'm sorry I missed mummy but I'm glad I didn't see Stuart. Can I open my present?" It was a games console. Peter took it to his room to set it up. Momentarily he had forgotten about Stuart.

Francine took John's hand. "The note was from Stuart wasn't it?" He nodded. "Do you think they have gone back?"

"I have no idea. It depends how long ago they came. They couldn't wait in an empty house forever. They did not know how long we would be away."

Francine turned to leave. "I'll ask around. Someone will have seen them arrive. Go and make sure Peter is ok."

John went into his son's room and closed the door. "You ok Peter?"

"It's got an English plug"

"I've got an adapter somewhere. Do you want me to look?"

"Later." Peter was quiet. John knew there was more. "They came to get me didn't they?"

"It looks that way."

Peter looked scared. "Will they try again?"

"I don't know, but if they do we will stop them. Remember what Thelma said, you are in control. That means if you don't want to go you don't have to."

Peter turned his head to hide a smile. "I don't want to go to school." John was taken aback. Before he could think of a reply, Peter turned back grinning. "Gotcha!"

John lunged forward. "You little..." He held Peter in a tight bear hug.

That was how Francine found them. "Everything ok?" She asked.

"Fine. Peter had been winding me up." Peter grinned.

"Arlene next door saw them arrive about two hours ago. She told them we were away till the end of the week. It seems they left about half an hour before we got back."

John looked worried. "That was close. Hang on Arlene doesn't speak English and Stuart doesn't speak French. How will they know we are not planning to come back for another three days?"

"She said she spoke to Cathy."

John nodded. "Cathy's French is improving. She went to evening classes." John was quiet. "I wonder why she bothered if she had no intention of coming here."

Francine whispered. "Not in front of Peter." She raised her voice to speak to both of them. "Thelma's on her way over. She can't stay as she has left Paula alone. She can come for supper tomorrow. Peter, she asked if you were ok for it to be family group therapy tomorrow."

"Of course. Daddy can you find that adapter? FIFA 2009 came with the console."

Thelma came in. Expertly she took in the body language of each person in the room. The adults were running on adrenaline that would soon run out. They needed a plan and they needed it soon. Peter was in denial hiding behind his new toy. It was the crisis that Thelma knew would come. She had hoped that she could help Peter build more resilience before facing it. She was in control of the therapy but could not control external events. It was imperative that Stuart did not return. This was already a major setback; a confrontation could do irreparable damage. "John, Francine said Stuart left a note. Do you have it?" John produced the crumpled piece of paper from his pocket and handed it to her. Thelma looked at it. "Please excuse me a moment, I have to make a phone call." When she came back she was considerably more relaxed. "It was a shame you had to cut your holiday short, camping in the rain is no fun. On the plus side, John has invited me to supper tomorrow. Peter, as we hadn't planned a session we could stay together and call it family group therapy. Actually I just want to hear about your holiday."

Near Calais

Cathy was scared. She had never seen Stuart so angry. She thought at first he was cross that she had brought the games console with her.

"I couldn't give a fuck about that".

She now knew what the problem was not. Whatever it was now put their life at risk. "Please slow down Stuart, you're scaring me." He ignored her. His phone beeped signalling an incoming text. He looked at it, almost hit the lorry in front and swerved into the outside lane. The car behind blared his horn. Stuart stuck a finger up. He tried to text a reply, almost hitting another car before throwing the phone on the floor. Cathy was crying. If she made it back to England alive she was leaving him. She even thought of hitching back to St Etienne alone if Stuart ever stopped the car. She remembered the lorry driver on the cross channel ferry and changed her mind. She went back to crying.

Things were unravelling for Stuart. It had not occurred to him that Peter would not be at the house. Now he was getting texts from other gang members. One it seemed had been arrested. Stuart needed to make sure everyone was covering their tracks. He could not access the dark web from his mobile; texts like this were traceable and risky. Finally they made it to Calais. Stuart handed over the passports. There was a pause while Border Control studied the screen in front of him. Several times he looked at Stuart. Eventually he returned the passports and picked up the phone. At the next checkpoint a British officer pulled them over. Cathy was expecting them to check the car. "Please turn off the engine, leave the keys in the ignition and step out of the car."

Cathy's anger towards Stuart changed to bewilderment and then to fear. Both passports were taken. A WPC was summoned. Stuart and Cathy were taken to different rooms. Cathy wondered if the car was being searched for drugs. An officer moved the car to a holding bay. Apart from a cursory check that there were no more passengers he was not interested. The WPC was making notes. "Let's start with your full name."

"Catherine Demelza Cartwright. My mother was a Poldark fan." Cathy always felt the need to offer additional information when she used her middle name.

"Where have you come from?"

"Saint-Etienne-d'Isle" The questions kept coming. Where was she going? When had she come to France? Why? What was her relationship to Stuart? She was separated from her husband. The man was her boyfriend. They were visiting her son. The officer was particularly interested in the last fact. She pressed Cathy on why they had gone, and why the visit was so short. Cathy explained it was a surprise visit for her son's birthday. They had returned immediately because he was not there. She supposed her husband had taken him on holiday.

Another officer entered the room. He handed the WPC some papers. He had searched Stuart and found the letters to Cathy from Peter and John. She changed tack.

"How would you describe your relationship with your husband?"

Eventually Cathy was told she was free to go. "Where is Stuart?"

"He is still being questioned. Who does the car belong to?" It was Stuart's. "Are you insured to drive it?" She was. "Then I suggest you take the car, board the ferry and go home."

"What about Stuart?"

"As I said, he is still being questioned."

"What about?"

"I am not at liberty to say"

"How long will they keep him?"

"I do not know." The WPC handed Cathy her passport. Her tone softened. "You are not obliged to return to the UK. You may prefer to go back and talk to your husband." Cathy went back to the car. There was a huge signpost in front of her. To the left was marked FRANCE. To the right FERRY. Cathy turned right.

Saint Etienne

"Goodnight Peter."

"Goodnight Dad" Father and son embraced. It was the end of a daily ritual that had lasted 12 years.

"Leave the light on" This was new. "Close the door". So was this. They did not talk about the day they returned from holiday but it hung like a shadow between them. John went back to the living room and snuggled up to Francine. He was worried.

Peter snuggled up to Pooh he tried to sleep. When it came it followed a familiar pattern. The humming in his head became a car engine. He was on the back seat. A couple sat in the front. They started as John and Francine then changed to Cathy and Stuart. The nest he had constructed was warm, but the warmth gave him no comfort. Cathy and Stuart were laughing. They were wearing fancy dress. Cathy turned. She was wearing a pig mask. "I'm Piglit" she squeaked in falsetto.

"And I'm Pooh" added Stuart in a growly voice. Both voices were wrong. Piglit was demonic, Pooh threatening.

"No you're not!" Peter screamed. "Take me home!"

"I am taking you home" growled not Pooh. Not Piglit laughed.

"I want daddy!"

"I'm your daddy, and I want you!" The car swerved as not Pooh turned pushing a grotesque mask into Peter's face. The warmth in the bottom of Peter's bed spread, its pungency repelling the aggressor.

"We're getting near Calais" squeaked not Piglit. "Where are the passports?"

"In the bag on the back seat." Growled not Pooh. Peter fumbled for the bag pulling out the newest looking passport.

Not Piglit pulled the bag on to her lap. "There are only two, yours and mine." Quietly Peter posted his passport through a gap in the window. It was caught by the slipstream and was gone.

"You stupid bitch, I told you to put them all together."

Cathy bit back. "No, you said you didn't trust me and that you would do it yourself."

Stuart jerked the car into a lay by. "Give me that!" He rummaged through the bag before throwing it back at Cathy. He jumped out of the car, opened the door and dragged Peter screaming on to the side of the road. The warm dampness that surrounded Peter's loins froze in the chill wind. Stuart pulled out the bedding dropping it in the puddles at the side of the road. Eventually he gave up rummaging. He pushed Peter roughly back into the car, throwing the wet bedding in after him. "We'll knock him out, cover him in blankets and hope they don't search the car."

Chapter 27
The interview

Peter woke screaming. He ran through to John and Francine's bedroom. John sat up and hugged him. "Nightmare!" Peter sobbed.

"I know. You've had an accident. Have a quick shower and I'll find you some clean pyjamas."

Francine jumped up. "I'll change the sheets." Both adults were naked. They gave no thought to Thelma's warnings. Peter had regressed. For him sex was something to be avoided at all costs. He drew the comfort of a baby from the skin contact. Out of the shower he jumped into the dry warmth of the big bed. His father's smell mixed with Francine's comforted him.

Francine came back. "Your bed's ready."

"Can I stay?"

"No darling, this is our private place. Daddy will read you a story in yours."

Peter listened to his pooh story then said "now I will tell you a story." He recounted his nightmare in meticulous detail.

John shared it with Francine. "The frightening thing is that if we had arrived a couple of hours earlier the nightmare could have been reality."

The next day Francine met Thelma in the library. She told her about the nightmares and the bedwetting. "It is exactly what I expected. He is behaving completely normally."

Francine was used to Thelma but even She was surprised. "How can it be normal for 12-yr-olds to wet the bed or have such night terrors? I've never seen anyone so frightened, even after he has woken up and knows it was a dream."

"Firstly it doesn't matter if he is asleep or awake. The nightmare represents a real and present danger. It is therefore completely normal to dream about something which could happen. He has to work out how he would cope in such a situation."

"What about the bedwetting? Surely that is not normal?"

"Absolutely normal, sexual abuse nearly always takes place in bed. Urinating makes the victim hope it will make them unattractive to the abuser."

"How can we help him?"

"First of all we have to remove the danger. That I have already done."

Francine was stunned. "But how?"

"I phoned Thames Valley. They put out an all ports watch. Stuart was picked up at Calais. They questioned on suspicion of attempting to abduct a minor. He was escorted to Dover and released on bail."

"Do you think he will try again?"

"Not without a passport. That is what you must help me make Peter understand."

"Will that cure the nightmares and bedwetting?"

"Eventually, yes, but it will take time. I suggest you buy a mattress protector and extra sheets."

That evening Thelma came for supper. It was still half term so Peter was allowed an extra hour before bed. Thelma proposed a board or card game. She brought a selection of Peter had never heard of. She didn't need props like this when she was working one to one, but she did find them helpful in family sessions. These were uncharted waters for John. Thelma loved watching father and son dance. It was Thelma's word to describe the way they interacted. Tonight she had a crisis to manage so he needed to choreograph the dance. Peter had the game sussed. "It's to get me to talk about my nightmares isn't it?"

"Yes it is, and to help Francine and daddy help you when you have them."

"They do help me. They give me cuddles."

Typically direct, Thelma came straight to the point. "Mummy and Stuart came to take you back to England."

"I know. I won't let them. They can't make me."

"That is why we are talking. We are here to keep you safe, to keep you in control."

"Stuart does things nobody expects. It is like he is two people. Pooh says he is like that because he never had people like you, daddy and Francine to look after him when he was little."

"Pooh is right. Pooh wants to help everyone. Just now we are concentrating on helping you. Fixing Stuart is someone else's job."

John and Francine sat and watched. Normally they both had plenty to contribute to conversation. Tonight they listened and learned from an old lady and a remarkable young man. "There's nothing you can do." Peter said. "Stuart does what he wants. He doesn't deserve to be fixed."

"Everyone deserves to be fixed. Not everyone can be."

"Now you sound like Pooh."

Thelma laughed. "Do I? That's the nicest thing anyone has said to me." She was serious again. "You are wrong about one thing; there is something I can do. I have made sure Stuart has gone back to England and stays there."

"How did you do that?"

"I told the police to arrest him and take his passport away."

"You can't do that!"

"I most certainly can, and I have. I am not just a doddery old dyke hiding in France with her girlfriend."

"You are not doddery, and don't say dyke, it's not a nice word."

Thelma smiled; it was the reaction she wanted. Having steered Peter in the right direction she continued. "The police want to talk to you about what Stuart did. I think you are ready to talk about it. It will be hard but we will support you."

"I'm not going back, even if the police want me to."

"You don't have to. They will come here."

*

It was mid November when a car containing two British police officers pulled into place de l'eglise. Peter was disappointed it was not a squad car. He hoped they would screech in sirens blaring. Thelma was expecting them. D. I. Jones was an old friend of hers. He greeted her warmly before turning to the others. "You must be Francine, pleased to meet you. My name is D. I. Jones, but you can call me Graham. This is D.C. Chandler."

The younger officer extended her hand. "Sophie."

John introduced Peter. "I expect he worked out who I was. He is a detective you know." Peter had broken the ice.

"Coffee?" Francine asked.

"Tea please love," Graham transferred from North Yorkshire twenty years ago. "Strong, two sugars". He had never understood the Home Counties. The liaison officer took him to task. "Graham, I know it's not intentional, but that sounds sexist."

"What, two sugars?"

"No, calling females 'love'." Now he did it on purpose.

John stepped in. "I'll do it; I know how Yorkshire men like their tea. What does everyone else want?" He took the orders and call Peter into the kitchen to help. "Are you OK Peter?" John asked when they were alone.

"Yes, Thelma told me what to expect. Will I have to undress?"

"Of course not! What made you think that?"

"Thelma said they might want medical evidence."

"Peter, they are just here to talk to you. If they want medical evidence then you go to a doctor, like when you are Ill."

"Will you be there?"

"I'll be in the next room with Thelma and Francine."

Graham drank his tea. "We need to set up somewhere private." Francine suggested Peter's bedroom. "As long as it is not where the abuse took place."

"So he has never been here?" Asked Sophie

"He came at half term but we were away. He left a note." Explained John.

"Was that the only time?" Graham asked?

"He drove one of the vans on moving day." Chipped in Peter.

Graham was confused. "Let me get this straight. Stuart assisted Peter's father in the removal of a minor from the UK. When was this?"

"August." Said John.

D. I. Jones turned to him. "He helps you move with Peter to France, then two months later he tries to get him back. Was there any attempt to persuade you to return Peter voluntarily?"

"My wife wrote to me. She said she wanted to divorce and that she wanted Peter back."

The police officer looked at Francine. She had put her arm round John to support him. "I'm not surprised."

Francine couldn't take any more. "Why are you taking Stuart's side? You make it sound like John is the baddie."

"Madam, I am not taking anybody's side, I am trying to establish the facts. Under the circumstances I think I should take statements from all of you."

Thelma stepped in. "Graham, could I have a word in private?"

"Of course."

Thelma continued. "Sophie, can you set the equipment up in the bedroom? It will save some time when we get back" D. I. Jones dutifully followed Thelma into the garden.

There was an awkward silence. "I'll fetch the equipment from the car." Sophie left.

Francine, Peter and John looked at each other. Peter was the first to speak. "Did you see that? The boss policeman was getting it all wrong and Thelma took him outside to tell him off like a naughty schoolboy."

"I don't think she was doing that." Said John, "She was just giving him background information so he can understand the situation."

"John, you always see the best in people. He was practically accusing you of abducting Peter. If you were sent to the guillotine you would be saying, 'I'm sure there has been a misunderstanding' as the blade came down. Why don't you get angry?"

John shrugged "Would it help?"

Francine looked at him. She still loved him to bits, but she was starting to understand why he had allowed the affair between Cathy and Stuart to go unchecked for so long.

Thelma came back into the room. She was smiling. "Peter, Graham has agreed that I can be in the interview with you. Are you OK with that?"

Peter looked relieved. "Of course." He had started to dislike D. I. Jones. He had been about to leap to his father's defence when Thelma took the policeman into the garden. Now they were back he could sense the dynamic had changed.

Thelma continued. "We are going to play a game. It's a bit like solicitors."

Peter's face lit up. "That's the one where you are not allowed to talk when someone asks you a question. The person on your right is your solicitor. They have to answer for you. If you answer you are out."

Sophie returned. "It's all set up so whenever you are ready."

Peter took Thelma's hand and led her towards his room. Sophie looked puzzled. Graham answered her unasked question. "Thelma is acting as Peter's appropriate adult. She will not speak once the interview has started. I will conduct the interview."

Thelma kicked off her shoes and stretched out on Peter's bed. "I am Paul."

Peter looked puzzled. "Who's Paul?"

Thelma sat up. "He is your twin brother."

"I don't have a twin brother."

"Peter, it's a game. I am pretending to be Paul. You are my solicitor. Graham will ask me questions, but I am not allowed to answer. You will answer for me. If I speak I lose."

Graham motioned to Sophie to start recording. Peter had one more question. "Give me some context."

Even Thelma was surprised sometimes by Peter's use of language. "I am Paul; I have just gone to bed. Stuart is babysitting. You share a bedroom with me. You are in the room, where would you like to be?"

"I'll be hiding in the wardrobe."

"Ok, but can you sit in front of the wardrobe and pretend to be inside? Sophie would like to film you."

"Sure thing Paul, pass me Pooh, you can keep Piglit."

Graham opened his notebook. "For the tape, I am D. I. Jones. With me in the room is D. C. Chandler. We are at Place d'Eglise, St Etienne d'Isle, 24520 France. It is Monday 17th November 2008. With me in the room is Peter Cartwright, a minor. Thelma Campbell is observing in the capacity of Peter's appropriate adult." He paused. "Peter."

"Paul" whispered Thelma.

Graham corrected himself. "For the avoidance of doubt, Peter has asked to be addressed as Paul for the duration of this interview." He turned to Peter. Thelma gave a slight cough and pointed to herself. Graham turned to Thelma and began.

*

Francine and John waited nearly two hours. John passed the time prepping vegetables for lunch. Francine started with the washing up. She swept then mopped the kitchen floor. The four others finally emerged from the bedroom. Thanks to John a three course meal was ready.

Thanks to Francine the grout between every tile in the kitchen shone white. Peter was smiling. "Don't ever play solicitors with Thelma, she would win every time!"

Graham could finally ask Thelma a question without calling her Paul. Furthermore he got an answer. "That is an amazing interview technique, where did you learn it?"

Thelma answered. "I didn't learn it. It comes from my latest book Uncovering historical abuse, how to avoid false memories."

"I would like to read it, can you give me the details?"

"It is not published yet, I am waiting for the peer review. If you wish I can give you the chapter on interview techniques, subject of course to the usual non-disclosure terms. You must be familiar with displacement theory when interviewing witnesses."

Graham was an old hack. He preferred traditional policing methods. He did not pay much attention when he was sent on courses. "Remind me."

Thelma continued. "After you have taken a witness statement, ask them to imagine they are viewing the incident from a different angle. You often find they remember details missed the first time."

"I heard about that!" chipped in Sophie.

Thelma carried on. "I have interviewed thousands of trauma victims. In many cases the patient recounts the incident in the third person. They cannot deal with the trauma happening to them, so they imagine it happening to someone else. I worked with a girl who was raped on a daily basis by her father. As soon as he entered her room she described leaving her body and watching the abuse from the top of the wardrobe. When he left she returned to her body, went to the bathroom and showered."

"Mummy always showers after sex."

John had forgotten that Peter was at the table. "Peter, how did you know that?"

"Dad I may be a kid, but I am not deaf and blind!" Thelma made a mental note. It was another important piece of the jigsaw.

The two police officers had booked into the local auberge where John and Stuart dined the night they arrived. The police accepted John's invitation to have breakfast with them before returning. They were saying goodbye. "It was a long way to come to conduct an interview" said John. "I do hope it was worth your while."

"Extremely." Graham replied. "We reviewed the tapes last night. I have never had such a consistent statement before. That is worth more than gold. The defence always search for inconsistencies to discredit prosecution testimony." He turned to Thelma. "With your permission I will recommend your interview technique."

Thelma hesitated. "It is for your personal use. As soon as the peer review is complete I will come out of retirement and deliver training."

Chapter 28
Christmas plans
England

The issue of Cathy resigning was resolved by her boss. She was sacked. She tried to go back to work after the French trip but her head was elsewhere. Sir Evelyn could not sack her summarily for incompetence so he asked HR to look for gross misconduct. They asked her for a doctor's certificate for the days she had taken off when she went to France with Stuart. When she couldn't provide one her boss called her in to his office. He came straight to the point. "Your performance recently has been appalling. I do not have time for the formal warning procedure. I am not interested in the reason behind your sudden change. The simple fact is that you are no longer on the game." He meant on *your* game. Cathy knew better than to correct him. "I have here a document for you to sign." By mutual consent her contract was being terminated with immediate effect. She would receive three months pay in lieu of notice. There was the usual small print. She skimmed through it and signed.

Stuart had gone to ground. When Cathy phoned all she got was a message saying number unavailable. She was not ringing because she wanted to see him. Nor was it to check he was ok. It was not even to ask him what the whole border issue was about. She wanted to tell him she was dumping him. Now he was even denying her that. She went to his house. There was police tape across the gate. A uniformed officer asked if he could help her. "I'm looking for Stuart Grayling."

"And you are...?"

"Cathy Cartwright." The name obviously meant something.

"Well Mrs Cartwright, we are looking for him too. Has he contacted you?"

"Not since we got back from France."

"If he does, please contact us immediately. Here's my number." He handed her a business card.

Back home Cathy had never felt so alone. Supper as usual was courtesy of the Raj. She pushed the food round her plate. The bottle of wine was nearly empty. When she ate with Stuart or John her partner for the evening generally drank the lion's share. When she started eating alone a bottle would last two meals. Nowadays there was not even a glass for lunch the next day.

The doorbell rang. She leapt to her feet knocking over the wine. Torn between dealing with the spill and opening the door for Stuart she grabbed a tea towel and went to the door dabbing the stain on her blouse. D. I.

Jones and D. C. Chandler stood in the doorway. "Mrs Cartwright?"

"Yes." They introduced themselves and asked to come in. "It's about Stuart isn't it? Have you found him?"

"No, we were rather hoping you could help us." Said Graham. "May we come in?"

Cathy continued to dab at her blouse. Sophie was watching her. "I think you should soak that, do you want to change?"

"Would you mind? I won't be long." She rushed upstairs to gather her thoughts as much as a new top. The two police officers scanned the room. They had no warrant but they gathered what information they could. They instantly recognised John and Peter smiling in the picture on the mantelpiece. There were no pictures of Stuart. Cathy returned. "Sorry about that, I am so clumsy."

Sophie produced the letters. "These were found on Stuart Grayling when he was arrested. They are addressed to you." She handed them to Cathy. She did not say that the police were already in possession of copies of the letters when they were recovered. Nor did she say that they also had on file copies of the letters Cathy had written to her son and husband.

Graham continued. "Can you explain how they came to be in Mr Grayling's possession?"

"I was upset when I received them. I was expecting my son to come home. He wrote to say he wanted to stay with his father."

"Please answer the question."

"I'm trying to. As I said, I was upset. Stuart and I are friends. I asked him to come round. I showed him the letters. He must have kept them."

"Please explain what you mean by friends."

"You've read the letters, we were lovers. You must have worked that out." Cathy looked down, studying her fingernails.

"This is just for the record." Graham looked towards Sophie.

"What was your reaction to receiving the letters?" The two officers had rehearsed who would ask each question. Cathy pointed out, none too politely, that she had already answered. Sophie ploughed on. "Did you expect your husband to refuse to return your son?"

"I don't know."

It was not Graham's turn, but he interrupted. "I find that hard to believe."

"I only read Peter's letter, not John's."

Back to Sophie. "Why was that?"

"After I read my son's letter I knew what my husband would say. I didn't want to hear it."

"Whose idea was it to go to France?"

"Stuart's. He thought if we talked to my husband and his girlfriend they would agree to Peter returning to England. I am his mother. Peter has only just met Francine. He has known Stuart all his life."

"Your husband made it pretty clear in his letter why he had no intention of allowing your son to return."

"Did he? I don't know, like I said, I haven't read it."

"I suggest you do. Finally Mrs Cartwright, I am going to ask you again. Do you have any idea where Mr Grayling might be?"

"No, his phone is not working. Maybe he has gone back to France."

"We have discounted that possibility."

Cathy was glad. Much as she wanted Peter back she didn't like Stuart's methods. "There is somewhere. He sometimes borrows a cottage in Devon. It overlooks the Dart. I have the address somewhere." It did not take much imagination to work out why Cathy knew about the holiday home.

Graham stood up to leave. "Goodbye Mrs Cartwright. Please let us know if Mr Grayling contacts you. In the meantime I hope you enjoy your Christmas with your son."

*

Devon and Cornwall police found Stuart at the holiday cottage. He was rushed to Exeter Royal

Infirmary where his stomach was pumped. Graham was down the following day. He was speaking to the doctor in charge. "I would not say it was a serious suicide attempt. Rohypnol is not very effective, even mixed with Paracetamol. There were several unopened bottles of Paracetamol. My guess is he took the Rohypnol with an open bottle of Paracetamol then fell asleep before he could get the lids off the other bottles."

Back in Reading Cathy put the phone down. She had been about to order a takeaway. She could not face eating another meal alone. She thought back to her university days. Boys then were like bees round a honey pot. Gradually each either moved out of her life or found partners. The two constants in that life were gone. Peter too. Friends had melted away. The harsh reality was that they were friends of John and Cat the couple. When they separated friends chose one or the other. With John cornering the sympathy vote Cathy was left with a few ex work colleagues. None lived in Reading. Since she lost her job she found it hard to stay in contact. She had followed Graham's advice and read John's letter. It brought little comfort. Stuart had never loved her. That was now clear. John had loved her. She had blown it. Now he loved someone else. She did not blame him. Peter loved her. She picked up her phone again.

John looked at his phone. "It's Cathy." He turned to Francine.

"Well answer it!"

"Hello Cathy, how are you?"

"Not too good. Can I speak to Peter?"

"He's in bed but I'm sure he is still awake. Hang on." He took the phone through to Peter's room, handed him the phone and left, closing the door behind him. He went to sit beside Francine. Neither spoke.

A few minutes later Peter came through. "She wants to speak to you."

"Hi Cathy, I've put the phone on speaker. Francine is here." Francine confirmed this with a 'Hello Cathy'.

Cathy found it difficult to find the words. "Peter would like me to come for Christmas. Are you still ok with that?"

"Of course." John and Francine spoke in unison.

"I don't want to stay with that batty old jam lady, can you see if the Auberge is open?"
"Stay with us. The loft is finished. There's no heating but I'll put a Calor gas stove up there and an electric blanket."

"Are you sure? Won't it be too awkward?"

John hesitated so Francine answered for him. "Not at all. It will be wonderful for Peter to have both parents with him for Christmas."

"If you are sure. I'll look up flights and let you know dates." She did not know what else to say. She asked to be put back to Peter to say goodbye. She put down the phone. On the one hand John had sounded as he had always done. On the other she could tell he had changed. The words in his letter came back to her. Find someone else to love. Better still learn to love yourself. In phoning to arrange Christmas she had taken the first

step. Now she would take another. She went to the bathroom to shower. She studied her naked body in the mirror. Not bad considering. She picked up her ladyshave. Carefully she shaved her legs, her armpits, and everything in between. She showered using her most expensive shower gel. It was a present from Stuart. She derived a small satisfaction from the thought.
Deliberately she walked naked to her bedroom. Opening a drawer she pulled out the smallest thong she possessed. Stuart had joked that it was a G string because that was the note it played when she farted. She pushed Stuart and the thought from her head. She would find someone else to love. Maybe then she would learn to love herself. She rummaged through her clothes until she found the outfit she had worn to Julie's hen night two years ago. Back then it got the same reaction from Stuart and John: 'Christ Cat, you going out in that?' Tonight it was two years tighter. Eventually she got the zip done. If either of them had been there they would have made her change. They were not. She was going clubbing in Reading on a Friday night. If anything this was understated.

Dordogne

Peter spotted Thelma's car pulling in to the square. He clattered down the stairs and threw himself towards her. "Mummy's coming for Christmas! I spoke to her on the phone!"

Thelma just avoided being knocked backwards. "That's really good news. I have news too."

"What?"

"I'll wait until we get indoors otherwise I'll have to say it again for daddy and Francine."

Inside, settled round the table Peter tried again. "Thelma has news but she won't tell me."

"I was waiting until we were all together, and a bit more private." She lowered her voice to sap some of the excitement from Peter. "Stuart has been found." She realised from the blank looks that nobody had been keeping them up to date. She backtracked. "He was arrested at Calais, transferred to Reading where he was questioned and released on bail. It appears he went straight to his house. He realised that his home had been searched before he had the chance to wipe his hard drive. Essentially he knew the game was up. He failed to report to the police station the next day. He was found a few days later in Devon. He had taken an overdose but it was not life threatening. After he was discharged from hospital he was remanded in custody. This time bail was refused."

There was a long silence. Eventually Peter spoke. "I hated him so much I thought I would be jumping for joy. Instead I feel nothing except maybe relief that he can't come here again. Will he be in prison a long time?"

Thelma answered. "Yes, he will stay there until the trial. That is likely to be a long time as there are other suspects and a lot of evidence to gather."

John looked at Thelma. "You said it could take years to come to trial. Will he stay in prison all that time?"

"Yes, but it seems I was pessimistic about it taking up to six years. The carefully constructed web his gang wove to protect themselves has unravelled very quickly. Stuart made a big mistake leaving the country. He was reliant on SMS messages to communicate with other gang members. Normally he would not do that but one of them was arrested when Stuart was here. Other gang members panicked when they could not contact him and resorted to insecure messaging services. One of them tried to get to Stuart's house to remove evidence but the police intercepted the message and beat them to it. The police got Stuarts computer before anything could be removed. They then arrested the paedophile who came to wipe the files. Three of the gang are now in custody. None have any idea what the others have said. To save their skins each is busy passing the blame to the other." Thelma was enjoying herself.

"That's awful" said John.

Francine disagreed.. "It's not awful, it's great news! They are finally getting what they deserve."

Thelma nodded. "I am not so concerned about them being punished. I am pleased that threats to young people are being removed. Tonight children who would have been abused will not be because the perpetrators are behind bars."

John was still troubled. "All the same I've heard about what happens to paedophiles in prison."

Thelma drew Peter into the conversation. "What do you think Peter?"

Peter thought. "I was thinking what Pooh would say."

"And what would he say?"

"He doesn't know. He is sad. He says he doesn't know why he is sad but he is going to be sad anyway. Piglit thinks he is sad because there are no bad people in the Hundred Acre Wood. Now Pooh knows there is a world outside he finds it too difficult for a bear of very little brain to understand."

Thelma Turned to Francine. "What do you think?"

"I think he deserves everything he gets. I think John is being forgiving when it is not his place to forgive. He was not the one who was raped."

Thelma looked at John. "Do you think you are being forgiving?"

He looked at Peter, he looked at Francine. Last of all he looked inside himself. "Francine is right. I can only forgive him for what he did to me. He didn't do anything to me."

"He did do something to you. He stole your wife." It was Francine who spoke.

"Everything happens for a reason." It was John's mother speaking inside his head. John replied. "If he had not I would never have met Francine. I would not be as happy as I am now. I have the most amazing son imaginable. He is already wiser than me. Wiser than most people I have met. I have the love of Francine. I cannot begin to describe that."

If Stuart had been a puppet master bending everyone to his own purposes, Thelma was one who imperceptibly drew each of them to their own healing place. Stuart was gone. He had wounded each person at this table in a different way. He could do so no longer. Gently she led them to a place where they felt neither sorrow nor hate. He was no more. It did not matter whether his attempt to take his own life had failed, nor would it if another attempt ended differently. For each of them he ceased to exist.

Chapter 29
Christmas Day

Francine prepared the loft for Cathy's arrival. The original plan was to make the upper floor into a guest suite. There was going to be a kitchen and bathroom up there, but they had run out of money. The bathroom was a dry loo, the kitchen a fridge, kettle and camping stove. Nevertheless the cavernous sleeping quarters enabled them to invite friends and family. The idea was for people to come in the summer taking advantage of free accommodation to secure a low cost holiday. Instead he and Francine had proposed it in the winter. Without central heating warming a little used part of a large old house was problematic. "It's not too bad when the fire is lit in the living room" said Francine. "If it's cold in the morning she will just have to get dressed and come downstairs."

John agreed. He had just installed a range in the kitchen. As the days grew colder he started the day by lighting it. He lit the living room fire in the afternoon. Tonight they sat staring into the flames. Peter had gone to bed. The night terrors were becoming less frequent as Thelma had predicted. Peter managed the bedwetting by changing the sheets himself. The main problem was keeping up with the washing. John was giving Francine a head massage as she adopted her usual position on the floor in front of him. She wanted to invite people over on Christmas day. "Won't they want to be with their families on Christmas day?" John objected.

"Most, yes, but some don't have any. Lee for example."

"I suppose so. We could ask him and see what he says." He thought before adding. "We always used to invite Jan and her girlfriend for Christmas"

Francine leant forward so he could continue the massage down her back. "That was when you were with Cathy. Inviting your ex's sister for Christmas doesn't sound very English. I thought Brits were hung up on stuff like that."

"We have already invited Cathy so she would be staying with her sister."

"She and her girlfriend would be staying with your ex" Francine reminded him. "In the same bedroom."

"It wouldn't be the first time, just the first time with this girlfriend. I'll phone Cathy and tell her that Jan and Alice are welcome to come too if she doesn't mind sharing with them"

"OK if you are sure. Is Jan going to be alright with you, remember you have just left her sister?"

"We are actually very good friends." Francine threw her head back to look at him. "Not like that. She's gay! I told her about Cathy dumping Stuart. I didn't go into too much detail. I also told her that I had left Cathy and was with you."

Francine raised her eyebrows. "She was fine. She declared that all men are bastards. She then excluded me from the list making me an honorary female. I think it was a compliment."

"Do you think she will be ok with me? She won't think I have taken you away from her sister?"

"Absolutely not. She made a point of saying that she blamed Cathy and wanted to stay friends with me."

"OK So that is us, Peter, Lee, Cathy, her sister and girlfriend, who else? I wanted to invite Thelma and Paula"

John totted up the numbers. "That would make nine. I think we can fit nine round the table."

"That's settled then. Are you OK cooking for that many?"

"I'll manage. It will be nice to have a house full. What are we going to do for entertainment?"

"We could have an evening of story telling. We will ask people to bring a Christmas themed anecdote or story."

*

When the meal was over Francine ushered everyone through to the living room. Thelma installed Paula in a corner near the fire and made sure she had a side table for her port. She went back to the kitchen to fetch a chair so she could sit and hold Paula's hand. Lee had wedged himself into the corner of the settee so he could drink himself to oblivion without falling over. Jan and Alice were enjoying being in company accepting of their relationship. Lubricated by the mulled wine they were wrapped round each other at the other end of the settee. Peter had gone to his bedroom to fetch something. Cathy came in. She could have squeezed on the settee in between Lee and the lovebirds but didn't fancy being that close to the old man. Francine gestured to one of the armchairs. "Are you sure?"

"Absolutely."

"Where are you and John going to sit?"

"John can have the other armchair, I'm just as happy on the floor"

Peter came back. He brought Pooh, Piglit and a wad of paper. "Are we doing the stories now?"

John was behind him, glasses in hand. "As soon as everyone is settled, everyone ok for drinks? I can do coffee or tea if you want."

Francine put her hand out. "Sit down darling, everyone's fine. I can do them later." Cathy was hurt by the 'darling' but was starting to get used to it. He and Francine had been very welcoming but they had made it very clear that this was their home. She wasn't sure where her home was, but was determined to find it.

Peter coughed. "Are you sitting comfortably? Then I will begin: Christmas in the 100 acre wood by Peter Cartwright."

There was silence. All eyes were turned towards Peter who had Pooh in one hand and papers in the other. "Chapter 1. Once upon a time, not so long ago, and in a country not so far away there was a wood. It wasn't so big, about a hundred acres, but to the animals that lived there it was their whole world.

"In the middle of the wood was a large tree with a door in it. Behind the door lived a teddy bear called Winnie the Pooh." Peter held up Pooh to emphasise the point

"Winnie the Pooh's best friend in the whole world was Piglit. This story begins in the middle of the coldest winter you can imagine. Pooh was sitting by a big log fire and on his lap was an enormous jar of honey. The clock on the mantelpiece said five to eleven. Time for a little smackerel of something.

"Piglit had just arrived wrapped in an enormous scarf and was feeling more snowy around the ears than he had ever felt in his life. "Hello Piglit, you are just in time for a little smackerel of something."

"What time is it?" said Piglit

"Why it is nearly eleven o clock"

"That clock stopped at five to eleven months ago"

"I know." Pooh smiled as he got up to lay the table. "Honey or condensed milk on your bread Piglit?" Neither. Do you have haycorns?"

Thelma sat like a proud teacher at a prize giving. Paula was lost in the story already. Thelma took the glass out of her hand before she dropped it.

"Chapter 2" Peter continued. "In another part of the forest, high in a rather grand oak tree sat Owl. He was doing what owls like doing best. He was opening his post. Owl wrote lots of letters to himself, so he also had a lot of letters to read. This one was different. It was not in his handwriting. Since he had not written it, Owl was having trouble understanding what it said." Peter paused for a reaction, Auntie Jan duly obliged.

"I really must get some new glasses" said Owl. "These have not been the same since Pooh sat on them" Owl decided he would take this important letter to Rabbit. Rabbit being one of the few other animals in the hundred acre wood who could read. It was some distance from the Wolery, where Owl lived to Sandy Banks, the comfortable hole in which Rabbit resided. It had stopped snowing, but it was very cold. Just the weather for making an important flight.

"Go away, I'm busy – oh, it's you!" This was what Rabbit always said when someone knocked on his door. Considering how large the rabbit warren was, the door was surprisingly small.

"You should get a bigger front door" said Owl, not waiting to be asked inside.

"That would only encourage certain honey loving friends to stay longer and eat more" replied Rabbit. Owl laughed as he placed the letter on the table with a flourish.

"What do you think of this?"

Rabbit glanced at the letter. "Wonderful news!" he exclaimed.

"What is?" said Owl

"Why this of course" said Rabbit, waving the letter. Owl was still unsure what they were talking about. "We must tell the others"

"Must we?" said Owl, hoping that things would become clearer.

"Of course, before it is too late" Owl considered reminding Rabbit that owls eat rabbits, but instead he tried once more to find out what they were talking about. "I'll fly and tell Eeyore, he lives in a very gloomy part of the forest, too far to go on foot in this snow. I can call in on Kanga, Roo and Tigger on the way back. You tell Pooh and Piglit." Now it was Rabbit's turn to wonder why rabbits were not allowed to eat owls. He wished he had thought of that first.

"OK, but I will have to take the letter with me" This made Rabbit feel important again.

Owl fluffed his feathers in a gracious, if rather condescending way. "Of course my dear Rabbit, but since you have the letter in your hand, remind me again of the exact words so I can convey the same message"

"The usual thing" said Rabbit. Owl ignored him.

"The EXACT words please Rabbit" Now it was Rabbit's turn to look important.
"Mr and Mrs Milne are delighted to announce the birth

of their son Christopher. Mrs Milne will be 'at home' from 4 p.m. on December 25th."

Owl breathed a sigh of relief which he tried to make sound like a sigh of pleasure at such delightful news." Peter paused surveying the room and checking that everyone was paying attention. They were, apart from Lee who had fallen asleep.

Peter continued. "Chapter 3. The clock was still saying five to eleven when Rabbit arrived. Pooh and Piglit were enjoying the doing nothing much that comes from a warm fire, full tummies and, good company."

Cathy interrupted. "A bit like us!"

"Indeed" said Peter before continuing. "The manner of Rabbit's knock suggested their time of doing nothing much was about to end.

"Hello Rabbit, we had just finished elevensies and were thinking about lunch. Will you join us?"

"No time. I am organising an expedition, and you are joining me."

"What is an expotition?" Asked Pooh "For I am a bear of very little brain and long words bother me."

"It is a long line of everybody with me at the front. Everyone has to bring things to eat"

"What are we looking for?" asked Piglit. The last time Rabbit had organised an expedition it was to find the North Pole. Today that did not seem necessary. To judge from the pool of melted snow surrounding Rabbit, the North pole had found him.

"Pooh did not mind what they were looking for as long as Piglit was looking too, and there was something to eat. Piglit however, being a very small animal, was less concerned about having lunch than being the lunch for the thing they were looking for.

"We are looking for a baby" said Rabbit importantly. Suddenly Piglit felt much better. A baby, even if it was the young of one of the more ferocious animals, did not seem quite so scary if Pooh was there too.

"Where is the baby?" asked Piglit, in his bravest voice.
"That is what the expedition is for." Said Rabbit "Come on!"

"With one last look at his warm log fire Pooh grabbed his scarf and large pot of honey before following Rabbit and Piglit into the snow."

Nobody spoke so Peter ploughed on. "Chapter 4. Owl finally reached the gloomy place where Eeyore, the old grey donkey lived. He had to admit that covered in snow it did not look nearly as gloomy as usual, and the house that Pooh had built looked positively inviting. Eeyore did not share this opinion.

"Three sticks were placed on the ground and Eeyore was looking at them. Two were touching at one end and a third smaller one was placed across them, half way up.

"What's that?" he asked, not waiting for the owl to greet him.

"Three sticks" said Owl.

"I thought you could read" said Eeyore

"Owl bristled, if it is possible for an animal that has feathers to bristle." This got a giggle from Francine.

Peter acknowledged her appreciation before continuing. "Of course" Said Owl, wondering if he had been rumbled. "Ah, I mean A" he explained quickly.

"I am repairing my house using the A-frame method of construction." Continued Eeyore

"Owl, knowing when he was beaten changed the subject.

"I have an important announcement" he hooted.

"Hold that" said Eeyore, waving a hoof at one end of the stick.

"An ANNOUNCEMENT" repeated Owl

"Eeyore looked at him. "There's is no need to shout, I am not deaf. What is your announcement?

"Mr and Mrs Milne are delighted to announce the birth of their son Christopher. Mrs Milne will be 'at home' from 4 p.m. on December 25th"

Owl's spelling may be wobbly, but his memory is excellent.

"But that is today!" exclaimed Eeyore before immediately resuming his gloomy expression. "Not that I have been invited."

"Of course you have" Said Owl. We all have. That is what "At Home" means, everyone is invited."

"I am at home. That doesn't mean I invited you."

Owl lost patience. "You are impossible Eeyore. I have to tell the others. I'll see you there" Owl was gone before Eeyore had the chance to ask where "there" was.

Alice stopped nuzzling Jan and asked "Did Peter actually write this?"

"I think so. He is very clever, but a bit obsessed with Winnie the Pooh. I blame his dad."

Peter raised his voice to make sure he didn't lose his audience. "Chapter 5. Kanga was busy counting Roo's vests while Tigger and Roo where playing hide and seek. As soon as Owl arrived, Kanga made them both come and sit at the table in the mistaken belief that Owl was both important and clever, and therefore someone to be listened to. Tigger knew better and simply ran round the table pretending to look for Roo even though he was sitting in front of him.

"When Kanga heard the news she jumped with excitement. This is not a good idea for a grown kangaroo that is indoors. Owl rubbed the bump on her head in an understanding sort of way, pleased that his news was much better received than it had been by Eeyore. "Come on Roo dear, Tigger dear time to go". Tigger was out of the door before you could say "sandwich", returning a moment later to say "where are we going?"

"Chapter 6" said Peter quickly in case his dad decided to say the story was too long. "Owl was the first to arrive, being the only one able to fly. Tigger was close behind not feeling it necessary to check on the progress of the others. Kanga at first allowed Roo to hop at his own pace before her excitement got the better of her and she bundled him into her pocket before bouncing to catch up with Tigger.

"Owl announced each arrival with the panache of a master of ceremonies, secretly glad that they had got there before Rabbit's party.

"A very frustrated Rabbit eventually arrived. He had covered twice the distance necessary by constantly returning to Pooh who was busy helping Piglet through the snow drifts. It did not help that Pooh insisted on carrying a honey pot as well. It was lucky that Pooh had eaten the contents near the beginning of the journey. When the snow became too deep for Piglit, he climbed into the pot and Pooh carried both. "I do love you Pooh" whispered Piglit. "So do I" said Pooh."

"Nearly finished" Peter reassured his audience. "Chapter 7. Christopher Robin's mother was feeding him when they all came into the room. She was not the least put out or even surprised by this strange array of animals. She knew, as only a mother can know, that Christopher Robin was special, and would be a special friend to all these animals. Even Tigger stopped bouncing. They were all completely silent, nothing being the correct thing to say when a mother is feeding her newborn child.

"When she was finally ready to speak to her guests Christopher Robin's mother asked each their name. When it got to Pooh's turn he proudly held out his honey pot. "I've brought Christopher a present" For a moment there was an awkward silence as everyone else realised that, in their haste, they had completely forgotten to bring a present. "How lovely" the mother exclaimed. "What is inside?" Pooh looked bashful. "It's empty. It did have Piglit in it when he couldn't get through the snow. Before that it had honey. It is very useful like that, you can put anything inside.

"A useful pot to put things in" declared Christopher's mother. Pooh looked relieved. "I love Christopher Robin" squeaked Roo.

"We all do, said his mother."

"Can I put that in the pot?" asked Roo

"Of course." Before Kanga could stop him, Roo had jumped into the pot and planted a big kiss on the inside. "Eugh, it's all sticky, just like extract of malt" Everyone laughed while Kanga helped Roo out again.

"I have an idea" said Pooh, "but I don't suppose it is any good"

"I'm sure it is" whispered Piglit.

"Let's all put our love in the pot for him so he will know that we are his friends."

"That is a wonderful idea" exclaimed his mother. "You will all be his special friends, but I think I know who will be his best friend." She was looking straight at Pooh. Pooh looked worried "but I already have a best friend".

Piglit squeezed Pooh's hand. "Pooh, your heart is big enough to have two best friends. Besides Christopher Robin is a different sort of Best Friend"

Everyone clapped. Eventually it was Thelma who spoke. "That is the best Christmas story I have ever heard. Can I just say Peter that like Pooh your heart is big enough to have two mothers. Cathy will always be your mummy, but Francine is a different sort of mummy."

Peter looked awkward. "It's not finished. There's a postscript." Every sat up and paid attention again. "Everyone was walking home, deep in their own thoughts when suddenly Rabbit turned to Owl. "What happened to Eeyore? Did you invite him?"

"Of course" said Owl "I wonder what happened to him?"

Sometime later, even gloomier that usual, Eeyore arrived. "Have they gone?" he asked.

"I am afraid they have" said Christopher's mother.

"Typical, it's just what would happen" There was an awkward silence. "Now that I am here, I don't suppose I could see him. If it is not too much trouble that is"

"Of course. He is sleeping, but while you wait for him to wake up I can tell you another story. There is a mother, and a baby, and lots of animals, but the most important animal is a donkey." Eeyore sat and listened, and for once in his life he was not gloomy." Peter waited for people to clap again. He saw that most of them were crying.

Cathy held out her arms. "Can I have a cuddle?" Peter rushed over and sat on her lap with Pooh and Piglit.

Chapter 30
Resolutions

Lee woke up. Francine tried to draw him into the festivities. "We are telling Christmas stories. Peter has done his. Who wants to be next?"

"I'll go" Said Lee. Francine looked doubtful. There wasn't much she could do about it. "Firstly I would like to say I am a liar. Don't believe any of this. Secondly every word of this story is true." He paused for effect. "I have met the Kray twins"

Francine whispered to John. "Who are the Kray twins?"

"London gangsters, before my time."

Lee continued "There was an older brother Charlie. He was in the gang too. He got done for smuggling ten years ago. He was 70. They shouldn't put old people like that in prison."

Nobody was sure where this was leading. Francine got up. "Everyone ok for drinks?" She asked.

"I'll have another beer please love" said Lee.

Cathy got up too. "I need to get rid of the last one first." She pushed Peter off her lap and made her way somewhat unsteadily to the bathroom.

Peter was glad of the change. The mulled wine had brought out too much of her mothering instinct. He had missed her terribly of course. He was overjoyed when she phoned to say she was coming for Christmas. Now he found her changed, or perhaps it was him. He had moved to an new country and a new school; he had a different role model in Francine. Most of al changes were taking place in his body. Cathy was still his mum, but events had changed her too. Thelma saw it all. She was holding Paula's hand. Like Lee, Paula had fallen asleep. Peter moved to John in the next armchair. He knew that if he too fell asleep he would be sent to bed. Francine came back with Lee's beer. She took Cathy's seat so she could un-cramp her legs. Cathy came back with a recharged glass to find she had lost her seat and her son. Francine was about to get up. Lee stopped her, patting the settee. "Plenty of room here Cathy" she hesitated. Emboldened by the wine she indulged him.

Francine got up anyway and put another log on the fire. "Is Paula ok?" She asked. Thelma smiled. "As long as I am holding her hand. I think I will get her back soon. She is not used to socialising."

Francine smiled. "Thank you for coming."

Thelma returned the smile. "It has been a privilege. It is not easy what you are doing, but you are doing a great job."

Francine was puzzled. "What am I doing?"

"Hosting a Cartwright Christmas."

The room had broken up into separate conversations. John was trying to persuade Peter he was tired. The girls where whispering sweet nothings. Lee had moved on from the Krays to a bullion robbery near Heathrow. Cathy had never heard of it. Lee put his hand on her knee. If she had not been maudlin drunk it would have freaked her out. Everywhere in the room were couples.

Paula woke with a start. Not knowing where she was she panicked. Thelma squeezed her hand and whispered. She stood up to go. "Thank you all for allowing Paula and I to share your Christmas."

Francine remembered. "I promised Paula we would play cards."

Thelma smiled. "Another time. We are both tired."

John took the opportunity. "Peter, the grown ups are leaving. Time to get ready for bed."

Peter felt honour had been maintained so complied. He did the rounds of good night kisses. Jan and Alice were included. He hesitated after kissing Thelma. She nodded so he gave a slight cheek brush to Paula too. She beamed. Last of all he went to his mother. Lee was encouraged by the lack of rebuff following the hand knee manoeuvre and had his arm across her shoulder. Peter pushed it away and gave is mother a long hug. Afterwards he looked at Lee. "Goodnight Lee." There was no way he was getting a kiss.

The party was breaking up. Jan and Alice decided to continue their intimacies upstairs. Lee saw Cathy's glass was empty. He called for Champagne for the lady. John said that he didn't have any. He did, but was saving it for New Years Eve. In any event Lee and Cathy had already had far too much to drink. "I have some Dom Perignon in the fridge at home. Would you like to share it with me?"

Cathy looked round the room. Her son had gone to bed. The scissor sisters were on their way to the bed next to hers upstairs. The old lady had already taken her partner home. Her husband would eventually go to bed with his mistress in the room below her. Cathy had to choose between an empty bed and Champagne with strings attached. She chose the latter.

Lee could not believe his luck as he walked out of the village with Cathy on his arm. The parts of his house he was prepared to show her were a monument to bad taste. Every decoration had been chosen because it looked expensive. He fetched an ice bucket and stand and took it into the bedroom. He gestured to Cathy. "Make yourself comfortable." He went back to find a bag of ice, Champagne and glasses. Cathy stood awkwardly. The only place to sit was the bed. Lee emptied the ice into the bucket. He clinked the glasses. "Real crystal." He quipped. He started to open the Champagne. Cathy looked round the room like a cornered animal. She had made some pretty poor choices in her life. This was about to trump them all. There were two doors. One she had just entered. The other she guessed was the en suite bathroom.

"I'll go and wash." Her voice was thin and distant. An echo from a past she thought she had escaped.

Lee listened to the shower. He stripped as quickly as the alcohol would allow. He kicked his clothes under the bed where they joined most of last week's discarded garments. He slid between the covers. Cathy scrubbed her entire body with whatever she could find. It could not wash away the inebriation. Nor could it remove the self loathing she knew she was about to experience. On the other side of the shower door was a man she barely knew. He was older than her father. Of all the thoughts that were waging war with the alcohol that was the one that scared her most. At least the man she picked up when she went clubbing in Reading was younger than her. The Purple Turtle had never been the most reliable supplier of fresh meat but at least Juan had lived up to his name. Eventually Cathy would have to step out of the shower. She washed again.

Opening the door she spotted a towel on the floor. It was almost certainly dirty. Using it would nullify what she had been doing in the shower for the last twenty minutes. She started to shiver, reluctantly picking up the towel. Had Lee been watching her she would not have hesitated. The imperative of covering her nudity would have trumped the disgust she felt using a towel he had used. This was nothing compared to what was coming. Mercifully Lee was not watching her. It was too much to hope the whole evening had been a nightmare from which she would soon wake. She located Lee. He was under the duvet and fast asleep. This should have been the cue for Cathy to dress and go home. It was not. She was still more drunk than she had been for a long while. That was quite an achievement. Recently she had been setting the bar pretty high. She had not paid any attention when walking to Lee's house. She was far from sure she would find her way back to the village centre. Suddenly she was overwhelmed by tiredness. Taking the utmost care to avoid any skin contact she slipped under the cover.

Lee woke with the mother and father of all hangovers. There was no trace of Cathy. At first he thought the whole affair was one of his regular fantasies. The opened but untouched Dom Perignon proved otherwise. John had seen his wife leave so he left the door unlocked. As dawn broke Cathy slipped into a sleeping house and climbed into bed.

Peter was the first up. He stayed in his room playing the computer games he was given for Christmas. Pooh and Piglit watched; Pooh was the first to speak. "The world is changing Piglit. I do not understand it any more."

"Only bits of it Pooh."

"Peter is changing, but only bits of him." Pooh continued. "That was a lovely story he wrote."

Piglit agreed. "We will always be in that story."

Pooh was puzzled. "Peter wasn't in the story, why was that Piglit?"

"Because he wrote it. You can't be in your own story."

Pooh scratched his nose "Why is that?"

Piglit looked at his friend. "Because Pooh, then it is not a story. It is real life."

Real life scared Pooh. "I think I will just be a story. I will be the kind of story that goes on the shelf until someone wants to listen."

John woke. He snuggled up to Francine. Cathy sleeping upstairs freaked him out. He had heard her come in. In a few days it would be 2009. A year ago he had made love to Cathy in this very bed hoping it would mark the end of Stuart and Cathy. None of them imagined what was about to happen. Stuart was gone but not in the manner John foresaw. The time before Francine seemed unreal. He turned to breathe her warmth. Without realising it he was creating this home for her, not Cathy. Now he understood. Before he was born Peter was part of his life, waiting for a body to inhabit. Francine was there too, waiting for him. The house was waiting for him. The house was drawing them back. It was telling him that there were past memories as well as stories waiting to be told. In each one of the people here yesterday played some part. The house was a vortex drawing souls to itself.

As the household woke the house retreated into its own stonework. It spoke in a voice so soft the stirring of a human soul would drown it. Plans were being drawn. Jan and Alice could only take so much of the quietness of the countryside. John ran through a list of the local attractions. The committee des fetes was hosting a children's tea party featuring Father Christmas. There was a carol concert in Sorges. Thelma and Paula had been invited to a free meal laid on for old age pensioners. Thelma declined on her partner's behalf. "But you will bring her for New Year's Eve. I promised her a game of rummy." Said Francine. Thelma thought she would be able to manage that.

None of these appealed to the girls. "We want to go clubbing" sulked Jan.

"You can. If you go to Perigeux" replied Francine. Bearing in mind their particular tastes she recommended l'Interdit. "It's a bit of a walk from the town centre. You need to cross the bridge and take the Bergerac road." John did not know which surprised him most. That there was a lesbian night club in Perigeux or Francine knowing about it.

Lee had gone to ground. Nobody was particularly inclined to invite him again. He was suffering from what he called 'a dose of the hurry-ups'. Being unable to stray far from a toilet gave him the excuse to duck out of facing Cathy to apologise. He was not sure what to apologise for. Was it getting her into his bed or him being too drunk to notice?

New Year came to the house on the square. Six of them sat down to play cards. Paula won. She remembered nothing of the evening a few days ago. In contrast she knew every rule in the game she was playing. including several that she introduced as the game progressed. "She's making them up" said Peter as he lost again to another new rule. Cards were put away. Thelma was preparing to take Paula home. Peter knew that meant he would be sent to bed. He played for time.

"We haven't made any new year resolutions! What will yours be Francine?"

"I am going to write the history of St Etienne. I will start by interviewing the old people who have lived here all their life. I also want to find out as much as I can about this house." She turned to John. "What about you my love?" Cathy winced but said nothing. John thought. "I am going to return to my hobby of brewing. If I can I would like to start my own business. Your turn Peter."

"To get a girlfriend."

Cathy instantly responded with "But you are too young! You are not even a teenager!"

"I wasn't talking about sex. People can be friends without sex. I want someone my own age to talk to. Girls are better listeners than boys."

Thelma responded. "It is good to have friends your own age you can talk to. Make lots of friends. Don't try and make one into a girlfriend. If you have friends who are girls one day one of them will become a special friend."

"What's your resolution Thelma?" Peter asked.

"I think I will come out of retirement. There's a lot I can do and still look after Paula."

John was delighted. "You have helped Peter so much. I hope you can help others too."

"My work with Peter is almost done. I will always be here if you need me Peter. We don't need to meet every week. That of course means I can take on new clients." Thelma was able to direct the comments without Cathy being aware she was the subject.

"Do you only work with children?"

"Not at all. If you are staying longer we can find a time to talk in private. I can explain better then."

"I was planning to stay longer. In fact that was my New Year Resolution: to move to France."

There was a stunned silence. Peter rushed up to his mother and hugged her. He would not let go. He was crying. Thelma knew exactly who was most affected. She reached for Francine's hand. Francine was not prepared for her own reaction. She was jealous. With her was the boy she had come to love as much as she loved his father. He was the man she had loved for less than two years and lived with for less than six months. The father and son had become her whole life. Were they about to do what they had come to France to do?

It was John who spoke. "What about your job?" He had worked it out long ago that she had never intended to resign.

"I was sacked." Peter released his mother. He understood that having two mothers carried responsibilities. He went and stood next to Francine. He inclined his head so it rested on her shoulder. He did not hug her, but he was there to be cuddled if she needed it.

John was scared of where this was leading. He was scared of the 'can we give it another go?' speech. Cathy looked at him. She could not deny that she had thought about it. She was released from Stuart's spell. She had become the girl John had fallen in love with all those years ago. She knew him in ways Francine had yet to learn. She loved him as she had all those years ago. She believed he loved her. Why else would he have done all he had done to remove her from Stuart? She would appeal to his sense of duty. He would do the right thing by his wife and son. Francine was nice but she would get over him. It would be as he had always planned it to be. They would be happy.

Part 4
The House

Chapter 31
New beginnings

Francine was trembling. Beside her Peter was inviting her to cuddle him. Behind was the man she loved more than life itself. In front the woman she had tried to help. Cathy held Francine's future happiness in her hand. Soon the two men in her life would be reclaimed by the person to whom they rightfully belonged. Francine would return to her flat, to the library. She would be nice to Pascal. She may even finish up as his carer. His mother would not live forever. Francine would become that nice little old lady at the library that everyone says is so helpful.

Cathy looked at her. "Now that Stuart is gone I am free to love again. John you tried to warn me. I should have listened. Well here I am. I am listening now. You told me to find someone else to love. The two people I love most in the world are in front of me. John you taught me how to love. I must use that to learn to love myself. Thelma from what I have seen of your work with Peter I think you could help me too. John, I love you.

For the first time in my life I know what that means. I cannot take from you what you have found. I cannot continue to share a life with you. That ship has sailed. You begged me to come aboard. I did not. I will not leave our son. Francine I commend them both to your care but I will not be far. Your loft is a little too close. I shall find somewhere nearby. I will learn to love myself. One day I may find someone to love half as much as I love you John. If that person loves me half as much as you once loved me it is more than I deserve. I will be happier than most people. Francine. I hope we shall be friends."

Francine was crying. She could not stop. Cathy did not expect it. She had just given her the two people she loved most in the world. Had she not understood?

She asked the question to Thelma. "She understands. She is crying from relief." Everyone gathered round to hug Francine.

Even Paula was stroking Francine's arm and muttering "There there". Eventually Francine calmed down.

Peter turned to Thelma. "What did mummy say to make Francine cry?"
Thelma extricated herself and Peter from the group hug. She held his shoulders. "Remember when I asked if you could have anything what would it be?"

He nodded. "I said I wanted Stuart t go away and never come back. I wanted to stay in France and live with Daddy and Francine. I also said I wanted mummy to live near enough to visit on my own."

"You have got your wish." Happy New Year Peter." He hugged Thelma then went back to hugging whichever mother would let him.

The clock struck midnight. Kisses were exchanged. When it came to Cathy's turn to kiss John she kissed him deeply. "For old time's sake" she whispered. "Go, and go with my blessing. Do not become a stranger." She handed him to Francine. "Look after him." Francine started crying again. Cathy drew her sleeve across her nose. "Don't start again or you will make me cry too. I might change my mind."

Francine reigned in the tears and managed a watery smile. "Don't you fucking dare!"

Thelma was finally able to say she was going. "You are the most remarkable family. I have never before been honoured to witness such an epiphany. Especially you Cathy. The others I have come to know well. I can see too we will become close friends. I can help you with your childhood if you wish, but most of the work you have already done yourself tonight." With that she and Paula left.

"Time for bed big fella." John went to pick Peter up. "Crikey you are getting big!"

For once he did not argue. "Goodnight." He turned to leave then looked back. "Epiphany is not till next week. What did Thelma mean?"

"Pooh will explain. Goodnight Peter."

The three of them sat round the table finishing the New Year champagne. They heard a taxi pull in to the square. The girls fell up the stairs into the living room giggling. "We have had such a good time! Thank you Francine for recommending it, you should go."

"Not my scene, but I am glad you liked it. Will you join us for a nightcap?"

"Thanks for the offer but we are going to bed."

"Goodnight!" they called in unison.

Alone again nobody knew what to say. Cathy had made her speech. It could not be unsaid. She remembered the dark times in her relationship with John. He had asked her directly if she still loved him. She had said "I don't know" That too could not be unsaid. She could not say she loved him, nor could she say she did not love him. She was simply stating the truth. That had not been good enough for John at the time. Now she was saying I do love you, but I do not deserve your love. It seemed a more honest thing to say. It was going to be hard for her. Every time she saw them together she would be reminded of what might have been.

John could not believe he loved two such different people. His love for Cathy turned to respect. She would be an amazing partner to the right person. That was not him. His love for Francine continued to grow. He remembered when she said that one day they would love each other more. He had not believed her. It did not seem possible. Now he did. He was in awe of her wisdom, her generosity, a heart so large it could hold all who came within its compass.

Francine was struggling to come to terms with the space she now inhabited. She had been happy to borrow

John in order to give him happiness and find some for herself. He was not able to do that. He did the English thing of making sure his ex was going to be ok before moving on. Francine had become English; she was unable to play the mistress. She wanted exclusive rights. She was willing to pay the price: dedication, loyalty, fidelity. She had seen the way Cathy kissed John.

Finally alcohol and tiredness got the better of all of them and they went to bed. The next day Francine woke. She caressed the sleeping body beside her careful not to wake either it or the sleepers above her head. When he woke they shared such intimacies as total silence allowed. Francine had yet to reach that place where Cathy was not a rival. She was confident in her abilities but this morning she was severely handicapped. When it was over she whispered "Did you enjoy it?" In answer he turned and kissed her. "I didn't mean just now, I meant when she kissed you."

John raised himself on his shoulder to look at Francine. "It was a goodbye kiss."

"You haven't answered my question. Did you enjoy her kissing you?"

"Are you jealous?"

"Yes. We have flipped. I have become your wife, and she has become your mistress"

"Francine, she has not become my mistress. Why do you say that?"

"Because you allowed her to kiss you and you kissed her back."

"I told you, it was a goodbye kiss."

Francine put her finger to his lips "Not so loud, you can hear everything upstairs"

"I did not make love to her."

"No, but you will."

"You heard her last night. That ship has sailed. Cathy and I will never make love again."

"Do you remember the last time you made love to her?"

"No. I suppose I could work it out. Why should it matter?"

"The first time matters. Everyone remembers the first time. Why does nobody remember the last time?"

"I suppose because when it happens you have no idea it will be the last time."

"She whispered to you when she kissed you. What did she say?"

"For old time's sake"

"Then you could have sex for old time's sake."

"No, because I do not want to. Francine I cannot prove it to you. I can say this: if it were to happen you would know. I couldn't hide it from you. You just have to trust me, just as I trust you."

"You trust me because there is nobody for me to be unfaithful with."

"And why is that? It is because you are not looking for anyone else."

"No I am not. If someone shows the slightest interest I let them know I am taken."

John held her gaze. "Francine, it is exactly like that for me. Cathy and I have a history, I acknowledge that but my future is with you."

Francine put her head on his chest "I'm sorry John, it is just that I cannot bear the thought of losing you. When Cathy started talking I thought I was going to. I couldn't cope when I realised she was saying the opposite."

He stroked her hair. "You are not going to lose me."

*

The holidays were nearly over. Jan and Alice thanked Francine for a wonderful time and went back to England. Peter finished his assignments under the watchful eye of Pooh and Piglit. Soon it would be the first day of term. Francine's holiday was also nearly over. She was doing the washing up when Cathy came downstairs. The tap was running so she did not hear her come in. She came up and put her arms round her. "Good morning Francine."

Francine jumped and spun round. "Good morning. I didn't hear you come in. John is out getting croissants he won't be long. Coffee?"

Cathy did not release Francine as she turned. "In a minute. I'm glad he's out. Can we talk?"

Francine gently extricated herself from Cathy. She dried her hands. "Of course. I think I am going to need coffee." She lit the gas under the pot. Taking Cathy's hand she sat with her at the table. The embrace at the sink was a peace offering. She had accepted that. Francine looked into Cathy's eyes, searching her soul.

Cathy held her gaze. She had nothing to hide. "John and I are not going to have sex."

Francine blushed. "You heard?"

"Yes. I was not spying, every sound travels through your bedroom ceiling."

"I know. I am sorry that I don't trust you. I am even sorrier that I don't trust John. I don't know why, it is so unlike me." The coffee boiled. Francine poured some. Cathy changed her mind. They both cradled the mugs in their hands. John had lit the stove before leaving but the kitchen had not yet warmed.

Cathy pressed on. "I can see why John fell in love with you. If I was like my sister I would fall in love with you." She laughed at Francine's surprise. "Don't worry, I am not bi!"

Francine laughed too. "That's a relief. I thought things were about to get even more complicated!" The tension was gone. Francine continued "You scared me New Year's Eve. It really sounded as if you had come to take John and Peter away from me. When I was a little girl I found a stray puppy. He was so adorable. I looked after him. We became inseparable. Then one day the owner knocked at the door. My mother answered. She just came into my bedroom, took the puppy and handed it back. I cried for a week. All my mother said was 'It is not your puppy, it never was.' That is how I felt when you were talking."

Cathy squeezed her hand. "I almost bottled it. There was a chasm I had to leap. I retreated to take a run at it. Back from the cliff edge I almost lost my nerve. I was back in the land of John and Cathy. Someone whispered in my ear 'stay, you can make John stay too. You can make him do whatever you want.' I believed the voice. I knew it would crush you. I didn't care."

Francine could hardly speak. "You were going to weren't you?"

"Yes."

"Why didn't you?"

"I would have crushed John too. I would have been living with a corpse. It was that thought which propelled me over the abyss."

"Thank you." The words were totally inadequate but Francine could find no others.

"I am sorry I kissed him like I did. It was wrong."

"You were saying goodbye."

"Yes I was."

Francine looked at her. "Thank you again. May I kiss you?" Cathy leant forward. Francine placed a soft kiss on her lips. John came in. "Breakfast is served!"

they were still kissing. "Crikey, for a moment I thought you were Jan and Alice!"

The girls pulled apart. Francine laughed. "No chance! Anyway that is my line."

"What, 'I thought you were Jan and Alice'?"

"No, 'breakfast is served'!"

John remembered their first morning. "Ah yes. Just don't say 'I'd better take these...'"

Francine shot him a look to stop him finishing the sentence. "John, that's enough!"

They sat pulling the croissants apart and dunking them in coffee. "John, I am staying in France but I can't stay with you. Also, without a job I am skint."

John had been meaning to talk to her about money. His business had suffered from the move. He had failed to pick up local clients. As he finished existing contracts subsequent phases were going elsewhere. "We have issues with your availability." Was how one client put it.

Francine had a brainwave. "You could have my flat in Thiviers. It's not very big but the location is ideal."

Cathy hesitated. "Are you sure? You would be burning your bridges."

"I burned them long ago. I was waiting for the tenancy to expire."

It was John's turn. "We need to make a decision about the house in England."

Francine stood. "That is something you and Cathy must sort out between you. If you don't mind I'd like to go to Perigeux."

Cathy looked at her. "Doing anything exciting?"

"For me, yes. The public records office is open. It's the first day since Christmas. I am at work tomorrow so it is the only chance I will get to start keeping my new year's resolution."

John remembered. "You were going to research the history of St Etienne. Enjoy yourself!"

"I will. Think about my offer of the flat. The keys are in the key box, you could look round together and Cathy can tell us what she thinks."

"Good idea." Said John. "I'll see if Peter wants to come too."

Francine picked up her car keys. Don't make him if he doesn't want to, he'll be fine on his own for an hour."

"Do you think so? You are probably right. He has grown up so much since I brought him to France."

Francine realised they were discussing Cathy's son without consulting her. "Sorry Cathy. What do you think?"

Cathy shrugged. "Your call, I am sure you will do the right thing."

Francine sat down again. "It's a joint call. Peter may be living here but you are his mother."

John added. "I think we should make him come with us. We can show him the spare bedroom. If he is going to have two mothers he may as well have two bedrooms. Also Francine is right. Anything to do with Peter is a joint call.

Chapter 32
The musician
1905

Francesca was bored. Her mother was helping her choose a new dress. She did not understand why she needed a new dress if they were leaving Paris. She was sure they did not wear such clothes in Bordeaux. The Domaine de Monplaisir was not even Bordeaux. It was somewhere north of Perigeux. Francesca's corset hurt; her waist was already tiny. "Make the most of it while you are young". Her mother's advice was tinged with envy. The dress the older woman had chosen for her daughter was yellow satin. The short bouffant sleeves were edged with Belgian lace emphasising Francesca's pale arms. The neckline was wide. It showed a generous amount of neck without drawing the eyes towards the breasts. These, her mother thought, were something of a disappointment. Francesca would grow, she decided. In any event she wanted her daughter to invite admiring glances, not improper thoughts. The tight bodice was richly decorated with swirling motifs designed to suggest what was not quite there. A décolleté in white broderie anglaise plunged to her navel drawing the eyes down to her tiny waist. From here the dress flowed to the floor overlaid with yet more embroidery and lace. Her mother approved. She produced a small phial, inverted it and removed the glass stopper. Dabbing on Francesca's wrists she motioned to her daughter. Dutifully Francesca rubbed her wrists together. Her rich auburn hair was gathered up, exposing the upper neck. She transferred some of the fragrance behind her ears. The light scent of jasmine and lavender filled the room. It was just the effect the older woman wanted. She hoped the ensemble would do its job of attracting a suitable husband. Whether such a person was to be found outside Paris was quite another matter. She had little choice. In Paris her husband had too much. Madame Lacroix was taking father and daughter away from the metropolitan distractions to the simpler pleasures of their Domaine in Perigord. Chateau Monplaisir would be well named she decided. Not for her the girlish fragrance of jasmine and lavender. Her own phial contained musk and civet. The animal fragrances were to would rekindle similar instincts in her husband.

Jean-Michel Belrose studied music under Gabriel Fauré at the Paris conservatoire. The maestro preferred composing to teaching. Jean-Michel was delighted therefore when he was invited to spend the summer with his mentor. They travelled first to Chartres then south. A new century had begun but the countryside had changed little since the revolution. Fauré encouraged his pupil to listen not to the notes, but the spaces between them. "When you play, you make the sound. It is God who makes the silence. If you wish to compose you must listen to God, not your echo. They had found silence in the great forests that stretched south from Limoges. Eventually they came upon a tiny village. They stopped to drink from the well. Behind them the Templar house was shuttered and abandoned. Its owner had returned to civilisation in Paris. The farm in front of them appeared equally abandoned. A church steeple peeped over the rustic roof. An old woman approached carrying her washing. They greeted her in French, she replied in Occitain. They pointed first to the Templar house behind them. "Paris" replied the washerwoman Jean-Michel pointed to the farm in front of him. She said the farm was no longer occupied. The occupier was captured at the battle of Mars-la-Tour in 1870. Like many of his compatriots in the Franco-Prussian war he had died in the smallpox epidemic that ravaged the prison camps. The farm had lost not just its tenant, but most of its labourers. The landowner had returned to Paris. His son had maintained the Templar house, but had no interest in the farm which was close to ruin. Jean-Michel was fascinated by it. He left Faure by the well and went to explore. There was little more than the church to identify the centre of the village. Jean-Michel stood looking at the farm with the church on his left. The barn projected into the village square. To its right was the path from the well. He imagined himself as the village's benefactor. He would build a façade on the front of the dwelling in line with the barn. There was space to his right for a school. He would build two classrooms, the second for girls. He would engage a schoolmaster to teach both sexes. If you educate the mother, you educate the child.

He saw it as his mission to bring enlightenment to these parts.

1910

Returning to Paris he did not have to wait long to realise his vision. He was an only child. His mother died giving birth; his father never remarried. Now he too was in failing health. On his death his entire estate passed to Jean-Michel. The musician returned to Saint Etienne. The few inhabitants that remained adopted him as their benefactor and rewarded him with the mayoral sash. With the energy of youth he set about regenerating the village. He tried, unsuccessfully to prevent the church steeple from falling. He added a large façade on the front of the farmhouse bringing it in line with the barn. The priest saw his opportunity and petitioned for a larger steeple. In this Jean-Michel indulged him. He had not discovered the cause of the demise of the previous spire. It was possibly a result of erosion. The region was riddled with underground rivers. One emerged only metres away at St. Etienne's well. Pragmatically he decided the priest could have his larger steeple, but that it would be at the far end of the church. There it would be away from the foundations that had already proved insufficient. If the new spire fell it would at least not fall on his new house. Away from the village he was introduced to the local gentry. Madame Lacroix approved. He found himself a frequent invitee to Monplaisir. Francesca's mother hearing of her visitor's musical credentials immediately explained her daughter's aptitude. That Francesca did not play was not an impediment. Had her daughter ever learned, she was sure she would have been a true proficient. Jean-Michel agreed, saying that Francesca was the perfect age to commence studies. He planned to found his own conservatoire in Perigeux. Until then Francesca was welcome to study at his new house in St Etienne, suitably chaperoned of course. Her father believed that learning in young girls was to be admired provided the subject was seemly. He declared that the violincello met this criterion. Her mother however questioned the manner in which the instrument was played and ensured her daughter had sufficient petticoats beneath the dress. The lack of exposed skin only served to fuel her teacher's passion but as befitted a gentleman of class Jean-Michel kept his attention strictly professional.

The shadow of another war was gathering in the East. The third republic was about to be threatened. The assassination of Ferdinand in Bosnia precipitated a chain of events which ended for Jean-Michel in Verdun. His work at the conservatoire excused him from military service, but he considered it his patriotic duty and volunteered anyway.

The day he left for the front he declared his feelings. When he returned he would seek an audience with her father to discuss his prospects. That he had sufficient means was obvious. His cultured refinement too he hoped was evident. When the honour of France had been reclaimed he would return a hero. Francesca would have come of age. Nothing could stand between them and a life filled with happiness and children.

Knowing Jean Michel was a musician his commanding officer, Noel de Castelnau secured a gift for his junior officer. It was a trench 'cello. The box that held it was the size and shape of an ammunition box. The instrument was rectangular and unpolished. Nevertheless the maestro was able two wrest from it a tune. General Castelnau thought it would be good for morale for the troops to be entertained from time to time.

Now was not such a time. The musician was huddled in a trench beside Pierre Leclerc, an Etiennoise who had travelled with him to the front. The French second Army were relentlessly bombarding the German fifth to control the high ground north of the Meuse. Jean-Michel craved silence. Unable to play he remembered the words of Fauré. For him the music of the spheres came not from the notes, but the spaces between them. In the space between each explosion Jean-Michel searched for his sanity. The bombardment had been going on for over a month. Crown Prince Wilhelm was inspired by his success at the second battle of Champagne the previous year. He would take the heights above Verdun and bombard the French army from an easily defensible position. His attack was hampered by poor weather. The French poured twenty divisions into the region. Noel de Castelnau dug his troops in. Little did either general know they were embarking on the longest and bloodiest battles of the Great War.

Stephan Leclerc had little affection for the cultured Parisian beside him in the trench. Jean-Michel never returned from Verdun. There was no family to mourn him. Only his students pondered whether a man of such talent might not be a greater loss to France than a simple peasant. One in particular died inside when she heard the news. As the war continued injured soldiers started returning. The Nunnery that dominated Thiviers was transformed into a hospital. Francesca worked alongside the Sisters. Pierre Leclerc had been injured in the same blast as Jean-Michel. He was evacuated to the convent. Francesca tended to his injuries. In doing so she learned about men's bodies. The man she loved did not return; the trench 'cello did. Mother Superior gave it to Francesca. She knew the young girl had been learning before the war. Besides, her name had been carefully carved on the back of the instrument. Knowledge of men's bodies was of no use if the man you love is dead. Instead she married Christ. He at least had survived death. Pierre Leclerc was visited before he died by his younger brother. Benjamin Leclerc should have been in Verdun with his brother. He lied about his age in order to avoid conscription. He learned from his dying brother that the bohemian bourgeois musician had died at the front leaving a magnificent restored building without an owner. Benjamin decided that Jean-Michel had bequeathed the property to Pierre. From this fabrication it was natural to deduce that his brother had passed it to him as his dying wish. Benjamin had some savings for just such opportunities. He prepared a generous donation before securing a meeting with the priest at the notaire's office. From the testimony of Father Thomas the notaire prepared deeds passing the entire property first to the deceased Pierre Leclerc, then to his younger brother. The notaire produced a bottle of wine. He poured three glasses. Leclerc passed a leather satchel to Father

Thomas. Without speaking or looking inside the priest raised his glass and smiled. God moves in mysterious ways he thought. Benjamin had not intended the leather satchel to be part of the bribe. He shrugged. He would get another.

Chapter 33
September 1942
The Collaborator

Herr Schneider sat at the large oak dining table. Notionally he was in Free France. There had been changes in the Vichy regime. Now German soldiers replaced the Gendarmes. The courtyard at the front of the Templar house was larger than the old farmyard near the square. This one opened almost directly on to Saint Etienne's well. Behind it the substantial building pleased the German commander. It was rectangular and efficient. There were no round turrets to suggest French romanticism. As a concession the roof at each end of the building was higher, suggestive of two square towers.

The Resistance were active in the area and posed a constant threat to the Oberleutnant's troops. It was a threat he faced with ruthless efficiency. Summary executions were frequent and public. Malefactors were shot where they were caught. Unlike most of his troops Herr Schneider was Nazi by conviction. His men were mostly raised in poverty. This drove their nationalism and xenophobia. The ruthlessly efficient Reich blamed the collapse of the German economy after the Great War not on the Allied policy of reparation but the immigrants the war had displaced. The ordinary German sought only a route out of poverty. The Herr Schneider had never been poor. He exploited nationalism of his troops feeding the cannons with the blood of his own men. For this he exacted retribution from the French with ruthless Germanic efficiency.

Stuardo rented the old schoolmaster's house built into the big one on the square. He arrived from Torano before the war. Then his experience as a stonemason was welcomed. Today his nationality was more relevant than his experience and was viewed with suspicion by the locals. Stuardo opened the shutter covering his front door. The square was empty. He turned left and slipped down the path beside the barn. Passing the well he approached the Templar house. The guard recognised him. He made no move either to acknowledge or challenge. The Italian passed under the carved Maltese cross above the door and into the room where the Oberleutnant was working. A few moments later Stuardo left empty handed. Payment was by result. He would return tomorrow.

Herr Schneider barked an order. An unteroffizier with two soldats saluted and marched out. They turned away from the village towards Blazon Noir. The isolated farmhouse was home to Guy and Bruno. The elderly brothers had survived the Great War to return to their village where they raised pigs. They had handed over two beasts to the Germans but managed to conceal the third. They had slaughtered it this morning. They were in the process of burying it when they heard the sound of Jack boots. The artillery fire from military service had rendered both men partially deaf. They heard the footsteps too late. Two shots cracked sending a flock of birds skyward. The soldats put their guns back in their holster. The unteroffizier pushed the corpses into the hole that was being dug to conceal the pig. He motioned to his subordinates to pick up the animal before the three returned. Another routine assignment had been completed.

Stuardo heard the shots. He had been told to return tomorrow for payment. The next day Francois, Pierre and Jean were also waiting by the well. Stuardo moved to pass him. They stepped to block his passage. Without a word the three Frenchmen bundled the Italian up the track leading to the woods. Eventually they stopped. Francis produced a rope to tie Stardo's hands. "Do we have proof?" Asked Jean

Francis looked at him. "Why do you always need proof? Guy and Bruno are dead."

Jean was suitably chastened. He looked at Francis. He was far too beautiful to be a man. Jean pushed the thought away.

Peter brought them both back to the matter in hand. "I saw him talking to the Bosh."

"What are you going to do?" Francis asked of Jean. Despite his criticism he admired the older man. Jean always knew the right thing to do.

"You could kill him." said Pierre.

Jean looked at his little brother. "We would be caught and killed ourselves. Even possessing a revolver is a capital offence. Executing an informer would see both our families massacred."

"You could make it look like an accident." Pierre smiled as he said it.
Francis handed Jean the revolver. "Take him further into the woods. I'll take Pierre home. He is too young to witness an execution."

Jean motioned to the Italian with his gun. There was a flash of hatred in the Italian's eyes. It upset Jean. He had gone out of his way to welcome the itinerant mason when he came to the village. The two walked in silence. Deep in the woods Jean placed a hand on the Italian's shoulder. He stopped. Jean applied slight downward pressure. Stuardo dropped to his knees. Fight had never been his preferred option. He considered flight then remembered the Frenchman's gun. He flopped, emptying his bowels as he did so. Jean untied the Italian's hands. Moving in front of him he spoke. "You have been found guilty of passing information to the enemy. The penalty is death. I should shoot you now."

"Then do so."

"Had you killed Guy and Bruno yourself the penalty would have been a much slower death. You would be hung from a tree until you died of asphyxiation. The executioner would ensure your neck did not break."

"Do you expect me to thank you?"

"No, I merely state the laws of the French resistance. I however answer to a higher Authority." He handed Stuardo the gun. "I give you three choices. You can run. I will say you overpowered me, took the gun and escaped. You will be captured, either by the Germans or the French. In both cases you will be killed. The second option is to shoot me. Your chance of escape will be greater. My compatriots will hear the shot and assume it is you that has died. It will give you more time." Jean turned to walk away.

"And the third?"

"I leave that to your imagination." He continued walking without looking back. A shot rang out. Death is never instantaneous. Injuries incompatible with life can be sustained in a moment. For the soul to pass in or out of this world takes longer. Jean took another step, then another.

*

Peter was quiet. Francine hugged him. Had she gone too far? The Winnie the Pooh stories with John were sweet but he was growing up. Francine wondered whether the stories were more for John's benefit. Her new year's resolution was going well. She had uncovered several interesting stories about the house. Peter asked about them. She proposed telling them to him instead of his Pooh story.

"I'm glad I didn't live back then. People were very cruel."

Francine agreed. "Life was much harder. War is a terrible thing."

Peter needed to know the truth. "Did the Italian shoot the Frenchman or did he shoot himself?"

"I don't know."

"But you must know, it is your story."

"Peter, sometimes it is the person listening who decides."

"That's a cop out. You are the story teller, you have to decide."

Francine gave in. "OK, this is what I think happened." She finished the story.

*

Jean stopped. The woods were eerily silent. He felt nothing. If the shot was aimed at him it had missed. He had taken the precaution of removing the other bullets from the revolver. He considered returning to the clearing where he had left Stuardo. The shot would undoubtedly attract Germans. It was better if he was as far away as possible. Leaving the path he made his way back to the village.

*

Peter was only half satisfied. "Now tell me what really happened. You said it was a true story."

"Peter, the truth is I don't know. I know Guy and Bruno were shot for hiding food from the Germans. I know that Jean Pierre and Francis were in the resistance. Stuardo was an informer. Jean died during the war. Pierre survived. Stuardo was never seen again."

Peter thought about it. "Those are the pieces you have found. You are guessing the bits in between. Here is my guess: Jean gave Stuardo three choices. Run away, kill Jean then run away, kill himself. He didn't run away immediately. He knew he would be caught. He didn't kill Jean. Although Stuardo is bad he is not a murderer. He could not shoot Jean in the back."

"So he killed himself?"

"No. He was too much of a coward. He fired the gun in the air. That would make the resistance think he was dead. Then he ran away."

Francine nodded. "Surely Jean would have checked to see if he was dead."

"I don't think he did. Your ending was right. He was scared of getting caught by Germans. I also think he didn't want to see Stuardo's dead body. Jean is kind. I don't think he likes killing people."

"You have a very good explanation. It is true until you find a new piece of information. That either confirms your explanation or you change it to fit the new truth."

"I love you Francine."

"I love you Peter. Goodnight." She kissed him softly.

Chapter 34
House for sale
Spring 2009

Francine returned to the living room. John was at his desk. One day they would knock through from the kitchen to the upper floor of the barn and create an office. For now the desk was set up in the far corner of the living room. She put her hands on his shoulders. "Work?" She asked.

"Sort of. It's a business plan for the brewery. Even a micro-brewery is very different to home brew. The equipment is very expensive."

"I'm not very good with money." Francine replied. "I can do family budgets but big numbers scare me."

John had stopped what he was doing so he could concentrate on her shoulder massage. "It's exactly the same. Just add some zeroes."

"That's the bit that scares me."

John smiled. He inclined his head on to her hand then kissed it. "I want to make it local, but with a twist. English real ale but brewed in the Dordogne."

Francine thought about it. "If you just do English beers the French won't like it. If you do local craft beers you will have a lot of competition."

"I'll do both. I'll give it a French name but say it is an English brewer."

"Have you thought of a name?"

"Yes. BASE? Bierre Artisanale de Saint Étienne?"

"You can't call it that!"

"Why not?"

"Base means basic. 'Une bierre base' is a weak flavourless beer. The kind of pression you get at a local event. Like the Brocante."

John was disappointed. "I'll have to think of something else then."

Francine had an idea. "I know. BAT. Bierre Artisanale de Thiviers."

"But we are not in Thiviers."

"Near enough. You can always put Brewed in St Etienne on the bottom."

John thought about it. "It could work. It makes it sound strong. You know, like a kick or a punch. I could put a cricket bat in the logo. That could be the English connection."

346

Francine was warming to the idea. "You could make it look traditional. What were those striped jackets the English used to wear?"

"Blazers. I could be W. G. Grace."

"Who is he?"

"The father of English cricket. I would have to grow a beard."

"Why?"

"I'll find a picture of him." John opened his browser and pulled up a picture."

Francine was not sure. "He's very handsome, but that beard would tickle."

"You like being tickled." He turned and put his arm round her searching for that spot just under her ribs.

She squealed. "John, no!" He picked her up and dropped her on the settee. He knew when 'No' meant 'yes'.

*

Peter still saw Thelma from time to time. She was working with Cathy now. Peter was singularly unsuccessful when it came to finding out what they talked about. He tried a different tack, his own New Year resolution. They talked about girls. The village was pretty poor as a source in that respect. Natalie was on his bus. She was a year older than him. "I don't think she even knows I exist." He complained. "She only talks to the big boys."

"Have you talked to her?"

"Of course not!"

"Then I am not surprised she doesn't know you exist. Peter, just talk to her as if she was a boy. A lot of girls like football. Talk about that."

"Nobody talks about football. They only play rugby here."

"Then talk about rugby."

"I don't know much about it. That is dad's thing."

"Then talk to him about it."

"No way!"

Thelma was surprised. "Why not?"

"If you get dad talking about rugby he doesn't stop. He tried to get me to do minis in England. That's why I joined the soccer team."

"What's minis?"

"It's what the little kids play. They throw the ball to each other. They are not allowed to tackle. You stuff a sock in the top if your shorts. If someone has the ball you try and grab their sock. If you get it they have to give you the ball."

"Sounds a good game."

"Not as good as football. Anyway we were supposed to be talking about girls."

"Peter, there is plenty of time. Next year there will be girls younger than you coming up from primary school. You will be one of the big boys."

"I guess so. Stuart put me off sex. It was like bullying."

Peter did not talk about Stuart much these days. That was the main reason the therapy came to a natural end. Thelma knew that from time to time it would resurface. "That was wrong, very wrong. So wrong he will go to prison."

"What's happening with that?"

"Not much. They want you to do a medical."

"Will they look at my privates?"

"No. I told them not to. It was so long ago they could not tell what he had done. They do however want to do a DNA test."

"Will I have to clean my teeth?"

Thelma was surprised. "It's better to take the swab before you clean your teeth."

Peter realised they were talking at cross purposes. "No, I meant..." He made the familiar gesture with his hand.

Thelma laughed. "No. You don't only get DNA from semen. All cells have DNA. They rub a cotton swab on the inside of your mouth. Skin cells come off. They use those. Anyway why do you say clean your teeth instead of masturbate?" Peter told her the story of the camping trip. They both laughed. Thelma was glad that John and Francine were taking her advice and being careful in front of Peter.

Peter, having got Thelma away from football and back to sex had another question. "When can I start shaving?"

"When you have body hair you want to shave off. There is no rule."

"Francine doesn't shave. Most women shave under their arms. She doesn't."

"That's a personal choice. Most men shave their faces. Some have beards."

"Daddy is growing a beard"

"Yes I saw. Do you like it?"

"It was scratchy at first. It's better now it has grown a bit. He used to have a beard when I was little. Mummy made him shave it off."

"Why do you think she did that?"

"I don't know. I don't think she likes body hair. She shaves everywhere. I mean really everywhere." This reminded Thelma to talk to Cathy about the reasons behind her grooming practices. It was not a conversation she was prepared to have with Peter.

Cathy was now going to therapy with Thelma. She was starting to understand the reasons for her promiscuity when she was young. She also understood that it had ultimately destroyed her marriage. Thelma was also helping her with her self esteem. The one area that was not working was finding a new partner.

"Give it time. It is still early days. John is right, learn to love yourself first."

Cathy sighed. "John is always right. It is the one thing about him that drives me nuts. It's not that he rubs it in. Quite the opposite, he always understands. I think that makes it worse." Thelma offered her a tissue and waited for her to go on. "I do meet other men. Not like the Lee incident. That really taught me a lesson. I make friends, but catch myself comparing them with John."

"It's natural. It often happens when a partner dies. If the survivor re-marries the new partner is usually very different. They have to be to get over the comparison phenomenon you describe. The difference for you is that John is still alive. You parted on good terms. He lives nearby. Those two things are excellent for Peter. They do however make it hard for you."

As usual Peter could call in at hid mother after school. It was the main reason she had taken Francine's old flat. He did his homework there and then went to the library just before closing to get a lift home with Francine. Today was half day at the library so Cathy ran him home. Francine used her half day to visit the public records office in Perigeux. John was alone. Cathy finally mastered saying hello to him. At first it was awkward. She didn't dare kiss him. One day she was upset about something. Now she couldn't even remember what it was. John hugged her. It was like old times without the sex. He was a friend. Now she could kiss him when they met without her stomach flipping. "John, we need to talk."

John remembered Tree's comment. 'yeah, women do that, it scares the shit out of me!' "What's up Cat?" He had been making supper. He put the knife down and sat at the table, motioning her to sit beside him.

"I'm skint. The money I got when I left work has all gone. The job at the tourist office doesn't start till Easter. I ought to be paying Francine for the flat but at the moment I can't afford it."

John too wanted to talk about money. Without capital he could not start his brewing project. "The house in England is just sitting there. Either we rent it and share the income, or sell it and share the proceeds."

"To be honest John, by the time we have paid management fees, half the net income would not make much difference."

John agreed. "The mortgage will be paid off in a couple of months. It is still our main residence so there will be no capital gains tax. Shall I get it valued?"

"Yes please darling." John shot her a look. "Sorry, old habits die hard. I'm not coming on to you."

"I'm glad." Cathy looked down. She was sorry she had said 'darling'. She was also sorry he was glad she was not coming on to him. He had moved on. She had not. She would talk again to Thelma. John continued. "We are going to have to go back to sort it all out. Are you OK with that?"

Cathy thought. She was more than OK. She was missing him. The thought of spending time with him made her happy. If there was sex that would be a bonus.

She kept the thoughts to herself. "I'm OK. Will Francine be OK?"

"I'll talk to her."

Francine said she was OK. She was not. She hated herself for being jealous. "It is so unlike me." She was confiding in Ariane over pancakes.

"Tell him how you feel."

Francine agreed. "You are right, I should. Usually I do. It's just I can't say to him I am jealous when he gives me no reason to be."

Francine dropped them both at the station. She hugged John. "Be careful, she still fancies you."

He gave a half laugh. "That is almost exactly what she said to me about you two years ago."

"She was right. I bet you didn't believe her."

"No, I didn't. Today I am older and wiser."

"Older yes, the problem with you John is that you are wise about everything except women." She kissed him again and turned to go.

*

John opened the door in Reading. Cathy went inside. It was as if the intervening two years had disappeared. Stuart too had disappeared. A shadow had gone. It was not just like old times, it was like the old times should have been. There was of course no food in the house. "Shall we go out for supper?" John asked. "We could go to the Cunning Man."

Cathy was not sure. "I don't fancy pub food. Maybe an Indian."

"The Tamarind? Garden of Gulab?"

"John, do you mind if we stay here? I just fancy something spicy from the Raj and curling up on the settee with you."

John was ok with a takeaway but not curling up on the settee. "Takeaway is fine, but just friends, ok?"

"Of course John. I will always be your friend."

"And I yours Cathy." She kissed him. He noticed she was crying. "What's the matter Cat?"

She fumbled for a tissue. "Nothing. This is just harder than I thought it would be." She blew her nose.

John needed to connect with reality. He knew that was back in France with Peter and Francine. Here he was surrounded by familiarity. He must not confuse the two. He picked up his phone. Peter answered. "Hi dad. Yes, Francine's here. She is playing rummy with Paula. Thelma's here too."

Francine concentrated on her cards. "Ask him if they had a good trip."

"He says it was fine. They have just got in. They are waiting for a take away. They are both tired so will probably get an early night. Do you want to speak to him? Dad? Hi, Francine says she is busy and will call tomorrow. She sends her love to mummy."

Cathy came in from the hall with the takeaway. "Are you OK eating from the box?"

"What? Yes, fine."

"Everything ok in France?"

"Yes, I think so."

"Francine OK?"

"I don't know. I spoke to Peter. He sends his love."

"Bless him!" Cathy sat as close to John as she could and still eat. The phone call was supposed to ground him in the reality of him and Francine. Instead she had cast him adrift. Reality was Cathy eating a takeaway beside him and drinking Indian beer from the bottle. Neither spoke. When they finished Cathy got up to take the empties through to the kitchen. She came back and sat on the sofa inviting him to spoon her as he always did. "Are we doing the right thing?"

John was struggling with whether something as ordinary as curling up on the settee together was OK. They had done it a thousand times. Now Cathy was asking if it was right. "No, I don't. You wouldn't sit like this if Francine was here."

"That's not what I meant. I meant are we doing the right thing selling our house? Anyway" she added "she's not here, I am." Cathy put her head back so it was resting under his chin. She pulled his arms round her. "Hold me" she whispered. He did not pull her closer. Neither did he push her away. He sat in a pool of his own emotions. Why had Francine not come to the phone? Cathy pretended to sleep. Eventually she looked up at him. "Thank you."

"What for?"

"Letting me sit like this." He squeezed her.

She smiled. "Time for bed. I'll go and wash."

Chapter 35
Reith Lecture

"Did you have a nice time?"

John had not seen Francine like this. Where was the young woman who wanted him to live in France with Cathy so she could be his mistress? "We didn't go to have a nice time, we went to sell the house."

"You can still do that and still have a nice time. You were away a week."

"We had to get rid of all the stuff we left behind. There was even a viewing before we left."

"Very nice."

"Francine stop it. Would you like me to say Cathy and I made love just like old times? Would you like me to say nothing happened? Which would you believe?" Francine picked up her car keys. "Where are you going?"

"I don't know."

"How long will you be?"

"I don't know. I don't know anything any more." She turned to go. "Don't phone me. I will come back when I am ready."

"Will you come back?"

"If you want me to. My whole life is here. I can't stop loving Peter just because he is not my son. I can't stop loving you."

John was stunned. "I never stopped loving you either."

"Not even when you were making love to her?" With that she was gone.

Peter came in. "Is Francine OK"

There was nobody else to talk to. John needed to talk. "Not really. She is upset."

"Is it because you and mummy had sex?"

"Francine thinks we did."

Peter nearly said 'Did you?' For him it was not important. He'd known for years that Mummies and Daddies had sex. He knew that he wouldn't be here today if they didn't. There it was. For his son it was not important. His lover had decided he had been unfaithful. In that circumstance whether he had was irrelevant. It only mattered that she thought it. John left it there.

Peter changed the subject. "I have a new assignment: Famous scientists." He handed his dad a paper. He had to research the life and work of a scientist.

There was a list of suggestions: Pasteur, Madame Curie, Ampère, ... at the bottom it simply said 'au choix.' "What does the last one mean?"

"It means you can choose"

"Can I choose another one if I want?"

"I don't see why not."

"Do they have to be French?" John could not see anything to say that. "I'd like to choose Schroedinger."

John was surprised. "Why?"

"Because he had a cat. I'd like a cat."

John laughed. "He didn't have a cat. Well, maybe he did, I don't know. Schroedinger's cat is something else."

"What is it if it is not a cat?"

"It is a way of explaining something quite difficult to understand."

"Try me." So it was that John found himself explaining a hypothetical paradox to a twelve year old. All the time Francine was on his mind. What had he done? What could he have done differently? What should he do now? Eventually the intellectual sponge that was Peter Cartwright was saturated. "I'll go and write some of that down so I can explain it to Pooh later. What's for supper?"

John had not thought at all about supper. "Egg and chips?"

Peter's face lit up. "Boys' night in?" He asked. Neither Cathy nor Francine considered egg and chips a proper meal. It was saved therefore for times when John and Peter were alone. The other concession was that they got to eat on their laps in front of TV. That was another practice frowned upon in female company.

"Yes, boys' night in." John confirmed. Given the manner of her exit he did not think Francine would be back for supper. John went to bed alone. He did not lock up in case she returned during the night.

*

The auditorium at the Royal Society was full. Madame Blanchard was standing at the lectern. "For the last of this year's Reith lectures our speaker will take us on a journey across not one, but many universes. Please welcome Doctor Peter Cartwright."

Peter walked in to enthusiastic applause. He placed Pooh on the lectern. In the front row Roo was jumping up and down making 'ooh I say' noises. Peter tapped the microphone to make sure it was working. "Tonight I want to talk to you about Erwin Schroedinger. Let's start with a word association game. I will say a word. I want you to call out the first word you think of. Ready? Schroedinger." In unison the auditorium shouted "Cat!" Peter unwrapped a piece of paper. On it was written in large letters the word 'CAT' "If I lose my seat at Cambridge I can always get a job as a magician!" There was a ripple of laughter. "That went well. Let's try again: Schroedinger's cat." This time half the auditorium shouted 'alive!' and half shouted 'dead!' Peter unwrapped another piece of paper. On one side was written. 'ALIVE' on the other 'DEAD' "I thought I should hedge my bets this time." More laughter.

As John slept the future Peter continued his tour de force. He effortlessly explained Schroedinger's wave theory to a teenage audience. They understood the real and imaginary component of the wave. He took them from Thompson's simplistic 'plum pudding' model of the atom to Schroedinger's wave model. Far from being confused by the uncertainty principle necessary to explain the behaviour of sub atomic particles his young audience understood it as clearly as Peter had when his father explained it to him as a twelve-year-old child. Now Peter took them on in a way his father could not. He connected the infinitesimally small to the unimaginably large. The cat that was both alive and dead ceased to be a paradox. It became as Schroedinger intended, a thought experiment. The universe ceased to be a single entity. The universe unveiled the founding principle of its creator: freedom of choice. When choice is exercised the Schroedinger principle allows for both choices to exist simultaneously. For this to happen both universes must exist. Each universe is arbitrarily large. Peter refused to use the word infinite. The supra-universe contained all possible universes. Few understand the concept; fewer still are able to explain it. Peter went further. The vast majority of random events create duplicate universes that are indistinguishable. Peter argued that when two universes became identical they merged. He distinguished between a significant random event and insignificant ones. The former produced discernibly different universes, the latter did not. For those able to follow he added another layer of complexity. Random events within disparate universes could render them identical causing them to merge. Peter likened each disparate event as a fork in a road. Choosing one over the other does not inevitably lead to a different destination. The journey continues. It cares not which road was taken to reach the present. Wherever one wishes to travel the journey can only start from the point where the traveller finds himself.

*

In one universe John and Cathy made love. In another they did not. In both they returned to France. The worlds merged the moment that for Francine it ceased to matter by which path they arrived. Silently she slipped into bed beside him. The normality of Francine's body beside him did not at first disturb his sleep. Then he was aware of the significance of her presence and was suddenly wide awake. Not knowing how late she had returned he left her to sleep. She was supposed to go to work today. He used that as an excuse to wake her. He slipped out of bed and made coffee. Putting hers on the bedside table he climbed back into bed and touched her arm. "I've made coffee. You need to wake up if you are going to work."

She sat up and whispered "Thank-you." The silence hung between them.

"Do you want to talk?"

"Not yet." She was not yet at the point where the two paths re-joined. Talking would mean discovering which path they were on. She was not ready.

"Would it help if I told you exactly what happened?"

"No John, it would not. If you try I will throw my coffee over you and leave. This time I will not be back any time soon."

"What do you want me to say?"

"Nothing."

"What do you want to do?"

"Drink my coffee, shower, go to work, come home, read a book, sleep. I want to repeat the cycle until my head catches up with the normality my body is giving it." That is what he allowed her to do. She was a zombie but she was with him. He did not know how long he would have to wait until she was ready, but he would be there when she did.

Francine remembered their first lover's tiff. It was New Year's Day, the morning after Cathy kissed him. He had been right when he said that she would know if he had been unfaithful. At first it was the not knowing that upset her. Forcefully she declared she did not want to know. She desperately did want to know. What she was saying was she could not bear to listen to him say it. Instead she created the worst case scenario. Cathy had done what she nearly did at New Year. She had reclaimed her husband. He had fallen in love with the new, Stuart-free Cathy. They had decided to stay in England and take Peter back.

The evidence did not support the hypothesis. Firstly they returned to France. A buyer for the house was found remarkably quickly. Francine saw very little of Cathy. She wondered if that was intentional on Cathy's part. It was. She had tried to seduce John in Reading. Back in France she knew it was wrong. How successful she had been changed nothing. She had broken faith with Francine. The sisterhood they almost found when they kissed in January was gone. That would be the last part to heal.

Apart from the actors only Thelma knew exactly what had happened. As usual she explained that the behaviour of each was totally normal. This was not to say it was acceptable. If you drop a vase it is normal that it breaks. That does make it acceptable. Actions have consequences. Some are not intended. Thelma's job was to help people understand behaviour and predict consequences. The journey she shared with Cathy was longer than Peter's. It had started longer ago. The trauma lasted longer. Cathy did not have Peter's support network. As a small girl Cathy flirted with her father. "All girls do that don't they?"

Thelma answered. "Yes they do. For most it is a safe environment to learn about human relationships."

"What I did was wrong."

"No Cathy. What your father did was wrong."

"I liked it. That was wrong."

"Did you like it?"

"At first yes. I liked the attention. I liked being his special little girl. I liked the cuddles."

"How did that change?"

Cathy tried to remember the sequence. Later events swamped the early memories. "He started initiating. It was as if he needed the cuddle, not me."

"Where did he touch you?"

"Everywhere. It was access all areas."

"Did you think that was wrong?"

"Why would I? He was my dad. He changed my nappy as a baby, he bathed me. It just carried on."

Over the weeks Cathy came to understand her father's behaviour. This enabled her to stop blaming herself. It took time for Thelma to probe the most intimate details. It was here too that Cathy blamed herself. "I wanted it."

"What makes you say that?"

"When he touched me it made me wet. That doesn't happen if you aren't ready for sex."

"Your body was protecting you. Suppose he penetrated you when you were dry. It would hurt. At that age it would have damaged you physically."

Cathy was crying. "Why did he do it?"

"Have you asked him?"

"Of course not. I did once. He said I was a slut and that I was leading him on."

"Did you believe him?"

"Naturally. Children always believe their parents."

There it was. Thelma had taken Cathy apart mentally. The parts that were malfunctioning she repaired. Now she had to put her back together. Her father's grooming practices were exposed. He preferred pre-pubescent girls. Cathy started growing up. Despite the abuse she was scared he would stop loving her. She removed her body hair to stay the little girl he wanted.

Thelma's phone rang. It was D. I. Jones. "Thelma, how is sunny France? Good. Look I need to check a couple of things. According to my notes the accused began his relationship with Mrs Cartwright when her son was a toddler."

"I believe so. He however waited until Peter was almost a teenager before abusing him."

"Yes, I've got that. The premeditation aspect features heavily in my report to CPS. Now I am more interested in the relationship with his mother. How would you describe her general relationship with men?"

Thelma thought. Exchanges with her client were confidential. The police, on a need to know basis, fell under the umbrella of confidentiality. "In a word Graham?"

"If you please."

"Promiscuous."

"I thought so. I suggest she wanted her husband to believe her relationship with the accused started after the birth of their child."

For Thelma the penny dropped. "Graham, am I correct in supposing you have a DNA report in front of you?"

"No flies on you Thelma! Look, I have to pass this to the defence or it will prejudice our case. There is no way we can keep it from Cathy or Peter. Since they are both your clients may I leave this little present with you?"

"You may, but I have to say I do not care for your presents."

The next session with Cathy took a rather different turn. Thelma tried not to sound judgemental. "Cathy, you said you had been trying for a while to conceive."

"Yes. I asked the doctor if I was getting too old. He said no."

"Did you think it might be a problem with John?"

"It crossed my mind but I never discussed it with him."

"Why was that?"

"Contrary to what my behaviour suggests I loved my husband. I still do. He wanted so much to be a father. I didn't want him finding out he couldn't."

"So he never had the test?"

"No. I thought it would be simpler just to get pregnant."

"Do you have an idea who Peter's father might be?"

"Thelma, if you eat a tin of beans do you know which one makes you fart?"

Even by Thelma's standards this was somewhat direct. "If you had to guess?"

The look on Cathy's face said 'don't make me do this' Finally she whispered. "Stuart."

"Did you know Peter was asked to do a DNA test?"

"Yes, he told me. That's what this is all about isn't it?"

"Yes, the police just phoned me with the results." She saw the look of pure terror in Cathy's eyes.

"Thelma, I beg you, please don't tell them. I have hurt them both so much already."

"That is not within my gift. The Police have the information. They are obliged to pass it to the defence. Peter and John are prosecution witnesses. Can you imagine the effect of them being ambushed with that in cross examination?"

Cathy was crushed. "Help me Thelma."

Most of the time Thelma found her job easy. This was not one of them. Part of the problem was that Peter worked things out so quickly. She found it hard to prepare the ground. She risked him working out the truth before he was emotionally prepared. It was the same with John. Notwithstanding his wife's infidelity he had never questioned Peter's paternity. The relationship between father and son was immeasurably precious. She was scared of compromising it. She decided to enlist the help of Francine. With typical directness she came straight to the point. Francine was still wallowing in the remnants of self pity. Maybe John had made love to Cathy. Probably he had not. Equally probably he had been tempted. That being the case she decided to string out her victimhood. This would make sure there were no repeat episodes. Thelma's news brought it all to an abrupt halt. Her love for John and Peter resumed their ascendancy.

"What can I do to help them?"

"Peter knows you are not his mother but his love for you is as strong as for Cathy. He is intelligent enough to understand that parenting has little to do with who gave birth to him. It has even less to do with which sperm won the race to fertilize the egg from which he grew. The most important thing for him to understand is that he has inherited nothing from Stuart."

Francine thought. "I am not sure what I can do except be there. And love them of course."

"Francine that is all I am asking for you to do. They must take the beating. You can help by being there to apply the bandages."

Chapter 36
Dinner parties

Francine invited Cathy and Thelma to supper. It was a warm evening so they ate outside. After the meal they repaired to deck chairs. Thelma started talking. It was getting dark; they watched the stars come out. By the time she finished the milky way was clearly visible. John and Cathy were still amazed by the number of stars. Back in England there was so much light pollution most were obscured. Thelma waited. Cathy was holding her breath. She wished with all her heart that she had made other decisions all those years ago. She was who she was. Her therapy sessions with Thelma made her realise why. She was starting to believe that it was not her fault. She found it hard. The crisis that now engulfed her came less from her promiscuity than from a desire to save her husband from hurt. In doing so she was hurting him now in ways she could not have foreseen. Francine was carefully rolling bandages as she had done in the Great War. This time her lover had returned. The surgeon was operating. Soon he would be handed to her care.

It was Peter who spoke first. "I saw a shooting star!" The earth was passing through the asteroid belt.

Next it was Cathy. "There's another one!" The meteor shower passed, but everyone was staring into the darkness, thinking of Thelma's words.

John was next to break the silence. "The Universe is so vast, does what happens on this tiny planet really matter?"

Thelma replied. "It matters to us because this is our home."

"My home is here. I have two Mummies and a Daddy. I am luckier than most kids."

"Yes you are Peter." Said Thelma.

"Thelma, I don't care what you said, Stuart is not my dad. He never was and never will be." At first Thelma thought this was Peter's first stage of grief. She waited for his anger. They would have to resume their counselling sessions. John too was going to need help. Peter got up and went to sit on John. He hoped the deck chair would take both their weights. "You are my dad. You have always loved me and always will. That is what makes you my dad, not some stupid sperm."

John hugged his son. "I could not have said it better myself."

Peter looked at Thelma. "I have a better test than DNA."

"What's that?"

"When daddy hugs me I feel safe. When Stuart hugs me I feel scared."

"That's a very good test."

Crises exist more in their anticipation than their execution. Thelma did not need to restart therapy with Peter. Although she kept an eye on John, Peter's speech under the stars seemed to have done the trick. If something came out later she would be there. The crisis had erased doubts in Francine's mind. What had, or had not happened between John and Cathy in England no longer mattered. Following the as yet un-postulated Cartwright phenomenon two universes merged. Francine found her own inner peace. It was possible that John had made love to Cathy, but she doubted it. He would have changed. She could read him so easily. She was sure he could have done it. She was pretty sure too that Cathy had tried it on. That was more difficult to forgive. Contrary to her previous attitude to relationships she was not prepared to share him. He meant too much to her. Cathy understood that. She could not find the courage to confess she'd tried to break faith with Francine.

*

Life moved on. Peter finished his first year at secondary school. There was no question of doubling. He had come top in maths. "That's normal!" He announced. He offered no explanation as to why he thought this.

John was busy spending his share of the proceeds of the house sale. He wrote a business plan and opened another bank account. He did not intend to ask for a business loan but presented the plan anyway. The bank manager was most disappointed John was not asking for money. In the end John took a loan he did not need. It was an interest free business development loan. Since it would cost him nothing he could find no reason to refuse.

Francine had her own project. She was aware that soon the war would pass from living memory. Already those she wanted to interview were only children during hostilities. Nevertheless they had memories of their parents, many of whom were combatant. Francine was well known and soon became an integral part of village life. She volunteered for the committee de fetes. At the first Assembly Generale she found herself elected as chair. The previous incumbent had been trying for years to pass the baton. It was an excellent way of getting to know the residents. Many had lived in the village all their life. Francine shared with the committee her wish to document the history of the village by interviewing the residents. She also enlisted John's help. She would breeze into the house and declare that she had invited someone to supper. John did not mind. He liked cooking. It was also a gentle way of demonstrating to a sceptical population that meat free meals were not just possible but delicious. He was not evangelical. He made it clear that it was his own choice.

Today Francine was particularly pleased Eliane had finally accepted an invitation to supper. Francine could not understand why such a gentle refined old lady was ostracised by the village. He asked Henri. Henri

Gagneux had succeeded Madame Guichot as Mayor. Francine suggested to him Eliane might have interesting stories to tell. Henri was dismissive. "You can talk to her if you want, but you will get a pack of lies!" Others had said similar things of Henri. Francine learned that there were two resistance movements. They corresponded, so far as she could tell, with the political left and right of the time. The Gauchistes supported the Russians; The Gaullistes the British and Americans.

Eliane sat upright in the chair Francine had provided holding her glass with delicate ease. "Yes, I was born in the village. The house is my father's. We had to go away during the war. My husband and I were lucky enough to be able to purchase it again when we returned from Algeria." This was typical of Francine's conversations. Snippets fell from the interviewee's lips in no particular order. Their connection was obvious to the speaker. Francine had to return many times to pick up more morsels that she could join into a coherent thread. Finally a story emerged. Eliane's father was a Gaullist; Henri's father a Gauchiste. The Allies were active supporting both resistance movements. Typically this took the form of air drops. As in any war intelligence was sporadic and often inaccurate. The RAF tried to get word to the ground of a planned drop. If they were lucky one of the resistance movements find out. If not the RAF simply made the drop and hoped the partisans would find it before the Germans. The drops took the form of arms, food or money. Bribery was a surprisingly effective weapon in guerrilla war. "Why did you have to leave the village?" Francine asked.

"I was fifteen. I had to leave just like that. I only had a suitcase. I went to Paris." Eliane had not said why she had to leave so suddenly. Francine assumed she was pregnant. "Do you have children?" she asked.

"Yes. I met my husband in Paris. He was in the diplomatic corps. We were stationed in North Africa during the Algerian war. My son was born there." The dates did not fit.

Perhaps Francine was jumping to the wrong conclusion about teenage pregnancy. "Did your parents go to Paris with you?"

Eliane looked troubled. "No. They couldn't." Francine could get no more information from her regarding her parents. It seemed however that Eliane never saw them again.

It was Henri who filled the gaps. "There weren't many Gaullists. We were the main resistance. The Gaullists wanted to split the drops fifty-fifty. We said no, we were twice the size. There was a money drop. The Gaullists got there first. Eliane's father denied it. He said there was no money. All I can say is if that is the case he must have a magic money tree in the back garden. We will not tolerate profiteering. We had no argument with the little girl, we let her go. The others had to be dealt with." Henri was a little younger than Eliane. His story must have been the version given to him by his father. Francine wondered if Henri and Eliane had played together as children.

Village life rolled on. The graveyard next door was long gone. A new walled cemetery was built just after the Great War not far from the Templar house. The houses built on the old graveyard were to accommodate those who returned from the front. The primary school founded by Jean-Mitchel closed from lack of pupils and became the new Marie. The old one on the far side of the church was renovated and let as apartments. Recently, in an effort to rejuvenate a dying village generous funds were provided by the European Union. In his annual speech Henri announced the village had secured funding for a new Salle de Fetes. He implied that by replacing a centre right mayor with his own centre left leanings he personally had secured the funding and provided the land. In fact the mayor had sold the land adjoining his house at a premium. He had also benefited from the generosity of the contractors anxious to secure the building project.

Peter took Thelma's advice and started talking to the new intake of girls at the school. He practiced his first kiss. At swimming parties at the lake he discovered that girl's bodies were surprisingly similar to Francine's. None of them interested him sufficiently to warrant a more detailed study. They did however serve to bring normality to friendships with girls. He had to wait another year before Susan arrived.

Converting the barn into a brewery also began. John wanted to maintain the architectural integrity of the building. Henri Gagneux insisted that the original barn doors stayed as they opened on to the village square. Inside it was completely transformed. The earth floor was removed and drains laid. Over this concrete was poured. The walls were skimmed and made washable.

John insisted that the structural beams remained visible with key parts of the stonework. Eventually the compromise that was reached satisfied the hygiene inspectors. He would soon be ready to start brewing, but his half of the house proceeds had gone. Much had literally been sunk into the venture as it concerned the well. John guessed that the water at the bottom of his well came from the same source as the well that gave the village its name. He did not believe in the magical qualities attributed to the water by the Saint, but he did want the brasserie to brew with Saint Etienne water. Francine enlisted the help of her estranged husband. He grew maize for animal feed. He had a ready market with both pig and cattle farmers. His crop needed constant watering. The region sat upon a vast underground reservoir. Mr Lefevre tapped into this reserve in order to irrigate his crops. He had all the equipment needed to flush the sediment from John's well. He ran a pipe from the well to the village well. The latter flowed continuously, except in they driest summers. Since both wells derived their water from the same source the mayor had no problem with John leaving the pumps running to flush the system. Francine arranged for a sample of the water to be sent for analysis. Many properties in the region still used water from their own wells as drinking water. They were supposed to have it analysed annually to check it was safe to drink. Not all did. They reasoned that as long as they didn't get sick they didn't need to. For the brewery it was different. The brewing process killed off any bacteria. Any that escaped were prevented from growing by the alcohol. Even so the first results came back 'non satisfant'. Francine phoned the lab to ask what they should do. John was ideologically opposed to putting additives in the water before brewing. The lab was sure that would not be necessary. They advised them to run the pumps for another week and submit another sample. This time it passed.

Another problem they ran into was registering the name. John and Francine were at the Chambre de Metiers et Artisans. Registering the name got them a Siret number which got them into the system. As soon as they proposed the name Brasserie Artisanale de Thiviers John was asked for his diploma. Not only did he not have a French diploma, he didn't even have an English one. John thought if there was a problem it would be saying Thiviers when the brewery was in St Etienne. The lady was fine with that. She was less fine with John starting a business without a diploma. There was not much she could do about it. Under E.U. law John was entitled to exercise his treaty rights and come to France and start a business. "You cannot" the fonctionnaire declared "refer to yourself as an artisan unless you have a French diploma. 'Artisan' is an appellation contrôlé. Also the company name cannot imply he is an artisan."

John understood. "We need to take the word 'artisan' out of the name?"

"Exact."

"Could we just call the company 'BAT'?"

The registrar thought. "No, I cannot allow that. People might think you were a builder."

"Why?"

"BAT could be seen as short for Batiment."

John turned to Francine "Brasserie Ancienne de Thiviers"

The registrar was about to say no to that as well. "You cannot call a new brewery in a new building Ancienne."

John was not going to give up. "The building is not new, it was built before the revolution."

Francine chipped in. "It is not brasserie ancienne, it is brasserie à l'ancienne. Brasserie can mean brewery or brewing. We use traditional recipes. It is not an old brewery; it is an old brewing process." The registrar gave in. She wrote "Brasserie à l'ancienne de Thiviers" in the company name. She was not deliberately trying to be obstructive, it was just that as a civil servant she had to get things right.

Chapter 37
The Birthday party

John and Francine still saw Cathy regularly but she was not as much a part of their lives as she had been. She started making her own circle of friends. Her French was passable, but she found it easier to socialise with the expatriates. Her work at the tourist office was seasonal. They liked the way she engaged with the English tourists. The job was not however as well paid as her job back in England. Peter was of course the main point of contact. They made a point of going to all the school events as a threesome. If a stranger asked Francine who she was she simply said Peter's mother. So did Cathy. They let them work it out for themselves. Afterwards they usually drove up the road to the Irish pub. It was a chance to debrief and talk about Peter. He was gifted so the main challenge was to stretch him. Learning in a second language did this but as he became fluent the teachers needed to find new challenges. At first the teachers dipped into course work from the coming year.

John was resistant to the suggestion that Peter simply jumped a year. "He would have to make a new set of friends. Besides, he may be functioning way above his chronological age intellectually, but emotionally he is still very young. I'm worried he would become isolated." Francine agreed. She had contacts at Saint Joseph in Perigeux. She invited Claude Agnew for supper. He taught Maths and Physics at the Lycee. He helped John prepare additional work tailored to Peter's needs. In class Peter kept to the curriculum but spent time mentoring the other students. In this way he unconsciously developed his own teaching techniques which he would use later in life.

Cathy and John were on to their third Guinness. Francine had a Pinot then switched to Perrier. She took the car keys from John. She had moved on from that time over a year ago when John and Cathy had gone to England to sell the house. She could see they had as well. They were close friends of course; there were moments when Cathy knew what John was about to say or what his reaction would be when Francine spoke. Cathy no longer exploited this for her own ends. They had become like brother and sister. She had not found a partner but no longer looked towards John for that. In any event tonight she had other things on her mind.

She stroked the side of her glass waiting for the porter to settle. "I am not sure it is a good idea for me to just use my half of the house money to supplement my wages. It may take ten years to run out, but it will eventually do so."

"What's the alternative?" Francine asked.

"I could buy into your brewing business."

John was surprised. "You mean as a sleeping partner? We are not capitalised formally. The books show the start up costs as a private loan."

"That's my point. John, you make fantastic beer. Francine you have all the local knowledge and contacts to market it. There is an awful lot more to a company than production, sales and marketing. I could do all of that. Starting with the bookkeeping, accounts, financial controls. I would be like a Business Angel protecting their venture capital."

John looked at his ex-wife. "That is the first time I have heard you refer to yourself as an Angel!"

"Cheeky bugger! Think about it. You need that second still. I learned a lot working for Sir Evelyn. I could work as a consultant for English start-ups in the Dordogne. I would rather do it for you."

"Thank you Cathy. I'll talk to Francine about it when I am sober. If it still looks a good idea and you are sure we may well take you up on it.

John did take her up on the idea. For the moment however he had a more pressing problem. It was 2011. Francine would be 35 in June. He wanted to mark the event with a surprise party. The first commercial bottles of BAT had rolled off the production line but John was still finding it surprisingly hard to organise a piss-up in a brewery. Ariane knew everyone so he enlisted her help. He was grateful he could leave her to manage the invitations. It was peak season for ice cream but the party was on a Monday so Ariane was less busy. She closed the shop early and brought the ice cream trike. John wanted to set up a bar in front of the barn. It needed to be done in advance and would arouse Francine's suspicions. He used the previous Sunday's Brocante as an excuse.

Francine, now chair of the Committee de fetes, argued that the village could no longer buy in commercial beer as it had its own brewery. The main objection was that the bar provided the lion's share of the profit. There was strong resistance in some quarters that a commercial enterprise could benefit from the village's flagship event. It was also the day the Committee de fetes made most of its money, mostly from food and drink. Others wanted to support a local business. Francine clearly had an interest and excused herself from the debate. The committee decided they would raise the price of the beer slightly. They asked BAT to supply the beer at a cost price and run the bar.

Francine 'took this back to the board'. It was her joking reference to talking to John about the brewery. In the beginning 'board meetings' often took place in bed. This practice clearly stopped when Cathy came on board. There was gossip in the village of course. There were whisperings that John kept two wives and the three slept in the same bed. When the rumour got back to John he laughed. "Now there's an idea!" He exclaimed.

"Yes, a very bad idea." Francine replied.

Cathy kept her mouth shut. She had done enough damage already. She wanted to bring this meeting to order. She was not happy about the brocante. "It's a lot of work. We get nothing out of it."

Francine disagreed. "We get the publicity. A lot of beer gets drunk at these events. It would be a great way to get our name out there."

In the end Cathy conceded. "Ok, but let me work out the true 'at cost' price."

John chipped in. "Don't include labour. Everything for the village is pro bono."

That concluded the Brocante discussion. John was thinking more about the party. Cathy was in on the secret, Francine if course was not. All he had to do was delay dismantling the bar. "We can sell to tourists." He argued.

"John, there are no tourists in St Etienne, just the occasional rambler or cyclist."

"You are probably right. I'll leave it up until your birthday and see how it goes."

Francine looked at him. "John, you are up to something."

He kissed her. "Francine, when you have a birthday coming you are not allowed to ask questions." This answered her question. She smiled and said nothing more.

On her birthday John and Peter gave her token presents over breakfast. They promised a special meal when she got home. She went to work, Peter to school. Ariane turned up as soon as they were both gone, bringing an army of volunteers. Tables and benches were borrowed from the Committee de fetes who took great delight in booking them out without the knowledge of their chair. It was unbearably hot with the morning sun beating down on the front of the house. Ariane was worried. "I'll need some shade for the ice cream. The freezer will struggle to cope in full sun. Can you borrow the gazebo?"

"By the afternoon the sun will have moved behind the house. If you turn up at 6 it will be much cooler. I had reserved it in case it rained, but I have to start cooking, at the last count over 40 people have said yes."

Ariane smiled "That's fine. Don't make too much food, people are bringing stuff." She had already sent out the invitations with 'auberge Espagnole' on the bottom. This essentially meant bring a contribution to the meal. She gave John a kiss. "I have to go, I need to open the shop for the lunch time customers."

"No problem. Thanks for your help." John was alone. He would do no work in the brewery today. Instead he started preparing the same meal he had done for their first night four years ago. She had not told him then it was her birthday.

Almost half the guests had arrived when Francine drove her monster truck into the square. The quart d'heure Perigordoin did not seem to apply if you were bringing food. People came early to help John. Ariane gave Pascal strict instructions. The first was not to tell Francine about the party. The second was to turn up. The third was to bring food. He managed the first by putting his finger to his lips every time he saw Francine. When Francine asked if he was ok he blushed and said. "I'm not allowed to say." Thelma helped with the second instruction by collecting him. The third he managed alone. He had brought a plastic box of sandwiches. It was his pride and joy. His English white sliced fitted exactly into the box. The cream cheese was spread exactly. Ariane reminded him that Francine was vegetarian. She told him not to put meat in the sandwiches. Pascal duly complied. As soon as he arrived he opened the box and started eating them. He had finished them all before Francine arrived.

Francine drew Ariane on one side. "How much of this is to do with you?" she asked.

"Not much, mostly doing invitations. I hope he won't mind but I've added Mary and Jake to John's list. They are English and have just moved into the area."

Francine was smiling. "Of course I don't mind. If their French is wobbly there will be plenty of people to talk to in English."

"That's what I thought. They don't know many people so this should be a good way to start. Their daughter Susan will be going to Peter's school after the holidays."

"I'll introduce them. He can talk to her in English about the school."

Peter was busy making sure Pooh and Piglit had good places to sit. "Where's the hunny" asked Pooh.

"I'll get you your own pot." He turned to go and bumped into Susan.

She smiled. "You must be Peter. Who were you talking to?"

Peter turned scarlet. "Nobody. That is, to myself. I was just saying that dad had forgotten to put the honey out. Francine likes honey. I was going to get some."

"Who is Francine?"

"My mum. It is her birthday. She is 35."

To Susan Peter looked like a grown up. "She must have been very young when she had you. Why do you call her Francine and not mum?"

"Because she is my step-mum. My real mum is called Cathy. She is here somewhere." He looked round for help.

"Where are the other children?"

"What other children?"

"You are doing a teddy bears' picnic. There must be little children here for that."

"No. Er, that is there were going to be but they couldn't come. I was just putting the toys away." He picked up Pooh and Piglit.

"Where are we going?" asked Pooh.

"Indoors Pooh, to look for hunny."

"Is it an expotition?"

"Sort of. Piglit will explain." He dropped them both on his bed and went back to find Susan.

The evening got underway. Francine was the perfect combination of host and guest of honour. She toured the table wine bottles in hand topping up glasses. If she saw a beer glass she directed them towards the bar where John was holding court. He only had two taps for pression so he put up a blonde and an ambré. The others he had, in true English real ale style, on trestles behind him. Francine engaged each person in conversation. She identified those with stories to tell. These she returned to later in the evening when alcohol had loosened their tongues. She kept popping back to John at the bar. "Thank you; I am having such a good time. This is the best birthday present ever."

He kissed her. "I am glad." Francine was looking round behind the bar. "What are you looking for?"

"Pen and paper, I want to write something down."

John found a notebook. "What are you up to?"

"Nothing. It is just there are so many interesting stories I want to write them down before I forget."

John laughed. "You never miss an opportunity do you?"

Francine put her arms round him and kissed him again. "No I don't."

Cathy came up. "When you love birds have quite finished, have you seen our son?"

John pointed. "He is over there talking to the daughter of that new couple."

"Yes I know. Her name is Susan. He has a glass of beer in his hand and he is giving her wine."

John defended himself. "I gave him half a pint of the weakest beer. He knows it is the only one he will get. I am in charge of the bar."

Francine pecked Cathy on the cheek. "Thank you for noticing. I will go and have a word." She went and put her arm round Peter. She smiled at Susan. "Hello, I'm Francine, Peter's mum. Well, one of them anyway!"

Susan smiled. "Yes, Peter explained." She was not sure what to do. "Do we kiss or shake hands?"

"We kiss, definitely." Francine leaned forward. For once she did not have to go on tip toes.

"How do I know which cheek comes first?"

Francine smiled. "I am sure Peter will teach you." Susan blushed. "Now if you don't mind I need to borrow him for a moment." She drew Peter away. When they were out of earshot she spoke. "Did you give Susan that glass of wine?"

Peter looked indignant. "It's not wine, it is water and wine, exactly like you gave me when I was her age."

Francine was relieved. "Ok, but that was not your call, you should have asked her mum or dad if they were ok with it."

"Francine, I am not a kid anymore. I know what I am doing."

She looked at him. "No you're not. And I believe you do." She hugged him. When she released him he turned to go. "One more thing." She said. He turned back. "There is no need to show off. You have made quite an impression already."

He gave her that special Peter smile. "I know!"

Eventually the numbers thinned out. Thelma had been there of course. She was the first to leave because of Paula. One by one the villagers left. Friends piled the empty plates and took them to the kitchen. John would sort it out in the morning. He had been drinking too much of his own beer to be able to face it tonight. Ariane took back the uneaten ice cream. "I'll count them when I get back to Vaunac. Just pay for the ones that were eaten."

Mary and Jake were the last to leave. They were sitting with Cathy John and Francine at one end of the table. At the other end Peter was explaining to Susan the difference between 'tu' and 'vous'. She also wanted to know when to kiss and when to shake hands. He demonstrated the kiss greeting. "What if you want to be more than just friends?"

Peter blushed. "You mean kissing on the lips?"

"Yes. I've never kissed a boy on the lips."

Peter was extrapolating from very limited experience. "Do you kiss your dad on the lips?"

"Not any more. He says I am getting too old."

"Remember when you did. What was it like?"

"It made me feel warm and safe, like I wanted to go to sleep. I suppose that was because he kissed me after my bedtime story."

"Kissing a boy makes you feel warm but not safe. It makes you feel excited like when the roller coaster is about to drop down. Instead of wanting to go to sleep you want to wake up."

Susan leaned into him. "Show me." She whispered.

Chapter 38
Dreams

Francine went to bed. Her head was swimming from too much wine and too much information. She hoped she would be able to remember all the stories she had heard about the village. By going through first the records of the Conservatoire de Perigueux, then the Convent in Thiviers she found a match. Francesca took Holy Orders at the end of the Great War but died of consumption soon after. Francine liked to imagine that she had died of a broken heart. Records of the resistance were less reliable. She was forced to rely on the oral tradition. The stories she heard tonight were as confused and contradictory as they had always been. Francine wanted to know what had happened to Jean and the collaborator. John slipped into bed beside her. Cathy was asleep on the sofa. John smiled and left her there. She could help him with the washing up in the morning. Despite a sleeping Cathy in the next room John fancied rounding off the evening with a cuddle from Francine.

He was out of luck. She too was fast asleep. John could tell from her twitches that she was dreaming.

*

Francis took Pierre back to the village square. He was not particularly religious, but was raised a Catholic. He took Pierre into the church. Neither had wanted Stuardo to be killed. He thought of the old pig farmers. They had survived the Great War only to be shot for a piece of bacon. Francis decided after all he did want Stuardo dead. Was that wrong? He went into the confessional. There was no priest. He hoped God was there to hear. God listened. The conversation about Stuardo was short. "He deserves to die" said the effeminate young man on his knees.

"Many deserve death" came the reply.

"The brothers did not deserve to die" continued Francis.

God was silent. In the distance a shot rang out. Francis had entered the confessional to confess a love that dare not speak its name. Instead he had questioned the omnipotence of a God who allowed the innocent to die and the guilty to go unpunished. God had forsaken them. Francis stood. He took Pierre by the hand. They left His empty house. He had not even furnished them with a priest to hear his confession. Francis would find his own salvation.

"Where are we going?" Pierre asked.

"To Stuardo's house, I want to look for information before the Germans get there."

The wood stove in the kitchen was still burning. The parlour next door was a mess. It would take hours to sort through. Francis reasoned that if the Italian kept secrets he would not keep them in the casual disorder of a bachelor's living room. "Let's look upstairs." Francis went into the bedroom.

"I'll check the loft." Pierre climbed the second flight.

Francis was still searching the bedroom when he heard a noise downstairs. He froze. They were trapped. He prayed Pierre would stay in the loft and stay quiet. There was no way he could warn him. There was a step on the stair. Francis pressed himself against the wall and pulled the bedroom door open to provide some cover. The intruder was muttering in Italian. Francis died inside. Behind the wall against which he was trapped was a bricked up door. One day he would kiss Jean in that doorway as he had done when it was first made. Those were other lives. Lives the Church denied. He was a woman. The Church denied this too. He was born with a penis. He loved Jean. That was also denied. He was an abomination. He held his breath. The Italian grabbed a few belongings before taking a knife from his pocket. He folded back the carpet and found the loose floor board. Prising it up he pulled out a wad of banknotes. He stuffed them into a bag with the random belongings he had picked up from the floor. Turning he looked straight at the door that concealed Francis. On hot nights Stuardo had to wedge the door to keep it open. Now it stayed open on its own. As he reached for the door handle he heard a footstep on the stair from the loft. He suspected a trap. Fight or flight? He chose the latter, hurling himself down the stairs. Hearing this Pierre quickened his pace. Francis had just enough time to come out from behind the door and grab him before he descended the second flight. Stuardo jumped on his bicycle and was gone. The bike was found at the train station in the next village; Stuardo was never seen again.

Pierre grasped the significance of the situation. "Stuardo is alive. A shot was fired. Jean must be dead." Francis was crying. The younger man took control. "I'll tell Corrine."

Francis nodded. "I'll stay here. I may find something."

"Don't stay too long, the Bosh will be here soon." With that he was gone.

Corrine was Jean's wife. Before her marriage she had been intimate with almost every man in the village. It was a useful source of information, not to mention revenue. She saw no reason why marriage should change this. Normally this would be condemned. War however changed that. Her special talent for obtaining information put it in a whole new light. Jean tolerated Corrine's behaviour figuring that the end justified the means. There was also the small matter of his feelings for Francis. Jean was not attracted to men but Francis was so feminine falling in love with him was like falling in love with a woman. Francis knew all of this. He also knew that it had all ended this morning. He curled into the foetal position and waited for the Germans to arrive. When there was finally a sound at the door he found he was not yet ready to die. He had to see Jean's body to accept what deep down he knew. He slipped out of the French window on to the balcony Jean had constructed when was a wealthy musician. He edged his way along to the next window. In this room as Francesca she had played the 'cello. Deliberately she raised her petticoat to give the maestro the tiniest glimpse of flesh. Now she was buried in the nunnery in Thiviers and her lover in a bomb crater in Verdun. Francis slipped inside.

Jean climbed the stairs. Entering the village a washerwoman had told him Stuardo had returned to his house. Jean opened the bedroom door. The French window was open. Something told him that it was closed when he approached the house. He crossed the room. In the next room Francis listened. This time he made no attempt to hide. He listened to the footsteps on the balcony. He watched the door open. Jean stood in front of him.

*

John could not sleep. Beside him Francine was swimming in very troubled waters. Gently he tried to wake her. It would release her from her dream. He might also get the cuddle he had hoped for when he came to bed. Francine turned towards him and hugged him. She did not wake. Back in her dream Francis threw his arms round Jean. Francis and Jean kissed. In the same room John and Francine kissed. She pulled herself out of the dream into wakefulness. The house took flight. The images it had been projecting into Francine retreated back into the walls. There was more to tell. The house would wait. It was neither malevolent nor benign, it simply was. It was accommodation. It accommodated souls, a repository for history. When stones had stood as long as these they became like sponges. Plays enacted within these walls saturated them. The stories leaked from the walls back into the lives of those that told them. Francine needed to finish the dream. "Take me John." She whispered. John thought of Cathy who had passed out on the sofa. John knew from experience that wild stallions could not wake her. He turned his attention back to Francine. She was clinging desperately to him. She offered herself to him as Francis had offered himself to Jean. The walls urged them on. Finally the ghost was exorcised. Cathy woke. She needed to rehydrate. Padding through to the kitchen she poured a glass of water, downed it and poured another. She returned to the living room. Silence had returned to the bedroom. The door was open. Cathy stood in the opening watching the sleeping bodies. She thought she had given her husband to Francine. She knew now it was she who had borrowed what was not hers. It did not make it easier. She returned to the sofa and did what she always did when she could not sleep.

Dawn broke far too early. It failed to rouse a sleeping house. This time it was Peter that made the coffee. He made lots. Everywhere he turned Susan was in front of him whispering 'show me'. While the coffee brewed he sorted the washing up into glasses cutlery and plates. Francine walked naked past a sleeping Cathy in the living room and into the kitchen. "Leave those darling. We will do it together when everyone is up."

Peter looked at her. He had grown out of his teenage crush. Francine was Francine. He was used to her disregard for convention. He wondered when Susan would walk into his kitchen like that. He turned to hide the effect the thought had on his body. "Go back to bed; I'll bring the coffee through. Is dad awake?"

"Yes."

"Mummy?"

"No, give her a bit longer. She had quite a night last night."

Peter smiled. "I think we all did."

Peter sat on the bed watching his parents drink their coffee. He sipped his own. His birth mother was sleeping a few feet away. Last night Susan asked if having two mothers was difficult.

"Not at all. Do you have brothers and sisters?"

"Two little sisters."

"Isn't that difficult?"

"Yes!" They had laughed.

John looked at his son. He had grown up. "Susan seems nice."

"Dad, stop fishing. Yes she is nice."

"She is a lot younger than you."

"She is nearly 12, I am 14. That is less than the difference between you and mum. Oh, and before you start, I don't need the talk."

Francine was glad he had not pointed out the age difference between John and her. She put her hand on Peter's. "She is very lucky."

"Francine, I have only met her once."

"Once is all it takes." added John.

"You're a fine one to talk. You were padding around after Francine for two years before you plucked up the courage to admit it."

"That was different. He was married to me." They all turned round. Cathy was standing in the doorway. "Mind if I join you?"

Peter made room. He looked at his father, then his two mothers. "Do you guys need to talk?" They did, but none of them knew what to say.

Eventually it was Cathy who spoke. "Sleep well?" The question was not directed at anyone in particular.

Francine answered. "Not really. I had the most vivid dream." She recounted it, stopping at the point where Francis and Jean made love.

Once again Cathy broke the silence. "That explains what happened next."

Francine blushed. "I thought you were sleeping."

"I was. You were very noisy."

"Yes you were." Peter confirmed.

Francine slid down the bed and hid under the duvet. When she peeped out, they were all smiling at her. "Aren't you jealous?" She asked Cathy.

"Not anymore, just envious."

Francine remembered when Cathy and John had gone to England to sell the house. "If it was me I think I would have killed you both." She stopped, remembering the dream.

"We are different" whispered Cathy. "It's not just us, it's the house. I think it's haunted."

"That's what I said when I first saw it." said Peter. "I didn't realise then that we were the ghosts." They all looked at him. It was a Damascus moment. The adults, yet again, had needed Peter to point out the obvious.

"You are a genius Peter." Exclaimed John.

"Yes I am. Just call me Professor Peter Cartwright MSBO."

"What's MSBO?" Asked Francine.

"Master of Stating the Bleedin' Obvious" he replied.

Chapter 39
The Fire

The clear up was mammoth but they all pitched in. Francine was glad to inject a generous portion of the banal into a turbulent twenty four hours. "I'll pop in to Thiviers and check Pascal is ok at the library. I can also pay Ariane for the ice creams." She made her way past the queue of customers. Ariane was serving, Nadine clearing tables. Francine waved her cheque book.

"Nadine, can you take over?" Ariane called. She drew Francine aside, pushing away the proffered check book. Holding her hand she looked into Francine's eyes. "There's been a fire."

"Where?"

"At your farm."

"Christ! Is everyone OK?"

"I don't think so. Benjamin called in. It seems to have started in the barn. His dad found it. Your husband pulled him out then went back to fight it."

"Is dad ok?"

"Yes. Smoke inhalation. Urgence checked him and released him."

"What about Jean-Mark?" Ariane looked at her. "O Christ! I must go."

"Is there anything I can do?"

"Can you tell the others?"

"Of course. Do you want them to go to the farm?"

"No. Just tell them not to worry but I don't know when I will be back."

Cathy had already left when John put the phone down. Peter, who was on study leave so thought he ought to do some studying and was in his room. He poked his head round the door. "Was that Francine?"

"Yes."

"I thought she would be back by now. Everything OK?"

"No. There has been an accident at her dad's farm. She has gone to help."

"What kind of accident?"

"A fire."

"Anyone hurt?"

"Peter, I don't know. You will have to wait till she gets back."

Most days John would be preparing supper when Francine came. Today there were so many leftovers he had nothing to do. He tidied, froze what he could, threw a lot away and prepared a plate of cold food and waited. Eventually her car pulled into the square. Both her men pretended they were not just waiting for her to get back. Both just happened to be in the kitchen as she walked through the door.

"Hug?" John held out his arms. She pressed her head against his chest, reassured by his heartbeat.

Peter came over. "Are you ok Francine?"

She smiled. "Yes. It is just a shock. I never really thought about him. He was just there, part of someone else's life. Now he is gone."

"Did you see him?" Peter was barely ten when his granny died. He was discouraged from seeing the body. John had simply said she was not there any more; it would be like looking at an empty shell. He had stayed outside. He wasn't sure whether he regretted it.

"I did, yes. At first I wasn't going to. I thought he would be disfigured. The pompier said no, he had died from smoke inhalation. I looked. He was just as I remembered him."

"He was here for your birthday wasn't he?"

"Yes. He didn't stay long. I hardly got to talk to him. I was going to go back but he had gone. A neighbour said he had a phone call from the farm and he had to go. I thought it was an excuse. You know, he was just putting in a token appearance and didn't plan to stay."

"What can we do?" John asked.

"John, you don't have to do anything. It's a shock because it was unexpected. It is sad because it is always sad when someone dies. It is not more than that because we were married. I told you at the beginning, we were never really married." She pulled away from him and smiled. "Now, what's for supper?"

"Leftovers."

"Yummy!"

That was it. She went to the funeral of course. Ariane's ice cream parlour was right next to the church. John, Cathy and Peter went to support her. They stood outside dutifully until the coffin arrived. Francine turned to them "Take Peter for an ice cream. You don't have to come to the service with me. You didn't know him."

"Will you be alright on your own?"

"Of course, I'm a big girl. Besides it won't look too good if the widow sits with her new boyfriend."

"I suppose if you put it like that..."

Francine's period of mourning was so short many judged it unseemly. The very next week she came home bubbling with excitement. "Guess who I've asked for supper tomorrow?"

Peter was trying out his teenage moody persona. It didn't suit him. "Some doddery old biddy who wants to talk about the war?"

"Peter that is very rude, say sorry." His dad's words were an echo of the time his parents had missed their flight. It was the night Stuart had planted the bomb in the back of his brain. Thelma had removed it and helped put Stuart behind bars. He had gone, removed like a gangrenous leg. The patient was healed but when he least expected it a phantom pain from the amputation came back to haunt him.

Tonight Francine was too excited to pick up on this. John thought he would see if Peter wanted to resurrect the Pooh stories. He turned his attention back to Francine. "Who have you invited?"

"Only Jean Nouvel!"

John had never heard of him. "Have I met him?"

"I don't think so or you wouldn't ask. He designed the latest Serpentine Pavilion in Kensington Gardens."

"What is he doing in darkest Dordogne?"

"He is on his way to speak at the Gallo-roman museum in Perigeux. He designed that too. I met him when it opened a few years ago."

"I don't remember that."

"You wouldn't. It was a few years before you came down."

"2003."

They both turned to Peter. "How did you know that?"

"I am a mine of useless information. The guide told us when mummy took me to visit. It was that summer we spent doing the house up. I recognised the architect's name."

Francine was impressed. John knew Peter was having them on. "Peter you are bright, but not a genius. You are making it up."

"How do you know? I am a genius, I just haven't reached my full potential. Anyway I had Francine fooled!"

"You did! By the way I worked it out, it was 2003. Maybe you are a genius after all."

"Told you." Peter had already shaken off the memory of Stuart. John looked at him and then at Francine. Peter was back to being Peter and Francine as always was being Francine. He ached with love for them both.

"I've invited two members of the société patrimoine, Claude and his wife Celine. They were on the dig that excavated the villa and are particularly interested in that period of history. Are you OK if Cathy Thelma and Paula come too?"

John did not mind but at bedtime Peter asked why they always included Thelma and Paula in their dinner parties.

"Because they are our friends. Thelma likes spending time with you."

"I think she is checking up on me. You know, to see if I am still ok."

"What's wrong with that?"

"Nothing. It is kind of her. She is special."

"Yes she is."

"I think she also comes to help Paula. She told me Paula is not able to go out much. She can handle coming here."

"You are right. Paula is much better than she used to be."

"Do you think Thelma is curing her?"

"I think it is just that Paula is getting used to us. Alzheimer's is not something that can be cured."

"Never say never. Good night dad."

Jean Nouvel proved to be a charming dinner guest. The mealtime conversation flowed easily. When Jean talked of architecture he made the complicated seem simple. They listened to him explain how form followed function. His extraordinary buildings flowed naturally from the design specification. When one looked at one of his buildings the first reaction was awe. When he explained the design the listener understood there was no other logical way for the form to evolve. John found himself wondering where he had witnessed this before. Thelma smiled. She asked a pertinent question on a subject totally outside her field. There was John's answer. She too had the ability to make complex ideas simple and accessible to anyone ready to listen. Peter sat soaking it in.

One day he would hold court with equal humility. Tonight he just tried to get into the adult conversation. "The mayor said we are going to have a new salle des fetes. Will you design it Mr Nouvel?

The architect tried to be polite. "I have not been asked. These things are usually planned years in advance."

John came to his rescue. "I don't think our little project is important enough for someone as famous as Jean" he then turned to Claude. "Are there many Roman sites like Vesunna?"

"I am sure there are. Human history has deep roots in the Dordogne, deeper than almost anywhere else on earth. When the Empire spread to Gaul it behaved as it always did. The Romans did not conquer, they overlaid. The ruling class could continue to rule as long as it paid tribute to Rome. The villa in Vesunna was inhabited by Gauls, not Romans."

"But it is a Roman Villa." Objected Peter.

"It was built in the Roman style by the local Gallic nobility. The Romans devolved power to those who already held it prior to their invasion. They built temples to Roman gods on Druid sites. After Constantine they simply elevated a Palestinian prophet to the status of God. They then built churches on the sites of pagan temples."

Jean Nouvel agreed. "When I build a modern structure over an ancient monument I am doing the same thing."

"The difference," said Claude "Is that when you built the museum on top of the villa in Perigeux it was to display the original structure, not overlay it."

Francine had an idea. Clearing the remains of the meal from the table she spread a map. The Church and Saint Etienne's well were marked along with all the smaller wells in the village. "Look at the line of wells. The Church is on that line."

Celine chipped in. "It has long been postulated that Saint Etienne's well was not the original source in the village. The site of the church is slightly raised but quite close."

"But it is uphill from the well. Water does not flow uphill." Objected Peter.

His father explained. "It is an artesian well. The water is forced to the surface through a natural fissure."

Celine agreed. "To the Druids it had magical properties. Firstly it came from the ground above surrounding woodland. As you say Peter, water does not flow uphill. Secondly it flowed even through periods of drought. Thirdly the water was always at 12 degrees. It would feel warm in winter and cool in summer. These provide plenty of reasons to build a temple."

Francine drew a line with her finger. She traced from the well to the church and on past the old marie. When she reached the site of the proposed salle de fetes she punched the map with her finger. "Imagine you are the head honcho in this part of Gaul. The Romans have arrived. You hold on to power by building a Roman temple on top of the Druid one and pay tribute to Rome. Now, where do you build your house?"

Chapter 40
The Villa

"Out of the question!" The mayor stood to make his point. Francine had taken her map to the Marie to ask permission to dig a test trench. It would establish whether there were grounds for a full archaeological dig. The vein on Henri's neck was throbbing. The standing position was to impose his authority and signal the meeting was already over.

Francine stood her ground. "For what reason?"

"It is private property. I am the owner. I do not give permission."

"You have sold it to the commune. It is public land."

"I have not yet sold it." He lied. "As soon as title is transferred it will be a construction site. There will be strictly no access on Health and Safety grounds." The next day the grounds man was erecting temporary fencing with notices to this effect.

Francine convened an emergency meeting of the Society de Patrimoine, inviting Claude and Celine back to the house. "There is nothing we can find out until the topsoil is removed."

Celine agreed with her husband. "As far as forcing anyone's hand we have a catch 22 situation. We cannot excavate without evidence. We cannot find evidence without excavating."

"The contractors will excavate" said Francine.

Claude pulled a face. "They will excavate the entire site in a morning. By then it will be too late, they will have destroyed everything."

Cathy popped her head round the door. "Peter about?" Holidays had started, she had promised to take Peter and Susan canoeing in Brantome.

"In his room I think." said Francine. Cathy went in without knocking. Susan sat up quickly rearranging her clothes.

"Ready?" asked Cathy.

"Nearly." said Peter.

"What have you been doing?" his mother asked.

"Looking for my canoeing shoes."

"I don't think you will find them where you were looking. Has Susan got any?"

"No Mrs Cartwright." The girl responded.

"Peter dig out that pair you have grown out of. I'll wait in the kitchen."

"Everything ok?" Francine asked.

John walked in "What's up?"

"Peter and Susan have been playing hide the sausage."

"Really? I'll have a talk to him."

Cathy relented. "It's ok, I'm exaggerating. I think he was just researching suitable hiding places for the day Susan finds it."

John smiled. "All the same she is too young to go looking."

"I know." said Cathy. "I'm taking them canoeing. I'll give him a refresher course on The Talk."

Peter and Susan came out of the bedroom. Both sported 'butter wouldn't melt' expressions. "Ready" they announced in unison. Cathy picked up her bag. "Fill me in on this construction project when we get back. Sir Evelyn was a property developer I may be able to help."

For now there was not much Francine and Claude thought they could do. They left it there for the moment hoping that Cathy was right.

Cathy was at the next meeting. Claude came alone. Celine's elderly mother had a hairdresser's appointment which clearly took priority. "Can we talk about the construction site?" Cathy asked. "As far as I understand it the Mayor and/or the contractors want to rush through the build so everyone gets paid."

"In a nutshell yes." Confirmed Francine.

"It is not unusual, if rather short sighted." Continued Cathy. "If it is a high profile find like the Globe theatre the payback in terms of kudos can outweigh the liquidated damages from the delay."

"This is rural France." Observed Francine. "Individual personalities play a big part. This is not the Globe theatre, it is some bloke's house."

"Two thousand year old house." Added John.

Cathy brought them back on topic. "Our objective is to secure a full archaeological excavation. To do that we need prima face evidence that there is something to dig for."

"Evidence which is buried on a site to which we have been denied access." Francine reminded her.

"How deep would any artefacts be buried?" John asked.

It was Claude who replied. "Once the topsoil has been removed, anything from zero to two, maybe three meters." John wanted to know why there was such a big variation. Claude continued. "There are lots of factors. Urban sites are often deep because rubbish accumulates more quickly. Many things of course are deliberately buried. Bodies for example, and artefacts buried with them. Riverside sites are also often deep. Rivers meander quite quickly. Sediment accumulates."

Francine was thoughtful. "This site does not fit any of those criteria."

"Exactly," continued Claude. "It is more likely to have been subject to erosion than deposition. Apart from bodies and grave goods there is a good chance that we will find something just beneath the topsoil. A pavement. If we are lucky, a mosaic. That would depend on the status of the owner."

Yet again it was Cathy that brought them down to earth, so to speak. "You were worried that groundwork would happen so quickly evidence would be lost before we have a chance to look for it." Francine agreed. Cathy went on. "I may have some good news. It is highly unlikely that they will remove subsoil on the first day. Topsoil is valuable and will be sold. Subsoil has to go to landfill. It costs money to get rid of it. The lorries will take away topsoil first and return another day for the subsoil."

John was working it out. "There will be a short time when undisturbed subsoil will be exposed. That is when we look."

"A very short time, probably overnight." Confirmed Cathy.

I'd like to involve Patrick Puissaud the curator of the Vesunna museum." Said Francine. "How will we know when to invite him."

"I can help with that" said Cathy. "Access to the village is severely restricted. Quarry lorries have to have permission to enter. It will be listed on the departmental website."

Thanks to Cathy detective work they knew when site clearance was starting. Patrick Puissaud was happy to renew his acquaintance with Francine. As usual John was prevailed upon to prepare supper. This one was barely 100 yards from the site they were meeting to discuss. "It is all rather exciting" said Patrick.

Cathy agreed. "Shall we wear balaclavas? I feel like one of those girls in the resistance, going behind enemy lines gathering intelligence."

Claude did not care for the analogy. "We are not at war. We are just trying to preserve our heritage."

Patrick was conciliatory. "We have enjoyed such a long period without conflict it is passing from living memory. That tends to a rather nostalgic view of our past. I agree with Cathy on one point, this is much more exciting than a curator's usual work."

"Shall we wait until the village is deserted?" Asked Claude.

"No need to wait" quipped Peter. "It is always deserted."

"Not today, with all those lorries" added John. "I'll pop out and check all the contractors have gone. If they have we can all go for an evening stroll."

"We need a dog." Said Peter. "Then we could pretend we were taking it for a walk."

"My dog is in the car" said Patrick.

Francine was put out. "Why didn't you say? You should have brought him in!"

"He is not very well behaved at dinner parties. He begs. It is my own fault, I spoil him." They all went outside and waited while Patrick fetched his dog.

"He's adorable" said Cathy. "I love spaniels. "What's his name?"

"Joe."

"Why Joe?" asked Peter.

"Because he is a Cocker." Peter looked blank.

John explained. "Joe Cocker was a singer."

Casually they walked past Henri's house and up to the building site. Both were deserted. Checking there were no cars Patrick let Joe off the lead. Casually he picked up a stone and lobbed it onto the cleared ground. Joe bounded after it. Since it was identical to all the other stones he could not find it. Instead he just sat down. "Oh dear, my dog has wandered off. I better get him back." Patrick ducked under the tape and squatted beside his dog. The others stood uncomfortably.

There was a shout. Henri came out of his house. "Hey! He called. What are you doing?"

"Walking the dog" replied Francine.

"That's a dangerous construction site. Leave immediately!"

Patrick stood. He slipped something in his pocket. Mentally he triangulated his position by estimating his distance from two corners of the site. "I am so sorry. My dog is not very obedient. Bad boy Joe!" He put him on the lead. Joe gave him a 'What did I do?' look.

Back at the house they all sat round the table. At Francine's insistence Joe joined them. Patrick took a small object from his pocket and placed it on the table.

"Are you going to clean it with a soft brush like they do on the TV?" asked Peter.

"Let's start by washing it" replied Patrick. He took from his other pocket an eye glass. Francine produced a bowl of water. Eventually Patrick was satisfied. He looked to the others. "I am as certain as I can be we have found our Roman Villa."

Cathy stared at the small object. To the untrained eye it was just a small stone, or perhaps pottery. To an expert it was a piece of Roman mosaic. "What now?" She asked.

"All construction work must stop immediately" replied Patrick.

"It is Friday. Works are due to restart on Monday" Francine pointed out.

"I cannot get an injunction to stop the work before then." objected Patrick. "Can we appeal to Henri's better nature?" Francine doubted it. She had two days to mobilise the village.

Everyone was up early Monday morning. Cathy contacted Sud Ouest and Dordogne Libre. Both papers sent a reporter and photographer. Francine had a live phone-in booked with France Blue Perigord. The Gendarme arrived. It was inevitable. Francine had spent two days telling every household in the village about the villa. "I want to lie down in the road in front of the Lorries" exclaimed Peter."

"Me too said Susan. If we are going to die, I want us to die together."

"Nobody's going to die" said Francine. "But get the high vis jackets from the car just in case."

Susan staying the weekend sparked a debate between the parents. "Do you think Peter is old enough to have a girl over for the weekend?" Cathy asked. This was a two mother conversation. Francine was fine with it, Cathy thought Susan was too young.

"We'll put her in the loft" said Francine. "If there is any hanky-panky we will hear."

"I know" said Cathy pointedly.

Now the two teenagers were lying in the road hand in hand. The press photographer loved it. The police pulled over the first quarry lorry to turn off the bypass. French lorry drivers were used to blockades. Usually they were of their own making. The photographer asked if the lorry could drive a bit closer. He wanted another shot of the sit down protest with the lorry in the background.

Francine was on the phone to the radio station. The protest had already made the 8 O'clock news. The D.J. flipped her mike. "And there is more on this breaking news story live on France Bleu Perigord right after this from Mika." The singer intoned softly 'Elle me dit...' while the D.J. threw another switch so she could talk to Francine. "I'll be with you in 2." She ran through the question she was going to ask. Francine was only half listening. Henri was marching down the road towards her. She interrupted Sophie to warn her. Ever the professional the presenter stayed calm. "Don't worry; we will play it by ear. I may change my questions. Just remember this is radio. You will have to explain things to listeners. If he talks to you go with it but say things like 'I have with me Henri Gagneux, mayor of St Etienne.'" Sophie regretted not getting a sound crew down. The situation had developed faster than she anticipated. If necessary she would have to ask Francine to pass the phone to Henri.

The Mayor was wearing his best suit and a red white and blue mayoral sash. He clearly intended to pull rank. The reporters were busy interviewing Francine when France Bleu phoned her. Now seeing the mayor they went off to get another angle. Francine was busy telling the local radio that this was a protest to stop the destruction of a newly discovered roman villa. Henri was handing out press releases. "This is a developing situation" He declared. "My house, I have just discovered was built next to the Villa of the first mayor of St Etienne. Legend has it that the Saint visited our village in the first century A.D. He converted my predecessor to Christianity. After the departure of the saint, the mayor wanted to give thanks to Our Lady for curing his daughter's deafness. He built a church on the site of our current one. We now know he built a house for himself in the Roman style. Thanks to my generosity, the site of the villa has been returned to the village. I was going to build a new Salle de Fetes for the benefit of the public. In the light of today's discovery I will spend considerably more to make the building a Salle Polyvalent. I have ordered a full archaeological excavation. When this is complete I will commission the architect who built the Vesunna museum. He will build an even more impressive example. Beneath your feet our glorious past will be visible through a glass floor. Above will be a fully equipped modern public building for the benefit of residents and visitors alike. It is all in my press report." He handed out the press release. It was all total bullshit of course.

Francine finished her interview with the radio station. She painted on a face she had not worn since entertaining Stuart in her flat years ago. "Henri!" she beamed. Deliberately she used his prenom to establish equal status before witnesses. "I am delighted you have taken my advice regarding the development of our site." He bristled at the words 'my advice' and 'our site'. There was nothing he could do, he was being watched. He took Francine's proffered hand. With her free hand she took one of the press releases. She had wanted to expose him as an unscrupulous opportunistic carpet bagger. She now realised she had got something more valuable: His permission for a full archaeological dig. He would take the credit. That was his price for cooperation. On reflection it was a price worth paying.

Chapter 41
The Hunt

The Villa was not the only thing over which Francine and Henri crossed swords. The mayor was a keen huntsman. As soon as the hunting season started he was out with his dogs and gun. Francine loved walking. She hated the woods being out of bounds every Sunday and Wednesday. Boars that were killed were taken back to the village where they were butchered and eaten. Hunters were obliged to follow wounded animals and kill them. Francine knew from experience that the law was honoured more in the breach than the observance.

On her husband's death Francine inherited a small piece of woodland. It would keep them in firewood and cepes but little else. It did however have a strategic value. She put up notices: Propriété privée, sanctuaire de la faune, chasse interdit. The land cut right across the mayor's prime hunting grounds. She went to tell him. He was not bothered. When it became clear her wishes were not being respected she went to the police. They were equally uninterested. Most of them also hunted. They asked if someone had been shot on her land. When she said no, what little courtesy she had been afforded evaporated.

Francine was not done yet. She went to the notaire. "I am afraid I cannot help you Mrs Lefevre. The right to hunt has been established. You cannot revoke that right."

"That's ridiculous, suppose an armed robber enters my land. How can he have the right to do so?"

"He does not. If he is a member of a registered hunt he does. The hunting associated meets to decide and record when and where they will hunt. If that includes your land they may enter."

"But there are sanctuaires de faune where hunting is forbidden."

"Those predate the hunting associations."

"Let me get this straight" said Francine. "One side can say we have the right to hunt, the other can say no. The one that wins is the one who said it first."

"In a nutshell, yes." Francine was not happy. It felt to her as if Henri had won. At least she had won the battle over the archaeological dig. Patrick took a great interest. With Francine living within yards he became a frequent visitor. Cathy too was often there, either to see Peter, or check out something with the brewery. At first John was surprised at Cathy's new found interest in archaeology. He assumed she just wanted to help, calling on her knowledge of construction projects. Now she busied herself on site ferrying new finds from the volunteers to Patrick in the tent. She helped him with the classification. Patrick spoke excellent English. Out of respect for Cathy he chose to communicate in her language rather than his own. When she was not needed she invented jobs like walking Joe. She did not think of herself as a doggy person but Joe got under her skin. There was something therapeutic about his acceptance of her. As soon as he realised she was willing to walk him he was her friend for life. She decided to buy herself a dog.

"I don't know why I didn't think of it before. He is a great companion. Walking dogs is also a great way of meeting people. Dog owners are very friendly."

Peter was the first to work it out. "I think mummy is in love with Patrick." John was surprised. Patrick was the diametric opposite of Stuart. He was impeccably polite. He was attentive to Cathy, but he was attentive to everyone. If he was attracted to Cathy he gave no sign. He was also very different to John. John always wore his heart on his sleeve. Cathy could read John. She could not read Patrick. It drew her to him. It drove her to understand this cultured aesthetic.

For his part Peter had no doubt that Susan was The One. He was sure too that his dad had found his life partner in Francine. He was sad that they had not met when they were young carefully ignoring the fact that he would not be here if they had. Instead he wondered why his parents fell in love, only for his mother to take a lover. Now she had set her cap at someone completely different to either his dad or Stuart. Peter had a natural gift for understanding the physical universe. He was aware now that love was force stronger than anything physical. He wanted to know how those closest to him viewed this mysterious force. In particular the way it paired souls.

"When you meet someone special, how do you know they were the one you will spend your life with?" It was a warm summer night. The special people in Peter's life were finishing of an evening together with a bit of star gazing. It seemed a good time to ask.

John answered first. "If you need to ask the question, they are not the one." Peter had no doubts about himself and Susan. It was a more abstract question.

Cathy went next. "If you keep asking if this person is The One there is a danger you just keep looking. You know, just in case there is something better out there. When I was a teenager I was shopping for a coat. The first one I saw was perfect. I went round all the shops. None of them were as good as the first one. When I went back to the first shop the coat had been sold."

Peter was not satisfied. "That's an allegory. It doesn't work because one is a person, the other is a thing. Relationships are different. There are two people."

Thelma agreed, but thought it was a useful illustration. "Don't confuse allegory with applicability. Everyone is different. You are different to the boy who first came to France. Teenage relationships are hard because both people change very quickly. Remember your jigsaw analogy? How would that work if the pieces were alive? They would grow and change shape."

Peter thought about it. "You are saying that people change. Two people that fit together now might not fit together later."

"Exactly." Thelma replied. "Young people change very fast, older people more slowly." She was trying to warn Peter not to tie himself down to one person too soon. Susan had reached for Peter's hand in the darkness and was holding it.

Peter squeezed her hand and carried on "Why do people change? People are changed by people, and events. If you set out to change someone it does not work. Like Stuart wanting to change mum. It breaks them. If you both grow without trying to change the other you both grow round each other. The fit gets better the longer you are together."

Francine was quiet. She and John were growing together. Peter was growing up. Soon he would have a life beyond this nest. The nest they had built together, the nest from which he would fly. When he had built his own he would return.

The house spoke. "You and John have returned. You will always return. When you are ready you will learn why." Francine was not ready. The most recent story was not finished. She was scared to ask how the story ended for Francis and Jean. She had no idea why she and John had been the same sex then. Today it didn't matter. Jan and Alice were a couple. So were Thelma and Paula. She knew a lot of gay men too, older couples hiding in the countryside at a time when society was less accepting of their lifestyle. Now they were accepted. It was 2012. France would soon formally recognise them by legalizing same sex marriage. England would follow suit.

*

Another year had slipped by. Last Christmas Cathy asked if she could invite Jan and Alice again. They declined. They said it was a bit cold. They fancied coming in the summer. They were all reunited in the summer of 2012. Everyone was going through old photos on their phones and passing them round.

"Your birthday party looks amazing!" Said Jan. "I wish we could have been here. You guys made us so welcome. Alice, wouldn't it be great if we could get married here?"

There was silence; nobody disapproved, it simply did not occur to neither John or Francine that they would want to do it in their house. When the penny dropped they were thrilled.

Peter had a more practical objection. "You are both girls. You can't!"

"Not yet" admitted Jan, "but one day it will be legal." Francine confirmed that there was talk too in France of gay marriages.

*

The new salle de fetes was finished. Henri claimed it would surpass the Vesunna museum in architectural splendour. He exaggerated. Jean Nouvel did not design it. "I believe in the maxim 'never go back'. Besides, I am in France very little these days. There is a building in Doha that requires much of my attention."

Francine was disappointed. "The dig is complete, could you have a look at the site and do a few sketches?"

"I will look, certainly. I will make some notes and send my assistant down. She is very good."

"Could she work from your drawings?"

"I don't do drawings. I prefer to think of myself as a conceptual architect. I have ideas, I put them in words. The engineers put the words into practice. If you start with a drawing you fix the form too early. The building must evolve." What evolved was a modern building that blended with the architecture of the surrounding buildings. The excavations were left exactly as the archaeologist left them. He identified areas where it was safe to put pillars that supported a glass floor. Once you entered the building you had the sense of entering a modern village hall. The excavations could be hidden or revealed with lighting.

Although Francine was disappointed Jean Nouvel was not more involved she was happy with the final result. She had other things on her mind. The dream she had after her 35th birthday party often returned. She needed to know how the story ended. She was fearful it would not end well. There were no graves in the graveyard but the records office showed Francis and Jean died the same day 'from enemy fire.' There was nothing for Corrine. It was as if she suddenly disappeared.

There was a familiar sound of a motorbike entering the square. Peter used his first bike to get to a holiday job near Brantome. An English couple had bought an old farm which they converted into a classic car centre. Robert gave Peter a job polishing the cars. With the money he earned he traded up to a larger bike. He was now able to give lifts to Susan. She was promised a job in the tea room next season. Today he came in to the living room, dumping his crash helmet on the coffee table.

"Not there." Francine had not even bothered to look up.

"Yeah, I'll put it in my room in a minute."

Francine was at the desk. He draped himself over her. "Ghost busting?" He asked, referring to her historical research. It was a reference to his comment about the house being haunted and them being the ghosts.

"Yes." She explained what she had found out about Francis, Jean and Corrine.

"Why are there no graves?" He asked.

"There are lots of reasons. Maybe there were no bodies. Like Jean-Michel who was killed in Verdun."

"But these all died in or near the village."

"In that case it would be because the Church did not allow them to be buried in the graveyard."

"Why would they do that?"

"If you have committed a mortal sin you cannot be buried in a graveyard. Graveyards are for people who go to heaven. The others go to hell."

"Some people have weird ideas" said Peter. "What mortal sin did Corrine commit?"

"She probably committed suicide. Saying she died of asphyxiation suggests she hanged herself."

Peter was shocked. "Why is that a mortal sin?"

"The bible says 'thou shalt not kill'."

Peter thought killing yourself should be an exception. "It is the one life everyone should have the right to end." He affirmed.

Francine turned round so she could hug him. She had to stand on tip toe to do it these days. He was growing up. There was no way she was going to stop hugging him. "You are too young to be troubled with thoughts like that."

"I can be young and adult at the same time. Men can multitask too you know!"

Francine smiled. "I love you Peter."

"Love you too Francine." He thought then added. "Do other families say they love each other as much as we do?"

Francine smiled. "Maybe not, but they should." Again they had side-stepped a part of their history. The Church had refused to bury Francis and Jean in consecrated ground because they were homosexual.

The breakthrough for Francine's research was when she tracked down a member of the Gaullist resistance who was still living. He was in an old people's home. Dordogne Libre had done a piece for Jean-Luc's hundredth birthday, describing him as a hero of the resistance. Francine arrived in Beaulieu notebook in hand. He was frail, but his mind was sharp.

"Yes, I remember Eliane. Pretty young thing. She went away. Such a shame. Still it was for the best." Francine waited for him to continue. When he did not she asked if he knew Eliane's parents. He returned from whichever place his mind had wandered. He looked at Francine as if he had only just noticed her. "Oh yes, her father and I did many sorties together." This could take a long time.

She cut to the chase. "There are stories that they were killed by the gauchistes. Is that true?"

"Not by the Cartel, by Lowell."

Francine was confused. "Was he not a gauchiste?"

"Oh yes, but he was a law unto himself. He returned from the Great War, but I think he left most of his senses at the front."

Francine pressed on. "His grandson says the Gaullists stole money intended for the resistance."

Jean-Luc made an irritated gesture. "The Gauchistes always say that. It is the politics of envy. Simeon did not need to steal. The family had money." He paused, drifting off into his own thoughts again. When he returned he spoke it was as if to himself. "War makes killing acceptable. You start by killing the enemy. Then you kill your own if they are traitors, then if they are deserters. Lowell killed his own men."

"You mean Simeon?" Francine asked.

"Not only Eliane's parents. He killed cartel members too."

"Why did he do that?"

"Because they were nancies. What do call them nowadays? Gays?"

Francine nodded. "Do you remember their names?"

Jean-Luc thought. "One was the husband of that Mata Hari girl" He paused trying to dig up the name.

"Corrine." Francine suggested.

"Yes, Jean was her husband. The other was that pretty boy."

"Francis." She whispered.

"That was it. Sent them off to ambush a non existent German patrol, followed them, shot them and claimed it was the Germans."

"How do you know there was no German patrol?"

"Because we had already ambushed them."

Francine was trembling. Later she would cry. Now there was one more question she needed to ask. "And Corrine?"

"They took her away. Quotas had to be filled."

So was Corrine Jewish? Francine knew about the Vichy government identifying Jews for transportation to Paris. The official line was that they were being sent to work in Poland. There were many French who shared Hitler's view on the Jewish problem. They were not interested what happened to them as long as they left France. She asked the question "Corrine was Jewish?"

Jean-Luc repeated his impatient mannerism. "Of course not. You did not have to be Jewish, it was enough that people thought it."

"So people thought she was Jewish?"

"Not even that. She had seduced enough husbands in St Etienne for a wife to claim what they knew to be untrue."

Chapter 42
The Wedding

It was now 2013. The UK had not yet legalised same sex marriage. Jan and Alice did not want to wait. They decided to marry in France. Cathy was being all big-sister. "You really do things the hard way don't you? It is not even legal yet."

"The law has been passed." Sulked Jan. "It was on the news."

"The act has been passed, she corrected her. I'll check when it is due to become law."

The next day Jan was back on the phone. "Did you find out?"

"End of May."

"Great. I love spring weddings. I'll pick a date and work on the invitations."

"Hold on Jan, you can't just get married like that, you have to be French." Cathy was not sure about that, but was trying to take a bit of wind out of Jan's sails.

"That sucks. France and UK are both in the EU. We should be able to marry in any EU country." Cathy promised to check. "I'll phone you tomorrow."

"I'm sure you will. Don't expect answers. I've got a ton of other stuff to do. I haven't closed the BAT accounts for 2012. John wants production schedules for this year, I can't even get him to do a full stock check. Don't get me started on the fixed assets register. I had to explain amortization to him."

"Cat."

"He has no idea what is the useful life of his equipment..."

"Catherine!"

She stopped. Jan sounded like their mother. "What?"

"It's OK. You have a job, I understand. I am grateful for what you are doing with the wedding. Take your time. It is just that being married officially means a lot to Alice and I. The homophobic stuff has changed. People come on to us with stuff like 'It's wonderful to see people like you in love.' what's this 'like you' shit? I feel like screaming 'You mean not like me', like it was, I couldn't get a man, so I got a woman which is the next best thing."

Cathy waited for the outburst to die down. "Jan, it's OK. I'll get back to you as soon as I can."

Francine was pleased to help. "The French love their rules and regulations. They also like ignoring them. The other thing to remember is that the mayor has a lot of power. It is important to understand the difference between power and obligation." Cathy looked puzzled so Francine explained. "Power is what the mayor *may* do. Obligation is what he *must* do. There is a huge area of discretion between the two. For example, at the moment the mayor has no power to recognise same sex marriage."

Cathy nodded. "He has to wait until the new law is enacted."

"Exact."

Cathy smiled. Francine's English was pretty much perfect now but she still had idiosyncrasies like saying 'exact' instead of 'exactly'. "So when the law is passed he must marry them."

Francine corrected her. "He *may* marry them, provided of course they meet other criteria."

"Like what?"

"The main one is that at least one of the couple must be resident in the commune."

Cathy pulled a face. "That could be a problem."

Francine agreed. "As soon as one of them has lived in the village for forty days the mayor may grant an attestation de residence. Notice I said *may*."

Cathy sighed. "What would influence his decision?"

"Lots of things: Do they have family in the village? Do they intend to live in the village after they marry? Do they have jobs locally?"

Cathy was on the verge of giving up. "There are so many obstacles, even if Henri was on our side. We fell out with him big time with the villa, not to mention your objection to the hunt. He is going to find any excuse not to cooperate."

"Then we must find a way of making him change his mind."

"How can we do that?"

Francine smiled. "Leave it with me." She was up to something, Cathy thought. She pecked her on the cheek and left.

Francine sunk back into her own thoughts. The thought haunted her that Francis and Jean had been murdered simply for being gay. She shared everything with John. This she could not. Peter had said that the house was haunted and that they were the ghosts. It was certainly haunted by Francis and Jean. Francesca too, and Jean-Michel were ever present. How many others? She did not yet know. A couple had stood in the bricked up doorway where Francis hid from the Italian. It was of course where she and John shared their first kiss. Francine did not think that was it. She found it hard enough to believe in ghosts from the past. That Francis sensed the presence of her and John in the future was too much for her to take in. She preferred to think that she/Francis/Francesca had been there before. Maybe it was when the original farmhouse was built. There were more stories to tell, that was certain. Why did she not share this with John? She did not know. Maybe he was too close. Maybe he was not ready. It was something he had to come to on his own. When he did she would be there. She would always be there.

Cathy had Jan on the phone. "How's it going?" her sister had asked.

"Complicated. Francine is working on it. She has something up her sleeve but she won't say. You will need to come over at least 40 days before the wedding. As an EU citizen you have the right to live in France. If you live in France, as a resident you have the right to marry here. When we get all the pieces in place we can ask the mayor to marry you. As soon as the gay marriage law is enacted of course."

Jan was delighted. She then remembered that relations with the mayor were strained to say the least. "You said ask him. Can he say no?"

"Yes, he could say no."

"But he doesn't like Francine. Will he say no to spite her?"

"It's possible. That is the bit Francine is working on."

"Alice and I are not very religious, but could we ask the priest to marry us?"

For once Cathy knew the answer without asking Francine. "No. Since the third republic church and state have been completely separate. Priests can perform a religious ceremony, but it is the state that marries."

Francine came into Henri's office with a smile. It was the smile of a confident barrister who has carefully prepared his case. She had a dossier and a book. Actually the book was a draft, held in a large ring binder. "My sister-in-law would like to get married."

Her husband Jean-Mark who had died in the barn fire, had no sisters. John had no sisters. Henri sensed a large degree of licence in the term belle-soeur. He let it pass. "And who is the lucky man?"

"Alice."

Henri raised an eyebrow. "Your, ahem, belle-soeur is lesbian?"

"Exact."

"Then I assume that by belle-soeur you mean your lover's sometime to be ex-wife's sister Jan." The intricacies of relationships within the large house on the square were a source of considerable fascination in the village. There was not much that Henri had not heard about the goings on there. Most were of course salacious fiction.

Francine smiled. "Would it help if I said that Cathy's sister would like to get married in the village?"

"Since Cathy lives in Thiviers and her sister in England I doubt that it would help much at all."

Francine produced two documents. One was substantial. It was the deed to the house proving John's ownership. The other was the one which John had insisted on signing at the same time. Francine showed it to Henri. "As you see, this is an attestation d'hebergement granting Cathy the legal right to live in her husband's house. Cathy has invited her sister to live here. I can show you the letter. It is in English. I can obtain a certified translation if you wish."

The domestic arrangements were becoming more interesting by the moment. The ménage a trois had invited a lesbian couple to live with them. It had all the makings of a porn movie.

"If and when Cathy's sister arrives your evidence suggests that I would have the power to sign an attestation de residence for her. Forty days after that, if and when legislation is enacted permitting same sex marriage, I could marry them."

Francine smiled "The ease with which you grasp such things is surely why you are such a capable mayor." The sarcasm was palpable.

Henri's eyes narrowed. "And what, in the name of all that is holy, would induce me to agree to such a thing?"

Francine slid the book across the table. "This. It is my book on the history of Saint Etienne. It is as yet unpublished. There are only two copies. One of course I have. This is the second which I give to the commune. As mayor you have the right to decide who reads it." The colour was starting to drain from Henri's face. Francine leant forward and spoke quietly. "You are a busy man, and the book is long. I will save you the trouble of reading it all by saying this: There is a chapter on the murder of Francis and Jean. There is substantiated evidence that your grandfather Lowell committed this war crime. He of course is dead. He cannot be tried. She whispered in French, quoting Exodus: God by no means clears the guilty, visiting the iniquity of the fathers on the children and the children's children to the third and fourth generation." Francine stood. "There is one more thing. I understand you intend to stand for re-election. I have announced my candidacy. I cannot remember the last time the office of mayor was contested. May you live in interesting times." She left with the ancient Chinese curse ringing in his ears.

Cathy was busy trying to explain amortization to John. "How long before you think you will need to buy another one?" Cathy had no idea what the piece of equipment in the ledger was for, or even what it looked like.

"Never. It will outlive me."

"I'll put 10 years."

"If you like, what for?"

"I need to value the fixed assets. I can't keep them at the same price you bought them."

"Why not? That is the replacement cost. In fact the replacement cost would probably be higher."

"It is not about budgeting to replace equipment, it is about estimating what they could be sold for."

"But I am not going to sell them."

"If you sell the business the value of the machinery is part of the value of the company."

"But I am not going to sell the business."

Luckily Francine came in to rescue her. "How did the meeting go with old misery guts?" She asked.

Francine added a smile to the self satisfied look she was already wearing. "OK I think. He didn't say yes, but I have given him an awful lot to think about."

John was relieved that it looked as if he was about to be let off the accounts. "Did you tell him you knew about his grandfather killing two of his own men?"

Francine did not realise John new. She had not talked much about it. It was hard enough managing her own emotions. She didn't want to hurt John. "Yes I did."

"I bet he was shocked." Put in Cathy.

"Not as shocked as when I told him I was running against him in the next election."

They both turned to look at her. "Really?"

"Yes really. It is about time he stopped having everything his own way."

John went over to kiss her. "You will make a fantastic mayor. I am surprised though. I thought you would have talked to me about it first."

Francine bristled. "I did. You weren't listening. Anyway I don't need your permission."

Cathy put her arm round both of them. "Don't start arguing. Misery guts has agreed to Jan and Alice's marriage and we are going to have a new mayor. We should be celebrating."

Francine pecked Cathy on the cheek. "You are right. Wine? I am sure you have both had enough of beer."

"Well the accounts anyway" said John. "That is what made me grumpy. I know I am preoccupied with the business, but I am sure I would have remembered something like you standing for mayor."

"It was last night. You were already asleep."

John gestured. "There you are. The defence rests its case."

*

Jan was delighted when she heard the news. She and Alice decided on late August to give them enough time to prepare. "We will still be the first English gays to get married." Cathy was going to point out that same sex English couples had been marrying in Sweden since 2009. She held her tongue. She did not want to spoil the moment. The two of them came over in May. It was an excuse for a booze cruise. They toured the Bergerac vineyards. "We want red, white, and rosé." They announced.

"Who's going to drink rosé?" Objected John

"We are!" exclaimed Alice. "You obviously know nothing about gay weddings!"

John had to confess that he did indeed know nothing about gay weddings. The girls toured the garden taking photos and planning where the ceremony will be.

"You won't be able to get everyone in the Marie" warned Francine.

"We will have close family in there and then parade out. We will cross the square and into the back garden." Jan wanted John to be the celebrant for that part. He was flattered. He asked whether they wouldn't rather have a woman. They reminded him that they had made him an honorary female years ago. "We thought about Cathy" Said Jan but I want her for my best woman."

"And I would like Francine to be mine." Added Alice. They had a whole retinue of bridesmen.

"I bet they are all gay" put in Peter.

"And what's wrong with that?" objected Jan. "As it happens most of them are straight. They will be the ones wearing dresses."

Francine was confident she could get the house ready for August. She was not sure the villagers would be. Jan and Alice had invited so many people from England there was no way they could fit in the locals as well. Francine suggested a lendeman de marriage. Jan and Alice would stay an extra day. The morning after the marriage the whole village, plus Francine, John and Cathy's friends would be invited.

A band was booked. Ariane's ice cream company was part of an association of food trucks. She suggested Chez René. It was an ancient Citroen van painted bright yellow with a large French cock on the side.

Peter laughed "That's the last thing they will want."

Ariane looked offended. "It is very French, I thought they would love it."

"I'm sure they will love the van, but they won't want the cock, they are lesbians."

Francine was shocked. "Peter, that's very rude! You are worse than your father!"

Peter looked hurt. He was trying to be funny. The phantom pain returned. Triggers were tiny and difficult to predict. He shook it off. "Won't dad want to do the catering?"

"Not for that many" said Francine. He is doing his signature dish, René is doing apero, served from the van. Crêpe 'n roll are doing French crepes served with Ariane's ice cream.

"What is crêpe 'n roll?" asked Peter.

"Another food truck" explained Ariane.

*

The day itself went exactly to plan. Francine was scared that Henri would make trouble. He was fine. "A little wooden" observed John. He also flunked a key line saying 'husband and wife' instead of 'wife and wife'".

Jan and Alice were not bothered. "Everyone gets that bit wrong" they said.

The band was Roma. All from the same family, three generations toured the tables in Italian troubadour style. The grandson was younger than Peter. He took a shine to Susan. The third time he came and performed a solo in front of her Peter growled. The band leader noticed. He whispered in his grandson's ear. The band was asked to stop. It was time for speeches. Cathy tapped her glass and called for Jan's best woman. In the silence before she spoke a 'cello played. All eyes moved to the balcony. A young girl in period costume was performing. When John looked up she smiled, pulling the hem of her frock above her knee. She finished playing, stood to acknowledge the applause then retreated into the bedroom.

Jan turned to Francine. "That was beautiful. What was it?" "Faure's 'cello concerto in D minor opus 109. She played the andante in G"

Susan looked at Peter. "Is your mum a musician?"

"Not at all, she doesn't know the first thing about music."

"Then how come she recognised that piece? Nobody remembers the opus number."

"I don't know." Peter did know, but could not begin to explain.

Jan was delighted with the performance. "What a wonderful surprise. Thank you. Who is she?"

Francine was shaking. "Her name is Francesca."

"You must ask her down so I can thank her."

"I don't think she will come."

"Nonsense. Go and ask her, the speeches can wait five minutes."

Francine stood reluctantly. She could hardly walk. She put her hand on John's shoulder to steady herself. "Too much champagne." Someone commented.

"I don't think it is that." John observed. Francine entered by Stuardo's kitchen and mounted the small staircase. The door she had hidden behind was gone. She paused in the old doorway to feel John's kiss. Crossing the kitchen she went into the living room. A figure was standing in the bookcase. John had moved the bedroom door to the corner to make more space. The original door was now a built in wardrobe. On the living room side it was blocked by a bookcase. The girl smiled. Holding out her hands she walked towards her. They looked into each other's eyes. The girl turned, took a step back, and merged into Francine's body. Francine entered the bedroom by the new door. She expected to find a 'cello. The room was exactly as she had prepared it. She and John had moved out, turning it into a bridal suite for Jan and Alice. She had scattered rose petals on the pillows. She stared. The petals had carefully been rearranged to make room for two more objects. On one pillow was a crucifix. On the other was a wedding ring. Francesca had placed them there before she went to play.

Francine returned to the wedding party. John looked up. Sensing something had happened he went to her. She was holding the ring and the crucifix. "Was that who I think it was?"

"Yes. She left her ring and crucifix."

"Neither Jan nor Alice are Catholic. Also, they both said they did not want rings."

"They are not for them. They are for me." Francine put the crucifix round her neck and went back to her place. "Cathy, do you mind if we do my speech last, I need time to gather my thoughts?"

"No problem. Love the necklace. A bit too Goth, doesn't really go with the dress."

"It is a family heirloom."

"Lovely. Your granny's?"

"Kind of."

"Where is the 'cello player?"

"She has gone."

"That's a shame."

"It is what she wanted."

It was time for Francine's speech. She threw away her notes. "One of the advantages of going last is that everything has already been said. Wedding speeches are usually filled with sexual innuendo and expectations of offspring. This wedding has had plenty of the former. I am not sure how Jan and Alice are going to manage the latter, we haven't discussed it."

"Neither have we" Quipped Jan and Alice together.

Francine continued. "Nor have I with John. This therefore will come as something of a shock to him. Peter is growing up. I am far too young to be a granny."

Cries of "behave yourself Peter!"

Francine raised her voice above the banter. "That is why I am delighted to tell you that Peter will not be an only child much longer." She slipped the ring on her finger. She was no longer married to Christ, she was married to John.